WRITE

YOURSELF

OUT OF

A CORNER

also by
Alice LaPlante

FICTION

Half Moon Bay

Coming of Age at the End of Days

Circle of Wives

Turn of Mind

NONFICTION

The Making of a Story: A Norton Guide to Creative Writing

WRITE YOURSELF OUT OF A CORNER

100 Exercises to Unlock Creativity

Alice LaPlante

W. W. NORTON & COMPANY
Celebrating a Century of Independent Publishing

For information about special discounts for bulk purchases, please contact W. W. Norton Special Sales at specialsales@wwnorton.com or 800-233-4830

Manufacturing by Lakeside Book Company
Book design by Marysarah Quinn
Production manager: Lauren Abbate

ISBN 978-0-393-54184-7 (pbk)

W. W. Norton & Company, Inc., 500 Fifth Avenue, New York, N.Y. 10110
www.wwnorton.com

W. W. Norton & Company Ltd., 15 Carlisle Street, London W1D 3BS

1 2 3 4 5 6 7 8 9 0

For Danica Wilcox and Matthew Clark Davison,
without whom this book could not have been written

When forced to work within a strict framework, the imagination is taxed to its utmost and will produce its richest ideas.

—T. S. ELIOT

Contents

SECTION 1:

Using Constraints to Generate Creative Work   1

SECTION 2:

Writing from Your Particular "Location"   9

SECTION 3:

Exercises   15

1. A Minor Irritation   17
2. I Am What Is Missing   20
3. Homecoming   23
4. A One-Sided Telephone Conversation   26
5. Aubade   29
6. Connecting the Dots   33
7. Difficult Communications   37
8. Pushing Readers into a Particular Emotional Space   41
9. Losing Your Senses   45
10. An Errand   49
11. Worry   53
12. Painful Beauty   57

13. Try to Praise the Mutilated World   60

14. Today, Five Years Hence   62

15. The Visitor   65

16. Dark Gifts   68

17. Grace Bestowed   71

18. Surviving the Plague   75

19. Running Late   77

20. Make It Rain   80

21. Despair and Peace   83

22. Passion for Solitude   86

23. Party Questions   89

24. 90 Seconds   92

25. One Hour   96

26. One Day   99

27. One Year   102

28. Nothing Personal   105

29. Not Guilty   108

30. Moving Toward Beauty   111

31. Maps   114

32. Love Lost   117

33. Sorrow   120

34. Black Box   123

35. Distracted by Scent   127

36. Toxic Touch   131

37. Time Travel   134

38. Things I Wish I Could Forget   138

39. The To-Do List   143

40. Suspense   146

41. Survival   150

42. Story Within a Story   153

43. Sins of Commission/Omission (Part I)   156

44. Sins of Commission/Omission: (Part II)   159

45. Clothes Make the (Wo)man   162

46. Sheltering in Place   165

47. Self-Sabotage   168

48. Second-Person Reflexive   171

49. Second-Person Complicit   174

50. Second-Person Direct Address of Character   176

51. Point of View and Truth   179

52. Life's Losses   184

53. Last Letter   188

54. A Fall in Slow Motion   191

55. Sister Ship   194

56. Think Big, Write Small   197

57. Bad Advice   201

58. Comfortable   204

59. Looking at Pictures   207

60. Ducks   210

61. Bitch Is a Word   214

62. Nonsense of Summer   216

63. Brevity and Intensity   219

64. Precious   222

65. Acting "Out of Character"   225

66. On Animal Friends   229

67. Not Guilty   232

68. Meet the "In-Laws"   235

69. Invisibility   238

70. His Terror   241

71. Caring   244

72. Controlling Chaos   248

73. Surprised by Joy   252

74. Sad Steps   256

75. Regrets   259

76. Heartbreak   262

77. Eating the Stars   265

78. Dramatizing Love   267

79. Capturing an Experience in Three Stages   269

80. Misalignment   273

81. Failing and Flying   278

82. A Brief for the Defense   281

83. Honoring the Shmita   286

84. Interrupted Journey   290

85. Not Ashamed   293

86. Heat   296

87. Grief   300

88. Forgotten 303

89. Accepting Yourself 306

90. A Month, Described 309

91. Beginnings 312

92. Expanding on Beginnings 314

93. Crushed 317

94. Earworm 320

95. A Visit to an Unpleasant Place 323

96. Silver Linings 326

97. Bad Sex 329

98. Unwelcome 332

99. Dueling Responsibilities 335

100. Hauntings 337

SECTION 4:

Afterthoughts 341

Acknowledgments 345

Glossary of Literary Terms Used in This Book 347

Notes 353

Works Referred To in This Text 355

Contributors 359

Permissions 363

WRITE

YOURSELF

OUT OF

A CORNER

USING
CONSTRAINTS
TO GENERATE
CREATIVE
WORK

Ask any artist. Most will tell you that nothing is worse than the blank page. Or computer screen. Same for the empty canvas (for visual artists) and blank staff (composers). The idea that creativity–and thus the artist–thrives in an atmosphere of complete, unadulterated freedom is widespread and romantic. But it's wrong.

For centuries, artists have used—no, depended upon—constraints. The haiku (three sentences: five syllables, seven syllables, and five syllables) forces poets to cut language to the bone. The Yadu, also called Burmese climbing rhyme, has rhymes that move from the end of the first line to the middle of the next. The Shakespearean sonnet (fourteen-line verses of iambic pentameter, with a rhyme pattern of abab / cdcd / efef / gg, compels poets to think within a rigid, almost mathematical formula. Yet look at the variety of spoils we've gotten from these constraints! From Shakespeare himself ("Let me not to the marriage of true minds"), to today's Rachel Eliza Griffiths ("Hymn to a Hurricane") and Francine J. Harris ("Enough Food and a Mom"), each poet embraces the constraints and makes them their own.

The same goes for other artistic fields. In music, form is also important. Mugham is a type of Azerbaijani singing or playing with strict rhythms. Its variations, or modes, are defined partly by the emotional states they evoke in listeners.[1] Jazz has its origins in the opposing rhythms of African music, especially syncopation, where all or parts of a piece place the stress on the off beats.[2]

The classical symphony (traditionally in four movements: an opening allegro, an adagio, a minuet with a trio, and another allegro) allowed composers like Mozart and Haydn to thrill us with their beautiful—and quite different—musical legacies. And then Beethoven arrived. Instead of complying with the constraints, he frolicked with them. For his first two symphonies he kept within the template. Then he started coloring outside the lines, playing and teasing his audiences. In effect, he was drawing new lines. Others who followed copied his new self-imposed constraints. That's why the final, majestic symphonies of Mendelssohn and Schubert open slowly and somberly in minor keys, advancing to movements characterized by transformational finales in bright, triumphant major keys. For these artists, following the constraints of Beethoven wasn't only a form of flattery, it was integral to their abilities to create great art.

Even painting has imposed its constraints on practitioners over the centuries (subject matter, color choices, composition, and so on), although—as in other artistic disciplines—such constraints are regularly broken and new ones promptly imposed by the next generation. A Parisian art critic, Louis Leroy, appalled at Monet's rendering of a harbor at dawn wrote scornfully, "An impression!" He was especially outraged by the incompleteness of Monet's images. "Wallpaper in its embryonic state is more finished!" he fumed. Yet within a year, Impressionism was an accepted term—and art form—in the greater world.[3] And soon after that, painting according to the Impressionists' constraints—broad brushstrokes, unusual color combinations, subjects depicting ordinary life—inspired new generations of artists.

What artists have known for centuries, scientists and engineers and mathematicians are now proving empirically. In an age where the words *innovation* and *disruption* echo through corridors in Silicon Valley, Bangalore, and Shanghai, businesspeople are wondering what spurs creativity and how they can force it to blossom in their labs and cubicle farms. Tune to the TED channel on YouTube and you'll find no shortage of talks on how to be more inventive, how to help employees be more innovative, and how to instill a culture of creativity within your organization. And it all comes down to constraints.

The idea behind constraints is a basic one: human creativity has never been about creating something from nothing but transforming existing materials into something surprising and new. About unusual combinations of unlike things. I'll discuss this in more detail later, but for now I'm asking you to accept the premise that creativity is strongest and most powerful when artists are pushed into a corner—whether by circumstances, emotions, events, or relationships—and forced to make use of what they have at hand.

Thus writers under pressure have always borrowed, even stolen (especially stolen) from others to avoid the absolute freedom of the blank page. With a few exceptions, Shakespeare did not invent the plots of the plays that he wrote for his acting troupe, the King's Men. Sometimes he used old stories (*Hamlet, Pericles*). Sometimes he worked from the stories of comparatively recent Italian writers, such as Giovanni Boccaccio—using both well-known stories (*Romeo and Juliet, Much Ado About Nothing*) and little-known ones (*Othello*). He used the popular prose fictions of his contemporaries in *As You Like It* and *The Winter's Tale*.[4] What exactly did he create—why do we remember him rather than the authors he stole from? New characters, new relationships, new emotional undercurrents, and, especially, new language were all Shakespeare's creative contributions to the world—all by making innovative use of materials already at hand.

Searching for the Creative Spark

But what is true creativity? As I've said, the notion that artists (or anyone) can conjure up something from nothing—and that the most creative people can do it at will—is (largely) a myth. (Never say never about the many ways humans create.) Today's consensus is that creativity builds on existing works by making fresh connections between previously separate objects, ideas, or theories. By making these connections, creative people come up with startling new insights about their worlds.

One often-cited example of this in the art world is Pablo Picasso's *Tête de taureau* (*Bull's Head*) sculpture, which he "found" (his word) in 1942. It is described by Roland Penrose as Picasso's most famous discovery, a simple yet "astonishingly complete" metamorphosis.[5] Picasso described the artwork to photographer George Brassaï this way:

> Guess how I made the bull's head? One day, in a pile of objects all jumbled up together, I found an old bicycle seat right next to a rusty set of handlebars. In a flash, they joined together in my head. The idea of the *Bull's Head* came to me before I had a chance to think. All I did was weld them together . . .[6]

Let's be clear, I am treading some well-known paths. These are not new ideas. Take *The Act of Creation*, a 1964 book by Arthur Koestler that examines the processes of discovery, invention, imagination, and creativity in humor, science, and the arts. Koestler believed that creative thinking was different from what he called "associative" thinking, which was "the logical application of a person's previous experiences, skills, or habits."[7] Associative thinking—or so Koestler posited—helps keep the world working, and in balance, and follows a strict pattern.

Koestler created a new word, *bisociative*, to describe thinking that "integrates two or more frames of reference," which he believed is required for true creativity. He wrote that the ability to simultaneously view a situation through multiple lenses is the source of all creative breakthroughs. But it can't be done logically, he argued. Bisociative thinking is visual, intuitive, and dreamlike. It operates on a subconscious level. Koestler wrote:

> The creative act does not create something out of nothing, like the God of the Old Testament; it combines, reshuffles, and relates already existing but hitherto separate ideas, facts, frames of perception, associative contexts. This act of cross-fertilization—or self-fertilization within a single brain—seems to be the essence of creativity.

Mihaly Csikszentmihalyi, a psychologist who studied creativity and authored the book *Creativity: The Psychology of Discovery and Invention*, also believes that creativity is about connections—about finding hidden patterns and making associations between things that aren't typically related to each other.[8]

He talks about going into a creative space that is a "kind of ecstasy or alternate reality," but stresses that a lot of hard work and knowledge—he calls it skill—is required in your given field to move into this space. In a TED Talk, Csikszentmihalyi labels this space—really a state of mind—as achieving "flow."[9]

But how does this research into creativity relate to constraints?

In ancient Greek and Roman times, it was believed that an actual muse would descend to spark creativity. The muses were nine goddesses for different aspects of literature, art, and music. Unfortunately, if you wait for a muse to descend with your fingers poised over a keyboard, you might be a long time waiting. Constraint-based writing replaces this idea of inspiration coming out of nowhere with being pushed into a confined emotional or intellectual space.

Csikszentmihalyi also said that constraints—he called them challenges—had to be appropriate to the skill level of the person. Too difficult a challenge, and the person becomes worried or anxious. Too easy, and the person gets bored or has too much logical control over the process to be truly spontaneous. The best state for creativity to get into flow is "arousal," he says, where the challenges force a person to stretch their skills beyond what they currently possess.

If done right, a constraint-based writing exercise will do this. It will force writers to put together things that otherwise might never meet—in a way that stretches their writing skills. Thus the key to constructing a good constraint-based exercise is to define those disconnected things precisely, while giving the writer enough wiggle room for spontaneity and their own inclinations, subconscious feelings and thoughts, and skill levels.

THE RISKS OF NO CONSTRAINTS

There are actually risks associated with a lack of constraints.

According to studies aggregated by the *Harvard Business Review*, when there are no constraints to the creative process, complacency sets in.[10] People will tend to go for the most logical or intuitive idea rather than having to struggle for a better one. Constraints, in contrast, provide focus and a creative challenge that motivates people to search for and connect information from different sources to generate novel ideas for new products, services, or even business processes.

In a 2015 study, Ravi Mehta at the University of Illinois and Meng Zhu at Johns Hopkins University found that people who possess abundant resources—read: freedom—simply have no incentive to use what's available to them in unusual or new ways.[11] But when people face scarcity, they give themselves the freedom to use resources in less conventional ways because they have to. The situation demands use of deep mental resources that would otherwise remain untapped.

Unfortunately, many of the writing exercises and prompts being used today are ineffective. Most of the time, it's because they are too simple. Too many consist of using a single word—an evocative word certainly, say, *grace* or *mercy* or *evil*—that is meant to trigger an emotional reaction in the writer. But these often fall flat. There's still too much freedom. Prompts that ask writers to describe or respond to images or photographs tend to work better, as they can contain more complexity. But there has to be an element of pulling the writer in at least two different directions for a constraint to really work.

And you also need to be mindful about imposing too many constraints. When a creative task is too constraining, if the space within which creative ideas are generated becomes too narrow, it is harder to form unusual connections and serendipitous insights. Hence, the key is to strike a balance between too much freedom and too many limitations.

In Homage to Oulipo

Inevitably when talking about constraints, we get to Oulipo. It's the very big elephant in the room when talking about constraint-based writing.

Oulipo is a French acronym that stands for *Ouvroir de littérature potentielle*, or a "workshop of potential literature"—a group of writers and mathematicians that formed in 1960 specifically to create literary works using constraints.

Here are some examples of Oulipo constraints:

- ☐ **Lipogram:** a letter (commonly *e* or *o*) is eliminated
- ☐ **Reverse lipogram:** each word must contain a particular letter
- ☐ **Mandated vocabulary:** the writer must include specific words
- ☐ **Acrostics:** first letter of each word, sentence, or paragraph forms a word or sentence
- ☐ **Abecedarius:** first letter of each word, verse, section goes through the alphabet
- ☐ **Pilish:** the lengths of consecutive words match the digits of the number π.

And here are some examples of Oulipo outputs:

- ☐ **In 1969,** French writer Georges Perec published *La Dispari-tion*, a novel that did not include the letter *e*. It was trans-lated into English in 1995 by Gilbert Adair, also without using the letter *e*.
- ☐ **The 2004** French novel *Le Train de Nulle Part* (*The Train from Nowhere*) by Michel Thaler was written entirely without verbs.
- ☐ *Let Me Tell You* **(2008),** a novel by the Welsh writer Paul Griffiths, uses only the words allotted to Ophelia in *Hamlet*.

The constraints in this book owe a great deal to Oulipo. But most are not the mathematical constraints Oulipolians enjoy the most. I believe in emotional prompts—prompts that push people into uncomfortable psychic spaces to imagine (or bring to the sur-face) situations, relationships, and character traits that would oth-erwise stay buried.

I am also less interested in weird results for their own sake than in where the constraints take us. An Oulipo poem might have some interesting theoretical points, but it rarely has the emotional movement that most of us look for in writing. Still, unusual word juxtapositions and uncommon sentences can spark something that can be useful for a writer to explore further or to integrate into a work in progress.

It is my sincerest hope that this book will help you generate fresh and exciting material in your own creative writing. Good luck on your journey!

WRITING FROM YOUR PARTICULAR "LOCATION"

Now, let's talk about your location.

I don't mean only the physical place you live—San Francisco Bay Area, New York, Japan, India, Nigeria, or Spain (where I happen to be located). But everything that has brought you to the particular space you occupy at this particular time. It's everything that has happened in your *life* to bring you here, in front of this book in this room (or outside space) on this date. Not incidentally, it also includes all the creative writing classes you have taken, the books you have read, the mentors you have been lucky enough to have, and everything you've written up to this moment.

But more importantly, it's your particular emotional state and your particular level of intellectual and character development at this moment of time due to *everything* that came before it. That's everything in your life.

So what you had for breakfast contributed to your current location. Perhaps your coffee was bitter and put you in a bad mood. Or you fell in love last week. Or the neighborhood you grew up in was rough. Perhaps you witnessed extreme violence or cruelty as a child. Maybe you have been ostracized because of your sexual identity, your race, your ethnicity.

What I'm trying to say is, everything you have experienced in your life (plus a little bit of genetics maybe) has culminated in bringing you here, now, to your current location.

Your location is utterly unique. No one else could possibly occupy it. How could they? They haven't experienced what you have experienced. They don't know what you know. No two people are in the same location. And your location is where I want you to write from when doing the exercises in this book.

We forget sometimes how remarkable our own locations are—and how interesting (or even helpful)—they can be to others if we write about them precisely enough. Think of all the rich human history each of us carries around! But we can think it's boring. Because it's not new to us.

And sometimes we dismiss our weirder or more unorthodox aspects of our location as too dangerous to write about. That revealing them will make us too vulnerable.

Yes, it will. That's why writing is a brave, difficult thing.

Ray Carver said, "Carry news from your world to ours." I would say, from your location to ours.

One of my heroes, George Saunders has said—and I'm paraphrasing wildly, he definitely used other words—that he goes over his sentences again and again to make sure each one could only have come from him. That's a tall order. Maybe you just want the waitress to bring the coffee to the table. How do you make that sentence your own? You might consider this impossible. But it's certainly something to aspire to.

Ask yourself when doing the exercises: What does everyone know about this topic? And what do *I* know?

Here's an example: Part of what I know about rural Spain (where I live) that I bet no one else knows—especially the tourists—is that if you're alone in an old farmhouse in the lonely Spanish countryside at night, things you can't see creep up and look through the windows at you. Watch you. That's part of my location. It might not be a pleasant part, but it's there, nonetheless.

Okay. Your location. Write from it.

How to Do These Exercises

Now I'm going to explain some of the instructions that you will see repeatedly as you go through these exercises.

THINK SMALL, AND PARTICULARLY

Often I'll say think small. Having trouble? Think smaller.

This isn't just me talking. It's Richard Hugo, from *The Triggering Town*. Think small, he advises. "If you have a big mind, that will show itself."

How does this work in practice? Let's say I want to write about death. No, I should recognize that's way too big.

How about: I want to write about losing a parent. That's better, but still rather large and abstract.

I want to write about how it felt to watch my father die. That's getting closer.

How about this?

I want to write about how my five sisters and I sang along to Louis Armstrong songs on Spotify over our father's body as he slipped out of life. How we told bad jokes and laughed and sang until the night nurse had to tell us to shut up.

Yes. Things are finally getting into focus.

Or, I want to write about the atrocities in Ukraine.

That's also too big—but how about writing about the Ukrainian woman giving sunflower seeds to Russian soldiers to put in their pockets, so when they die, the fields will bloom profusely with Ukraine's national flower? That's a small detail, but oh, so very big.

THINK CONCRETELY

Another thing you'll hear me ask you: How does this manifest itself in the world of the senses?

That's because the biggest mistake I see in writing is abstraction. Characters are fearful or happy or surprised or dumbfounded. But those are abstract qualities.

We should always be asking ourselves, *How can I anchor these abstract thoughts and feelings with images that can be perceived by the five senses?*

She was afraid. She began to shiver uncontrollably. (A little overused, but better than an abstraction.)

He was happy. His hands opened and closed. He began tapping his feet.

I'm always reminding myself of what Flannery O'Connor said: "We are made of dust and if you scorn getting yourself dusty, then fiction isn't a grand enough job for you."

Or (my favorite) William Carlos Williams: "No ideas but in things." By this, he was protesting the abstract nature of the poetry of his time. Writers need to focus on *things of this earth* to get their ideas across, he insisted.

Keep those quotes in your head as you do these exercises, and you'll do great.

AND WHEN I ASK YOU FOR A "SCENE" . . .

For the purposes of this book, we'll just say simply that a scene is something happening at a particular place at a particular time. That's kind of a guardrail I'm putting on some exercises to keep you from ruminating without grounding the exercise sufficiently in a tangible world.

Don't get me wrong. Narrative—or telling—is good, is truly wonderful. For example: "It is a truth universally acknowledged that a single man in possession of a good fortune, must be in want of a wife."

That's great narrative that opens *Pride and Prejudice*, by Jane Austen, unanchored by a scene. So, yeah, I'm all for narrative.

But in some cases, I'm going to be asking you to specifically write in scene. Take that instruction seriously to get the most out of those exercises.

NEVER WORRY ABOUT WHETHER IT'S BORING

I mean, of course we all worry about whether what we're writing will be interesting to anyone else. But when generating stuff, we have to forget about that concern.

I can't tell you how many writers give me dull, unengaging prose without sufficient detail because they think too much detail will be boring. Put it in. Put it all in. Later you can take some of it out. But when you're generating stuff, anything goes.

"Let a man get up and say, Behold, this is the truth, and instantly I perceive a sandy cat filching a piece of fish in the background. Look, you have forgotten the cat, I say," wrote Virginia Woolf in *The Waves*.

SHARE THE SPOILS!

I hope you enjoy these exercises, and that you get as much out of them as I did, and as hundreds of other writers have over the years.

Get fabulous results? Have an idea that will help others? Have a complaint? Want to share any other thoughts? Feel free to drop me a line at my website: www.alicelaplante.com.

These exercises are not ordered by type or theme, although there are a few multipart exercises that should be done in sequence. These are clearly marked. The rest of them are meant to surprise, even startle you by their variety. In other words, the random nature of the exercises is intentional, so anyone going through the book systematically will have a varied experience that continually stretches them in different directions. Or you can dip in at will. Either way, I hope these push you in fresh ways so you can delight others while surprising yourself.

How to Approach These Exercises

For the purposes of this book, I've identified four different types of exercises that are based on constraints, or specific limitations:

1. Limit inputs (for example, you cannot use the letter *e*)
2. Impose inputs (for example, you must use the words *cloud*, *petite*, and *green*)

3. Impose processes (for example, you must follow these three steps)

4. Make explicit output demands (for example, the result must exhibit specific characteristics or achieve specific goals)

Most prompts use a combination of these constraints. But if they're too narrow and try and constrain writers too much? They won't work. I've tried to be careful in how I constructed them for this reason.

Do you, the writer, have a hypercritical attitude toward yourself or others? Are you allergic to failure? Then, again, this way of working won't fly.

To help you out, I've included introductions to each exercise that tell you what point of process or craft is targeted. I've included an example of a finished exercise for each one, many of which are from past students. And I've written a short analysis of how the example fulfilled the requirement of the constraint.

The goal is to reach inside yourself and find out what you really have to say about the conditions of the world you live in. And most of these exercises can be repeated over and over again, to get fresh results. Try them. See which ones trigger the best responses. And (again) good luck!

1.

A Minor Irritation

We're always looking for ways to peer inside our characters. Of course, when big things happen to them, their reactions can reveal a lot. But often you can get at their traits and emotions more subtly. Make minor things go wrong. Impede them in some small way. How do they behave? What does it reveal?

Of course, that will depend on many facts, including their exact location (as we've discussed). But it can be fun to play, to throw small things at your character and see how they respond.

In this exercise, you will do exactly that. As you'll see, this is an excellent exercise for scene-building.

Exercise

1. Write a piece in which you are (or a character is) trying to overcome a nagging issue. It can and should be small (the toilet is plugged, the milk has soured).
2. Describe what happens in detail. Do not worry (for now) about whether it is boring.
3. Somehow, the issue gets resolved (either actively by you or the character, or passively just resolves itself).
4. How do you (or your character) feel upon resolution? Is it satisfying? Not satisfying? Why or why not? Tease out what happens.

HINT: Ask yourself how the emotions related to both the irritant and the resolution would manifest themselves in the physical world, using as many of the five senses as you can.

Example

The tube had been extra awful this evening. It was raining and those who might normally have walked or waited for a bus had scuttled underground instead and now here they all were packed in like steaming sardines. She managed to get a hand on one of the rails, shifting her weight and ignoring her squelching feet—another pair of tights ruined—and settled in. She counted off the stops: Tottenham Court Road, Oxford Circus, Bond Street and then her, Marble Arch. It would never fail to delight her that she lived here, amongst the streets picked directly from the Monopoly board of her childhood. A quick stop in Marks & Spencer to pick up what she needed for the evening. Chicken and leek pie, some baby potatoes, a token-gesture bit of broccoli, and last but not least a jam roly-poly and a carton of custard. Check. She fast-walked the five minutes to the flat, impressed at her own dexterity in damp heels. She had been so looking forward to this evening. The flat to herself, a proper meal, and the new Barbara Trapido she had been saving.

The smell and the note taped to the kitchen door hit her at the same time.

"Think TP might be finished unless you stashed some away. Someone left the milk out.

I think the pilot lights gone off. You should just come down the pub."

Why would Lizzie just go off knowing that the flat was filling with gas? It was so irresponsible. She was so mad she actually stamped her foot, which served to make her even more angry as cold, damp rainwater squeezed between her toes, knowing all the while that she would have done the exact same thing. Left a note and gone out because wasn't this why they were in London? Living in this flat they could barely afford, working jobs that were just one step above clerical? Nothing wrong with that, but what had been the point of university then? The point was to have fun, and a good friend would never deny her best friend that. A few dramatic sighs later and she had forced open the kitchen window and propped it open with the silver ladle that belonged to Lizzie's grandmother. The dear lady would have been mortified to know that it had only ever been used for two things, this and for stirring fruity floral punches that definitely got the party started. She opened the oven door and stiffened.

Sickly sweet, the siren smell of her nightmares. The ones from which she woke with her heart thudding so hard that she is surprised it is still in her chest. The ones in which she is standing in her nightie in the kitchen doorway and someone is screaming and there is a shape of a body with no head crouching in front of the stove and the air is thick with the smell of decaying flowers and a hissing that calls you into the void.

She struck a match from the half-empty Swan Vesta box and used it to light a long, rolled-up piece of newspaper, squatted by the stove, and thrust it inside, waving it around blindly until there was a soft pop. Leaving the groceries on the floor, she went back out to the hallway, peeled off her tights, pushed her feet into a pair of olive wellies, and, slamming the door behind her, went to meet the others in the pub.

—NIRMY KANG

Advice

What's nice about this piece is how grounded it is. We're almost on sensory overload—as befits a description of a young person trying to make it in London—with this young woman's sensory percep- tions. This particular young woman's competence in dealing with the mess, the smell, and the potential danger is impressive. Through these irritants we get a glimpse of her character, as well as many potential plot points. What happens when she goes to the pub? What plays out between her and her roommate—that night and in the future as they perhaps question what they're doing in London, barely making ends meet despite working hard and scrimping on niceties.

2.

I Am What Is Missing

In his poem "Keeping Things Whole," Mark Strand talks about having the feeling that he "completes" every place he goes to or occupies. How he makes a place whole with his presence. "Wherever I am, I am what's missing," he writes. It's a lovely concept, and it allows us to try something creative that's different (and difficult): trying to render a sense of happiness without sentimentality.

Exercise

1. Think of a time you (or a character) felt at peace in the world. That you (or they) felt you really belonged, at a specific place at a specific time.
2. Describe that place and time in intimate detail. Do not worry about it being boring.
3. Begin your description with the words "Because I am here . . ." and write in a way that conveys how much you belong to where you are, how comfortable you feel, without outright telling us.
4. Try to avoid being sentimental and going for "easy" images like beautiful nature scenes, waterfalls, rainbows, and so on. Try to delve into the more surprising details you (or your character) might find comforting.

Example

Because I am here, we are four—this cousin, that cousin, my sister, and me.

Don't eat the blueberries, my grandfather yells. The four of us—sandals barely strapped to our feet, overgrown mops of brown hair, skin darkening in the June sun—fling open the back door and run. We are at the age where hand-me-down threads drift between us. So, I wonder—whose basketball shorts graze my scraped legs? Whose oversized T-shirt covers my chest?

Over the stone patio, through freshly mowed grass, and out to the corner of the yard. We run. Don't eat the blueberries, he yells, they're for the birds!

The blueberry bush is sparse this early in the season. The branches are dark and sturdy, but the shoots look stringy, skeletal. Some bear green leaves. Even less bear fruit. Most of the berries are an earthy green, freckled in purple—the same purple as the bruise that covered my sister's knees when she fell while rollerblading. She leads the way, past the blueberry bush and toward the oak tree. My sister is two heads taller than the rest of us; three emergency-room visits braver. She leads the way.

A handful of berries have turned blue, like the fruit that comes in plastic containers from the supermarket. But different. These entice us more than any produce-aisle find. If it were two weeks later, if the ratio of blue to green were higher, my sister would look back toward the ranch house. Then, ensuring we were no longer in sight, she would reach out and pluck the ripest, bluest berry. She would hold the fruit on her tongue like a secret, letting it settle for a moment or two. Then, she would bite, the tart running, seeping, onto a hungry tongue. She would nod. And the rest of us would pluck too.

But it is too early in the season for tasting. So, instead, we climb. We think the old oak tree grew here, in the corner of the yard, just for us. The branches, sprouting like prophecies, the morning of each birth. My sister is the bravest, the tallest. She kicks off her sandals. She reaches, arms then legs. She claims the highest branch. Then, this cousin, then that. I am the youngest, the smallest, the most afraid. The one who wakes up at six a.m. most Saturdays, reads stories to a Beanie Baby audience. The bottom branch belongs to me.

My sister drops a hand to pull me up; her pale fingers grip my tanner ones. She did not inherit Puerto Rico in her pigment like I did. But I will not think of this inheritance yet—at five years old I am just sun-kissed. I am just tan.

From here we can see the top of our grandparents' ranch house, cutting through the trees. Two decades later, when I am grown, I will think of it as the *made it* house. My grandfather, finally—his dream job at a hospital on Long Island. Finally—a house to own. An office; a big kitchen; a backyard where the kids can run. My mother will grow from tween to teen here. She will go off to college, then graduate school. Then her brothers. Then us.

Here, my grandfather will never talk about Puerto Rico. When I am grown, I will ask questions—about his family, their move to New York, his siblings, his father's bodega in Harlem. But he will only close his lips, change the subject. All of that is in the past. He is a doctor, now, a Long Island man.

But on this June morning, I do not ask questions. The ranch house is just a ranch house. The tree is sturdy. The lowest branch is the perfect height for me, the perfect cushion for my bony limbs. I will sit here, with my sister and my cousins. We will not eat the blueberries. When we grow bored, we will climb down. We will strap on our sandals. We will run back inside.

—EMMA ZIMMERMAN

Advice

The narrator, a third-generation Puerto Rican American, combines images of playing with her sister and cousins at their grandparents' house in the country with what she knows about their struggle to reach a point of economic security. She doesn't know much. So she concentrates on the world around her—the blueberry patch, the trees to climb, and what emerges is a lovely sense of belonging and contentment ("the lowest branch belongs to me") despite coming from a background so economically uncertain that her grandfather won't talk about it. What makes this work is the focus on concrete details to carry the emotional resonance.

3.

Homecoming

"Home, I said / In every language there is a word for it," wrote Mary Oliver in her poem "The River," portraying home as an inviting and comforting space. Contrast that with Phillip Larkin's "Home Is So Sad": "It withers so," he wrote, "having no heart to put aside the theft"—the theft, he implies, of the people we loved who once lived there, who are there for us no longer.

Many of us have complex feelings of home. (By definition, complexity comes from being pulled in at least two directions at once.) The idea for this exercise is to dig deeper than Norman Rockwell–esque views of Thanksgiving or Christmas with our families, but to zero in on the nuances, good or bad, of home. We might decide, like Larkin, to investigate the darker or more melancholy aspects. Or go in a different direction, and try, as Mary Oliver does, to seek out what is beautiful and human in the idea of home but without being sentimental.

NOTE: *Sentiment* (feeling) is good. But we don't want to be *sentimental*, which is when we deploy cliché or otherwise overused imagery and language to try to evoke "canned" emotions in our readers. If you're being sentimental, you're attempting to get an emotional payoff without doing deep or original work.)

Exercise

1. Write 1,000 words (about two pages) about a time you (or a character) were longing to go home.
2. Keep in mind that "home" can mean many things, not just a physical place.
3. Your first constraint: Your character has just made

a decision to take an action. Try to make it small. Not "I've decided to leave my partner" but "I'm not going back to the store to get the milk I'd forgotten."

4. What they decide to do, that action (unexpectedly) conjures up a longing for home. In other words, something about the act triggers an association. (Associations are very important in fiction and poetry.)

NOTE: Your character doesn't actually have to go home, just long for it.

Example

I drove by our old street on a whim. I had just accepted a job at a large tech company in the Valley—a decision I had mixed feelings about—and it made me remember the extraordinarily busy yet happy years of working independently while raising the boys. How full life had been then!

Our house is gone. Vanished. The house that has replaced it is large and gray, dominating the small lot on which it crouches like a giant toad. Its windows are just twelve inches away from the walls of the neighboring houses. It could be considered a grand house, I suppose, if it weren't so ugly and out of place among the small wooden bungalows that otherwise line the street. It is three stories high, with an impressive, portentous portico at the front. There isn't enough ground left on the plot for shrubbery or trees, but grass has been planted on the little ground that wasn't devoured by construction.

The giant fir trees in the back of the lot are gone. The oak tree next to where the old garage once stood is gone. We had hung hummingbird feeders on its wide-spreading branches so we could see the shimmering birds as we ate breakfast. Gone is the white picket fence. Of course the century-old wisteria that framed the front porch is gone, as is the porch itself. I lived on this spot for fifteen years. I raised my family, my two boys, in the small, eight-hundred-square-foot white bungalow that preceded this monstrosity. Over the years, running feet battered the wooden floors, furniture marked up the white walls, and we ate uncountable meals together at the small kitchen counter— something I always insisted on over the years, no matter how busy the boys were with their basketball or violin lessons or homework.

After my youngest son followed his brother to the state university across the bay, my landlord gently broke the news that she was selling the house to cash in on the real-estate boom. She gave me six months to pack up my life. I found a one-bedroom apartment on the other side of town that was going for 2.5 times the rent she'd been charging for the house. I had to give or throw away a lot, of course, to downsize. One thing I didn't realize until years later was that somehow in the packing and the visits to the dump and Goodwill, I'd lost something precious: the cardboard box in which I'd kept the boys' refrigerator art over the years. I didn't realize it until my oldest stopped by the other day with his daughter's first family portrait. I was in the foreground of it, tall and skinny, with arms raised as though I were about to fly away. I tried then to find my sons' own early family drawings, only to realize they were gone forever.

Advice

When writing your own piece, it might help to think of the Welsh word *hiraeth*. No comparative English word exists. It means a kind of homesickness that is a combination of longing, nostalgia, and yearning for a home that you cannot return to, no longer exists, or *maybe never was* [italics mine]. It can also include grief or sadness for whom (or what) you have lost, losses that make the home you encounter today not the same as the one you remember.

The reason this constraint includes making a decision is to focus your mind concretely on what is happening to you (or your character) in the present, as this example does. That way you avoid this exercise merely rendering a flat description of a house, or other dwelling. Keep in mind that in any exercise, *putting your character or characters in motion* is always a good idea for generating usable material.

4.

A One-Sided Telephone Conversation

In this excerpt of a play by David Mamet, *The Museum of Science and Industry Story*, a young man, Albert, is at the named museum (located in Chicago) as closing hours are announced.

> (ALBERT is seated at a phone, has dialed, and listens
>   to ringing.)
> ALBERT: Hello? Where are you?
> Albert.
> Albert Litko
> (As ALBERT talks, we see the lights, section by section,
>   being extinguished in the museum.)
> At the Museum.
> Waiting for you.

It turns out Albert has been stood up. He asks the unnamed person (whose gender isn't even revealed) What are you doing tonight? What are you doing tomorrow night? I'm not hurt, he insists, after being shot down again and again as he tries to make a date with the unnamed person. although clearly he is. Through this one-sided conversation, we learn everything we need to about the characters, the situation, and the story. It's a fun read, the entire play. You should read it (or attend a performance, if that is possible).

Exercise

1. Write a section of one-sided dialogue in which you (or a character) are having a conversation on the phone but we can only hear your (or your character's) side of the conversation.

2. You can use narrative in the form of "stage directions," (the wind blew the paper out of his hand, the sun is going down) but that's all. Otherwise, everything has to be dialogue only.

3. Make sure the conversation fulfills the following two constraints:

   a. There is a disagreement between the character and the person on the other end of the phone about something (it can and should be a small thing).

   b. The other person (the one not heard) has the upper hand (more power) in the conversation.

Example

(In the recreational room of an old-age home, an elderly woman is on the phone)

"Thank you. But my birthday was yesterday, my son."

"Of course I am sure. I am not that senile." (gives a little laugh)

"No, dear. I am not confused. Yesterday, the fifth of March was my birthday."

"No, today is not the fifth of March."

(Checks the date printed in the newspaper that she has been reading. It reads March 6.)

"I am not implying that you are lying, my son. But thank you for calling anyway."

"No. I never . . . I did not mean to insult you . . . I am sorry I made you feel that way."

"Really, I am so sorry, my son."

"Hmmm. Perhaps."

"Yes. Perhaps. Maybe I am mixing up the dates. Today is, indeed, the fifth of March."

"Yes, I thank you, my son, for remembering."

(Puts the phone down with a sigh. "Today, March 6. . . ." the TV host says in the background)

—SARVESWARI SAIKRISHNA

Advice

The goal of this exercise is to practice dialogue that tells the reader everything about situation and character without spelling it out. As a general rule, facts don't belong in dialogue. It sounds too artificial that way. "You know the doctor told you that you had to cut out meat because of the results of your cholesterol blood test" would never fly in dialogue, for example.

If you do have facts that can't be adequately implied in a natural way, put them in narrative (just tell the reader directly).

Another point to keep in mind: a scene like this (an event or inter-action that starts and ends in a specific, defined place and time) should move a piece forward, both in terms of plot (what happens) and sub-text (what it means).

In this example, an argument over the date exposes a power play between this mother and son. In effect, the son is gaslighting his mother—trying to convince her she is wrong about something she is very sure of. That he pulls out all the stops and acts hurt because she won't agree with him tells us a lot about his personality—and his relationship with his mother. That she gives in, and admits in effect that she is not completely compos mentis tells us a lot about her—that she will deny reality to keep peace with her son, who seems like a bit of a bully. There is a lot packed into these few words of dialogue. See if you can do the same.

5.

Aubade

An aubade is a morning love song (as opposed to a serenade, which is an ode to the evening). Traditionally, it is a song or poem about lovers separating at dawn. It has also been defined as a song "welcoming or lamenting the arrival of the dawn," according to the Poetry Foundation.

"Good morning to what's left and what has gone," W. S. Di Piero begins his poem "Aubade" as he talks about saying goodbye to the dark things of modern life, "my mood, gunfights," and "our murderous American sunshine." What he wants from the coming days, he says, "grace and mercy around us, plainer talk."

It is actually more difficult to write about positive than negative things, because there's always the trap of easy sentimentality to fall into when writing about lighter or happier emotions; there are too many clichés within easy reach. And we must be careful to avoid all clichés—of language, of character, of situation. Read Di Piero's lovely "Aubade" and see how he avoids all these potential pitfalls.

> *Good morning to what's left and what has gone.*
> *No more of my dense cries and heavy songs*
> *about time's hardships, my mood, gunfights in schools,*
> *our murderous American sunshine.*
> *I want a looser grip, a sweeter lightness*
> *and grace and mercy around us, plainer talk*
>
> *while my neighborhood's wild parrots squawk*
> *and flash their smart immigrant finery*
> *and acute green wings over treetops and roofs,*
> *and Jimmy starts his Tuesday picking through*

trash bins, fifteen years now, set your watch.
Buongiorno, too, you kestrel in the blue,

ignorant of tech genius and real estate.
It's a happy day to begin happy days
to come. My friends won't have to remind me
to say thank you, excuse me, please, how nice.
The glory of the casual and destined,
last month's blue moon, the orbed orange shade

of last week's eclipse. Good morning in
the afternoon to the cranked-up cockatoo
outside my café, on my neighbor's shoulder,
my constant strangers, each day at 4 P.M.
I love morning's unmenacing purpled beauty,
its silvered extremities, how it tamps beginnings

but cheers us through sunrise's slow ascending
flannel blue. Say this, say that, this fair hour
we want to feel as hope, as I write now
past midnight: I'm not waiting for day but know
it's here, a California sun rising on
our Americas, on schoolkids, gun nuts, nomads,

and megachurch and gospel choirs that sing
to heal the hearts of shopkeepers and cops,
poets, snowplow drivers, unionists.
I shout morning blessings on them, O world
of chronic pain and tenderness. Dear day,
protect me and our common. Sponsor us.

Exercise

1. Write an aubade in either poetry or prose—your choice.
2. Use any definition of aubade that you like.

3. Constraints: make sure to include the following two
elements:
   a. You are saying good morning to what has gone.
   b. You are also welcoming what is coming in the
   day. Be specific! Avoid abstractions, and, as
   always, keep things grounded in sensory images.

Example

Lockdown.
Before the goldfinches
in high nests tucked on hawthorn branches, awake,
shaking tiny petals to the ground, the warmest snow.
I stand in my stocking feet breathing in the stone's cold.
Descend from sleep-soaked chambers searching for
   answers to questions no one knows
Before the new reality comes tumbling down, and we
   learn what we should not.
I am listening to other news.
The tiny smooth buds have unfurled from the fig trees
   overnight.
Almond flowers have turned to fuzzy green fists holding
   fruit.
The snail moves across the moss wall in the dark, leaving
   a slippery shadow, taking his home with him.
Defying orders.

Advice

Spring in 2020 after COVID-19 hit was one in which everything was
on hold. People around the world were stuck at home, locked down
and fearful, and the daily news seemed apocalyptic at times. But for
this very reason, the flora and fauna were thriving—and nature, as
the poem notes—was defying the strict lockdown orders that the rest
of us were under.

See how this writer avoids sentimentality by the surprise of the images she chooses, and the language she evokes. "Stocking feet breathing" and "Sleep-soaked chambers" use personalization to bring the scene alive and give it movement. And the last line, "defying orders," reminds us of the physical restrictions that were imposed on most of the world in 2020.

6.

Connecting the Dots

This is a reworking of an improvisational theatre exercise used for many years by the Second City comedy troupe in Chicago. It can be done multiple times, using different paired words, either the ones I've suggested or ones you create yourself. The important (and fun) part is that the words have to pull the writer in two different emotional directions, yet the piece has to come together at the end.

Exercise

1. Start by writing a sentence containing the first of the paired words you choose from the list below. Note that it is a noun, and singular, although you can make it plural if that works for you. As always, you can write about yourself, or about a fictional character.
2. Do a free write of 500–1,000 words. You must end with a sentence containing the second of the paired words in a way that makes both logical and emotional sense. That is, as you write your way from one word, you have to strive to somehow find a connection to the next word, and earn it through associating images, thoughts, and feelings.
3. Write about anything that comes to mind, as long as you follow the constraints.

    Mother (or father)/comic
    Car/sweet
    Boss/lifelike

Cat (or dog)/career
Shoes/deadly
Sister (or brother)/light
Accident/reflection
Vacation/evolve

Example

Shoes/deadly

I always lose my **shoes**. Usually they're under the bed or in a closet somewhere in the house. In good weather, I find them outdoors, under the magnolia tree or to the side of the clothesline—the same line my mother hung my baby clothes from. Now that I'm back home, it's easier to find them. There are the usual spots. While I was away—at university, at work in the city, that was another story. I'd slip them off in the taxi and forget them. I'd visit a friend in the same apartment block and leave them there, walking back down the hall to my apartment in my socks. The problem is my feet, they're too big and bony. It's hard to find comfortable shoes, so I always take them off at the first opportunity. My mother had the same problem when young. Then, on top of that, her big toe began growing in the wrong direction when she was in her sixties, about the age I am now. On her left foot. It headed right and curved like a scimitar. Like it was attempting to hitch a ride. She endured it for years as it slowly grew more and more deformed. She had to eventually buy two pairs of shoes, in different sizes, one for her normal, right, foot, and one for her increasingly grotesque left one. Since her regular shoe size was a women's 11, it was difficult. She had to mail order size-13 shoes from special paper catalogs (this was before the Internet, of course). Finally, in her seventies, she broke down and went to a doctor, a podiatrist. I was away at the time, so I don't know how he worked his magic, but he operated on her foot and somehow managed to tame the wild toe. The next time I came home for a visit, it looked perfectly normal. I couldn't even see where it had been surgically sliced and put back together.

I am hoping that this doesn't happen to me. I am sensitive about my feet anyway, as large and knobby and awkward as they are. You would think this would cause me to keep my shoes on, but no, I still take them off at every opportunity. Anyway, it doesn't matter much, now. Here I am, my career over before I was ready for it to be, pushed out because my seniority made me too costly for the young men and women in accounting, back in the old house, which I never sold, despite the entreaties of the realtors in town. As old and dilapidated as the house is, the land on which it sits is extraordinarily valuable. But I won't sell. No.

My neighbors are all young, seemingly bitterly determined to succeed in this hard, hard world. They are not around during the day. Their children are shunted off to daycare, or to school, and the parents to work, and so the streets are dead while the sun shines. These streets, which when I was young were filled with children on bikes, children with balls, children running from whoever was designated "It." Now everything is silent and I look forward to 5:00 when the nannies drop the children back home, and the moms and dads drive up and the lights go on, and there is some noise, the clatter of pots and pans, and the calling of children to bath and bed. I then sit on the couch reading as the clock ticks—that **deadly** sound— until it chimes midnight and sends me to bed, shoeless always as I climb the stairs.

Advice

The trick in this exercise is to always be pushing to find the next sentence that will move you incrementally from the first toward the final word. You can't do it too suddenly; that would miss the point of the exercise. But to gradually shift the subject, logically, rationally, evocatively, to something that can include the final word. Bear in mind poet Richard Hugo's advice of what to do when writing a poem: when you run out of things to say, move on. Make the subject of the next sentence different from the current sentence. It will always belong because, "in the world of your imagination, the next thing always belongs." That's because it comes from your particular and very individual imagination and subconscious.

One way to do this exercise well is to figure out the general tone you are aiming for. Obviously, with *deadly* as the target adjective, the mood of this example exercise would be dark. But choose a pair with a lighter target word, and you would have to keep the tone brighter, more optimistic, funny, even, as you work your way toward it. You can make up your own pairs of words to do this exercise. The trick to that is to pick two words with no discernible association between them, the first one always being a noun. It's harder to do than it sounds. But give it a try.

7.

Difficult Communications

In fiction (or nonfiction, for that matter), we sometimes want to portray difficult conversations between characters. Difficult either because of the subject matter or because of a complicated relationship. The challenge with dialogue is that subtext is so important: what's not said usually matters more than what is. People are nervous, they skirt around the point, they dissemble, they might even lie.

And here are four points to remember every time you write a line of dialogue:

1. Dialogue is (mostly) not for conveying facts.
2. Gesture is a part of dialogue.
3. Silence is a part of dialogue (a non-response is a response).
4. Dialogue is what your characters *do* to each other.

In this exercise, you are going to write a scene where communication is difficult, yet something of importance must be conveyed.

Exercise

1. Write a brief scene in which you are (or your character is) trying to urgently convey something very important to someone you/they are close to.
2. This conversation takes place in an extremely crowded, busy environment. The other person is having difficulty understanding what is being communicated because of distraction.
3. Describe the environment as well as render the con-

versation (in dialogue) and show how the tension of being interrupted and unheard affects you (or your character) physically, verbally, and emotionally.

Example

The smell of chlorine burnt Luca's nostrils. High-pitched screams of excitement came in never-ending waves. Lukewarm water splashed his feet. He could see Chloe floating in a large red innertube, her dark hair slick, laughing as the water rocked her. He didn't know how she found comfort in a pool of screaming children. When he was off the clock he didn't want to be anywhere near the water or even think about anyone too young to vote. But not Chloe. The second her break started, she'd go from the lifeguard stand to the pool, as if the community center didn't provide them with a break room. She somehow managed to find joy in things, and Luca really admired that. He didn't want to dim that joy.

"Chloe!" Luca called out, but his voice was drowned out by cackling tween girls running behind him. He fought the urge to reprimand them about the no-running rule, reminding himself that he was also on break. He moved around the pool's edge in an attempt to get closer to her. He positioned himself at the western corner of the pool; she was drifting in that direction. But at the last minute a trio of soccer moms attempting to swim laps redirected her course. She didn't even seem to notice the jostling. "Hey, Chloe!" he called again. Her sapphire eyes finally opened. She looked around at the bodies convulsing in the water before she found him.

"Oh, hey," she called. "Is our break over already?" Her face changed from smiling to concern.

"No!" he called back. "You got a phone call!"

The lifeguard on duty, finally noticing the running girls, blew her whistle in three repetitive bursts.

"You have to make a phone call?" she asked as a group of kids in a chicken fight positioned themselves between their line of sight.

"No," he said as one of the boys on his friend's shoulders yanked his opponent off another pair of shoulders, producing a loud splash. Chloe laughed as she covered her face.

"Someone called for you!"

"For me?" she didn't seem to understand. "Who was it?"

"They didn't say! They just left a message!" he yelled over the squealing. He bit at his lower lip. "Maybe we should talk inside!"

"Huh?" she called, but finally slipped herself off her floatation. She waded toward him, looking hopeful. He went to repeat himself but was cut off before the first word left his mouth by a boy screaming "Cannonball!!!" as he ran at the pool, hurling his body into the water and producing an eruption of water.

"Chloe! Get out of the pool!" Luca yelled, louder than he had anticipated. He could feel his frustration pooling in his face. Nearby faces looked at them, maybe concerned, maybe afraid.

"What did I do?" she asked, getting to the pool's edge, looking like an injured puppy.

"Nothing." He sighed, thankful that she was close enough that he could speak at a normal volume. He tried to remove his irritation from his face. "It's just—"

The sound of laughter and feet slapping on the pavement rang in his ears, immediately followed by the feeling of a tiny body ramming into his back. Before he could fight it, he went over into the pool. World turned upside down. Head submerged in water. Body weightless, embraced by the aquatic chill. Mouth and lung searching for air but sucking up something else entirely. His employee polo shirt floating around him like it was trying to escape. He took his arms, scooping at the water around him, kicking with his legs. He forced himself up to the water's surface. Coughing and gasping.

He was face-to-face with Chloe, who was laughing. "Now you're in the pool? I thought you wanted me out."

"It's your mom," he said, still working to keep himself afloat. "There's been an accident," he said.

—TreVaughn Malik Roach-Carter

Advice

The reason this constraint works is that it puts additional stress on what is already a tenuous situation: someone is attempting to communicate something of importance, and the environment gets in the way. This brings out aspects of personality and character that would otherwise go unrevealed. We learn more about Chloe and the narrator than if they'd tried to have this conversation under different, more normal, circumstances.

Note that we're never told exactly what either Chloe or the narrator is feeling. Everything is conveyed through dialogue, gesture, and imagery. This isn't to say that you couldn't use narrative—telling—to be more direct about what the characters are thinking and feeling. But this writer chooses not to.

8.

Pushing Readers into a Particular Emotional Space

"I was on a bus to Washington, D.C.," Tobias Wolff wrote once, to illustrate what short-short fiction was. He did this, cleverly enough, by writing a short-short story as the explanation. "Two days I'd been traveling, and I was tired, tired, tired," he wrote. "The woman sitting next to me, a German with a ticket good for anywhere, never stopped yakking."

Wolff goes on to describe a "moment" where he looks out the bus window and observes a couple with a baby:

> There is something between them, something in the instant itself, that makes me sit up and stare. What is it, what's going on here? Why can't I ever forget them?

"Tell me, for God's sake," Wolff entreats, "but make it snappy—I'm tired, and the bus is picking up speed and the lunatic beside me is getting ready to say something."

What Wolff is doing is describing what to him was an unforgettable image. Keep in mind that in writing, an "image" is something very specific: it is a person, place, or thing that can be rendered concretely with one or more of the senses. And so when creating an image, don't limit yourself to visual descriptions only. Try to include other senses: smell, touch, taste, and hearing.

Exercise

1. Do a quick scan of your mind (don't try too hard). Choose one of the many images that will naturally (and probably illogically) present themselves to you at this particular moment in time. It can be a memory of your mother putting a Band-Aid on your knee when you were small or a quick recollection of how a BMW cut you off on the expressway this morning on your way to school or work.

2. Describe the person, place, thing, or event in detail. Be concrete. And here are a series of constraints in the form of don'ts.
   a. Don't tell us how it makes you "feel."
   b. But don't try to be "objective," either, in your description—in fact, be as subjective, and honest, as hell. (Your mother's hands were bony and cruel and caused pain as they applied the band-aid. The BMW driver was a beautiful, unconcerned redheaded man.)
   c. Don't worry about it being interesting. Really. I can't stress that enough. Just describe the image as best you can.
   d. And, especially, don't try to interpret the image, or explain or analyze it. Just place your reader there.

What you're trying to do is to render the image in your mind on the page to evoke emotion in your reader. But you don't want to come out and tell the reader what the emotion is. And it doesn't have to be a static image—as with Tobias Wolff's piece above, it can be a "moving image"—an event in which you encounter, interact with, and even speak to other characters.

Example

There was that girl on the train. This was maybe twelve months ago. I was on my way to the second week of my sixth month of my first job after college, a horror of drudgery, where I spent eight hours a day writing clickbait for a dubious website. One weird trick to losing all that weight! Hollywood stars as you've never seen them before! I was living with my parents in the burbs, taking the train to the city every day. Then there was that moment that illuminated everything. I was sitting in my usual seat on the train, scrolling through social media posts on my phone, seeing my friends from college tweeting from Wall Street, or Silicon Valley, or Tibet, crowing about their achievements, their incredibly full and exciting lives. Just that morning, my mom had patted me on the shoulder as she put a plate of eggs in front of me. Not the way we thought things would play out, she'd said, and her face was sorrowful. I was trying to get that image out of my mind when it happened. We were stopped at the last station before entering the city proper. The surrounding houses and apartment buildings were already taking on the crowded, grimy look of downtown, the lawns had already shrunk, the litter on the streets and sidewalks more visible. A bunch of suits got on. And then her. She was dark, maybe of East Asian, or perhaps Arabian, descent. By dark I mean dark. Black skin, black hair, black eyes that showed nothing as she walked into the car and sat down in the seat facing me. Arrogant? Shy? It was hard to tell. She looked natural, not painted like those girls that apply makeup with a shovel. Her lashes! Her lips! The whiteness of her teeth as she yawned before taking out her phone and studying it! I had never seen such beauty. There was a tiny scar on her chin, a thin white line in sharp contrast to her dark skin. It only accented her beauty. The train jerked, and her right knee bumped my left one. I felt as though I'd been shocked by an electric current. Sorry, I mumbled, hoping she would say something so I could hear her voice, but she only nodded somberly. When the train arrived at its destination, she got up first and headed toward the exit. I sat in my seat and watched her out the window as she walked toward the terminal. Since that day I've held my breath every time we make that particular stop, but she never got on again.

Advice

This exercise forces you to identify what is on your mind now. From your current location. The goal is to render it honestly and completely, but without interpretation or telling what it means. If you do it well, you will identify something that is, for whatever reason, emotionally urgent, and get it on the page using only concrete imagery. The hope is that it will force you to avoid abstractions and unnecessary explanations when you write.

What do I mean by "location"? As I explained in Section 1, it's a word sociologists use to sum up everything that happened to get an individual (or a group of people) to a particular place, at a particular time. For you, it would be everything that happened to you from birth to this exact moment, including what happened in your childhood, your teenage years, what you had for breakfast, and whether your partner was kind to you when you woke up this morning. Your location. The physical and emotional space you inhabit at this very minute. When I asked you to give me an image from right now, it would reflect your exact location in time, in place, in the universe.

The nice thing about writing from your location is that it's all yours. No one else inhabits this space. They couldn't possibly—it belongs to you. And that's what writing is all about—communicating what the world looks like from your very individual, particular place on the planet.

9.

Losing Your Senses

This is an exercise in imagery. Being able to render things of this world precisely, using as many of the senses as you can, is a requirement for any type of creative writing: fiction, creative nonfiction, poetry (especially poetry!), and hybrid work.

Most of us, when we first start describing a person, place, or thing, use sight. That is, our descriptions are mostly visual. Even when we try to infuse different senses into a scene, or section of narrative, we mostly revert to visual descriptions as foundational to what is being described.

So I'm going to take the sense of sight away from you. You are going to write as though you don't have that sense. If you are vision-impaired, this exercise might be easier than for those of us who have taken sight for granted all our lives.

A word about metaphors: You will probably find yourself using a lot of metaphors and similes when doing this exercise. (Remember a metaphorical statement is a comparison of two unlike things.) It's virtually unavoidable. In Michael Ondaatje's poem "The Cinnamon Peeler's Wife," the narrator describes a loved one based on her scent, and he mostly uses metaphors to get across the sensual feelings he is trying to evoke.

If you decide to take this route (as many of you undoubtably will), be careful that your metaphors themselves do not use comparisons to visual objects or things. You will write this as if you have never seen any of the world.

NOTE: I am *not* asking for you to render a sight-impaired character as your narrator or subject. That is a different exercise altogether. Write a detailed description, but as if you had only four senses.

Exercise

1. Think of someone you love (or a character's beloved object).
2. Describe them in a way that makes us understand the depth of your affection.
3. Use any (and every) sense except sight.
4. See how far you can take this. Try to get 500 words out of this.

And, as in all exercises in imagery, as you are writing, do not worry about being boring! Describe the loved one so thoroughly that your readers will be in love with them, too.

By the way, this exercise can be done in all sorts of ways. Take out any of the so-called essential writing tools from your toolbox and attempt to write without them. It's a way of strengthening your weaker descriptive powers.

Example

When you cuddle up next to me like this I think back to how my mama would let me crawl into her bed at night when I couldn't sleep. I would lay my head on her shoulder, my cheek smushed against the soft and taut plain of her chest. I'd listen to the thump of her heartbeat dull as we'd both fall back asleep. So, when you told me you needed to be held tonight, I opened my arms and assumed the position so you could curl into me.

My love is muscle-memory, inherited from one generation to the next.

As I wait for sleep to take me under, I think of today, of the explosions as manhole covers shoot into the air due to air pressure from underground fires. Of how the apartment was filled with the buzz of electric wires and the blare of fire trucks. Before I could launch into my rant about how California is a hellscape—burning above and below the ground—you placed your thumb in between my brows and massaged my frustration away. Your warmth cooled me down.

Don't start, you said. And I didn't.

You have a certain tone about you when you're trying to keep me from going off the deep end or, sometimes, trying to pull me down with you. It's like molasses, or like the *rush rush rush* of water that poured from the busted pipes on our street. I have no option but to go in your direction. That's how we ended up here. Three months ago, in your sweet tone, you suggested we move to Long Beach. *Folks like us are meant to live by the water—Lesbos, Fire Island, San Francisco—it's only natural,* you said. So we moved . . . to all of this.

Despite it all, today, as we sat with the windows open, it was not the scent of burning asphalt, sewage, and a distant smokiness of another wildfire that caught my attention, but the smell of your Victoria's Secret perfume. The one that smells of strawberries and cheap rosé. The one we found in a Marshall's discount bin. The one you insist on still wearing despite being thirty-one because, as you say, *Life is about the little things* and smelling sickeningly sweet is one of your little things.

My life is about the way you pop your toes when you're anxious. It's about the way the comfortable hum of our silence drowned out the sounds of Long Beach's terrible infrastructure. It's about how the softness of your skin engulfs me. It's about how your drool is pooling on my collarbone and slipping to the back of my neck. And how it doesn't gross me out, but instead I look forward to it crusting over in our sleep so I can show you in the morning and feel your laughter explode like manhole covers.

—LONDON PINKNEY

Advice

Note the wonderful imagery that this writer was able to render without using visual cues. We had sounds, touches, and smells to evoke a wonderful sensory scene. We don't miss the images that come from sight because what is here is so rich. The writer could have added the sense of taste as well, but chose not to.

Doing this exercise can teach us an important lesson about how most of us are dependent on visual imagery—or metaphors based on visual things—and how that actually limits us in our descriptions. A whole new world opens up when we use all of our senses.

10.

An Errand

In this exercise we're working on the color of our language. We know that when we view the world through the point-of-view character—whether that's ourselves (nonfiction) a first-person persona (first-person narrator) or close third-person narrator—the world gets slanted. No one sees the same red ball. No one experiences the rude taxi driver in exactly the same way. An emotional state can influence a simple walk down the street and help us see magic in the ordinary, as Dylan Thomas shows us in this section from *Under Milk Wood*.

> Now behind the eyes and secrets of the dreamers in the streets rocked to sleep by the sea, see the titbits and topsy-turvies, bobs and buttontops, bags and bones, ash and rind and dandruff and nailparings, saliva and snowflakes and moulted feathers of dreams, the wrecks and sprats and shells and fishbones, whale-juice and moonshine and small salt fry dished up by the hidden sea.

Exercise

1. First, conjure up either a memory or a current pre-occupation that has a deep emotion attached to it. Anything at all—a recent breakup, a fight with your mother, falling in love. This preoccupation can be positive or negative. Joy, happiness, fear, anger, and so on. And as usual, this can be autobiographical or made up. Write this down (briefly).
2. Now, with that memory or preoccupation in mind, take an imaginative walk down a street. Make it a

populated and busy street—with people and things
going on. Most important, walk down a street with
an errand to complete. Anything—a trip to the
drugstore, grocery, or bakery . . .

3. Write down exactly what you see and what happens as you proceed on your errand. What people are
   doing, what's happening in the shops or playgrounds,
   and so forth. Don't worry about it being boring.
   But keep that memory or preoccupation in mind
   at all times. Don't be afraid to write down associative thoughts as you record what is happening in the
   street ("the man on the corner reminded her of her
   father when he was young, anxiously consulting his
   watch"). Above all, try not to be too direct. Try to
   slant at the material.

4. Complete your errand. Try to render how you (or
   your character) feels upon this completion. Try to
   not tell us (not, "she felt relieved,") but show us ("her
   shoulders relaxed and she proceeded to her car at a
   slower pace").

Example

It is my wedding anniversary, but when I think of that day ten years
ago today, I think of my sister Nara, not my wife. At the reception,
Nara found me on the dance floor and we threw our hands up and
legs out in a delayed mirroring of the other, a game we'd played when
we were kids in Nairobi. She leaned close to my ear, and I buried my
face in her coarse reddish hair, hugging her close.

Married! she said. I love you, brother.

Even though the music was loud, I heard her.

I am rushing to the post office before it closes to pick up my wife's
anniversary gift: an expensive blender she's wanted for years. I park
the sedan and turn to the kids in the back.

I'll just be a minute, guys. I just have to get Mommy's present.

This is the closest spot. Do not tell your mom. I smile. You guys will be fine here. Read to Samira, Ri. Samira and Riad nod without looking up, heads already together over a book.

I close the car door, engaging the childproof lock after opening the front window a sliver. I wave at them, pointing my thumb at the white building with the large wide steps ahead. Starbucks cups and discarded mail overflow the trash bin in front. An American flag flaps above the building, making a loud snapping sound. I pull up my coat collar against the wind.

My wife would be furious with me for leaving the kids in the car. I take the steps up to the post office doors two at a time. Looking back, I see their frizzy dark heads close in the backseat, curly strands floating upwards together like black-seeded dandelions in the sunlight.

Nara's halo of hair had been the same. We used to joke she was adopted, her lighter skin and reddish ringlets compared to my dark looks and black frizz. She has been gone for five years, and I still dream about her. I slip through the revolving door into the marble lobby, cavernous and nearly empty, save a silver-haired woman standing in line, leaning on a metal frame with wheels.

I file in behind her. She is holding a largish box. It has the name Genevieve Jones and an address in Chicago scrawled in sloping ballpoint pen marks on the label. Every generation has different handwriting, a language within language.

Can I hold this for you, is it heavy?

I indicate the box, and she smiles, passing it to me.

Thank you, it's for my sister. The woman says. She shifts her weight heavily against the cart and laughs revealing beautiful teeth.

We're turning ninety-five next week.

Twins? I ask.

Yes. The woman says.

I take the box to the window for the elderly woman, then return to the line to wait my turn.

When I return to the car with the box my kids are laughing together, the way only siblings do.

Advice

A man is picking up an anniversary present for his wife, but he is pre-occupied by nostalgic thoughts of his dead sister. He is not thinking about the pleasure his wife will get from the present but about her anger should she know he left the kids alone in the car, and about a time of intimacy with his sibling.

In this state, he encounters the old woman in the post office and finds out she is a twin who misses her sister. Because he was preoccupied, that's the only thing he tunes in with the old woman, rather than anything else he could have focused on, like what's in the parcel, or the place it is going to. Then when he comes back to the car, his children are close together.

Note that everything is reminding him of his sister on this day, it affects everything he sees or thinks. It is his particular filter at this particular time. That's why a walk down a street on one day can be totally different from a walk down that street on a different day. It's all about your (or your character's) location. I can't emphasize that enough.

11.

Worry

This is another exercise in imagery (you really can't do too many of them) in which you explore the different aspects of a landscape that come out based upon different moods of your character.

In her poem "I Worried," Mary Oliver creates a list of things she was worried about in the world. Notice how she ends her poem—on a different note altogether.

I WORRIED
BY MARY OLIVER

I worried a lot. Will the garden grow, will the rivers
flow in the right direction, will the earth turn
as it was taught, and if not how shall
I correct it?

Was I right, was I wrong, will I be forgiven,
can I do better?

Will I ever be able to sing, even the sparrows
can do it and I am, well,
hopeless.

Is my eyesight fading or am I just imagining it,
am I going to get rheumatism,
lockjaw, dementia?

Finally I saw that worrying had come to nothing.
And gave it up. And took my old body

and went out into the morning,
and sang.

What we (or our characters) worry about reveals tons. Sometimes worries are realistic (my rent is due and I don't have the cash), sometimes less so (I live in California and we could have a major earthquake today). How we perceive the world around us with our senses (always) can change dramatically based on what we are worrying about.

Exercise

1. Write down five to ten small things that your character worries about. Not abstractions like "death," but concrete things like "my knee cracks when I stand up" or "I need to lose ten pounds," or "the mortgage is due, and I don't have the money."
2. Write a short descriptive piece of that character walking down the street while worrying about some (it doesn't have to be all) of these things. What do you/they do? What do they say? What do they see?
3. Next, imagine that all worries have been magically lifted. Do a second piece, describing yourself (or your character) walking down the same street. What's different about what they see, do, or say?

Example

Five Small Worries

☐ What are we going to do with all of these persimmons?
☐ If I tear down the shed I built for the goat, will the cow miss scratching her ears on it?
☐ Should I wear my new boots at risk of scuffing them?
☐ Even if I'm technically not grinding my teeth, am I still clenching my jaw too much?

☐ I was eating well but then the holidays happened and now more holidays are going to happen. Each decision seems reasonable but with so many holidays what am I supposed to do?

River Walk—Worried

Jacob Manus stepped carefully over uneven bricks beside the river that ran through his adopted West Texas town. His boots had cost six hundred US dollars and the idea of importing them from England only to scuff them on poorly kilned American brick generated a sour taste on his tongue.

As he reached the edge of the bumpy bit and stepped onto flat concrete, he noted that he ought to feel more comfortable spending money. He could afford a cobbler.

He gazed up from his boots. The view down the river afforded a simple metal bridge with a low arch, an open stretch of brown water, and a blue-pink evening sky. Restaurants that served the same thawed patties on the same thin bread, and pubs that served the same two flavors of American pilsner dotted either side of the river walk.

It had been a year but Jacob still didn't feel like he lived here. He was familiar with his surroundings, and he had found that butcher who sold blood sausage, but there was something about the dry air and the way people talked to each other here that made him sick.

River Walk—Unworried

Jacob Manus stepped across a patch of broken bricks and onto the flat concrete path that led along the river. The river was pretty, the sunset in the sky arresting, and the scene of the bridge over the water caused him to pause and stand in place.

It was a strange thing, being British in this old American town. He still dressed like it could rain at any second, but it had taken surprisingly little time for him to adjust to enjoying his surroundings. When

Londoners came to visit, he could still crack jokes with them—but his heart truly seemed to warm simply from walking down the street these days. It was very un-British.

He walked on. There were lights strung along the path, with small-linked chains hanging between them. He stepped closer to examine the function of the chains but found there was none. The chains were simply for decoration. Delightful.

Past the bridge, he came to the old railway and stepped up to walk from plank to plank, pleased by how nimble he was in his new boots.

There was a group of teens at the end of the gangway. He trusted them, for no reason at all. Free of worry, he saw the best in them: giggling about something that surely was funny, their big ears and cheeks flushed like ripening fruits.

—JOHN DIDDAY

Advice

Bouncing thoughts off your (or your character's) environment is a way to show emotion without flat-out telling your readers what your character is feeling. This is a time-honored exercise that demonstrates how things get infected with emotions (in this case, worry), or, alternatively, how a lack of worry can imbue surrounding objects and people with a warmer light—and even influence events (plot).

In the first version of this piece, the writer makes sure that everything takes on a negative or even ominous tone—the narrator feels out of his depth, not at home. Yet in the second version, these objects do not carry the same emotional weight and are even viewed warmly, with affection. This is a great example of how, when trying to evoke emotions in a character, you should try to concentrate on physical things whenever possible. As William Carlos Williams said, "No ideas but in things."

12.

Painful Beauty

In her celebrated poem "Tulips," Sylvia Plath writes about being in the hospital and receiving a bouquet of tulips as a gift. Despite the fact that this would ordinarily be a pleasurable experience, Plath writes of experiencing pain "The tulips are too red . . . they hurt me." She uses metaphor, compares them to an "awful baby," and says they are a "dozen red sinkers around her neck."

This works well because of the surprising nature of it. It goes against our expectations, of flowers being beautiful and a source of joy, especially when given as a gift. This working against expectations is always a good thing to do, in particular when a twist like this reveals something about a situation or a character that might otherwise stay hidden.

Exercise

1. Write a brief piece in which your character encounters something (or someone) remarkably beautiful yet which causes acute anguish.
2. Describe the beautiful object or person in detail.
3. Make sure to write how the anguish is manifested in concrete physical detail. (What does your character perceive with their five senses as a result of encountering this beautiful person or thing? What associations to other times, other things, or other people do they have?)
4. For the purposes of this exercise, try really hard not to tell us how your character feels. "She felt bad, she felt sad". . . No. Just put everything into the images.

HINT: When dealing with situations of intense emotion, sometimes you want to underplay rather than overplay it. So use language judiciously.

Example

On nights like this, nights when you can't sleep, you slip away to the pier. As you walk out to the end you can feel it sway beneath you, but this is not concerning. The churning black ocean. The wind pushing against you. You've learned how to take all this motion for rocking and let it soothe you. Instability is something you learned how to live within once your pupa left, or rather, once you left him.

You can only visit your pupa in memory. One of your favorites from the place in Trelawny is the day your pupa told you the elders thought your muma was a vessel for a god: Oya—meaning *she tears*. Meaning you're some kind of Jamaican Hercules, born to a human and a god. Your muma was outside on the patio hanging clothes on a line. From outside the window you can see a billowing pink cloth and her thin arms.

You remember your pupa whispering this revelation to you and you can still feel his breath curve around your ear. Then louder, your pupa said, *Your mutha's a god*. Through the window, she laughed and said, *Mi dat that mi*. She ran into the living room and hopped onto your father's back. She began to sing "When the Lights Are Low" by the Paragons. Her voice was bright and filled the room. Even that young, you could tell she didn't sing for the sake of singing. She loved the audience of you and your pupa. *What happened to that woman who loved to be seen by you?* As she sang, she nuzzled her head into your father's and stroked your cheek with the back of her hand. The memory ends before she can get to the chorus.

You thought you'd never love your muma again for ruining this and the infinite happy moments your family could have had. She pulled you away from all that joy for what—to be lonely? For private schools and immigration court dates? For ESL classes even though you fucking knew how to speak English? Belt whooping? To be

picked up late from the Boys & Girls Club? Everywhere and everything reminded you that you are different and you must contort yourself, get a piece of paper, remember a song, in order to be better. The
present you wasn't enough. That in the future, somewhere down the
line, if you worked hard enough, you could be accepted. You just
have to be patient. These were your early lessons.

And your teenhood——times filled with bickering, feeling unloved,
feeling the growing pains of your father being a continent away. It
was hard to love her until you remembered what your pupa said. And
it may be hoodoo shit, but hey, you realized if your mother really is
a vessel for Oya you couldn't be mad at her. Oya. Goddess of storm.
After years of trying to wade in your muma's waters you saw that she
is a roaring ocean stitched up with skin. Now are you gonna blame
an ocean for drowning you, for doing what they do? You learned how
to accept who she is and what she fabled herself into: your mother.
Whose attributes she had no road map for.

You never felt like you could share this with your muma. Not
then, or now. You can never tell her how you view her or how lonely
you get; you can let yourself feel all of this. You're not closed off out
of malice but because you can't trust her with yourself. You are her
audience. Her son. The shore to her ocean. You've learned how to
love her from that place, how to be happy when she reaches out to
you. But on nights like this, you struggle.

—LONDON PINKNEY

Advice

This beautiful but painful memory of growing up with an elusive and
seemingly self-involved and impulsive mother is grounded in the concrete. Again and again I quote William Carlos Williams: "No ideas
but in things."

13.

Try to Praise the Mutilated World

In his poem "Try to Praise the Mutilated World," Adam Zagajewski describes a world that is beautiful but imperfect. "Remember June's long days," he says, and describes wild strawberries and wine, but also "the abandoned homesteads of exiles" as he attempts to be honest about what the world is really like despite the beauty he finds in it.

Trying to capture contradictions is the essence of good writing. Things are generally neither all good nor all bad but something in the middle. Still, we can have mixed feelings (guilt? shame?) like Zagajewski does about seeing beauty in a world in which there is so much suffering.

Exercise

1. Think of a scene (a particular place at a particular time) where the world was beautiful to you (or your character).
2. Think of a way that, despite its beauty, it was deeply flawed.
3. Write a short piece (or poem) that praises the particular place at a particular time while acknowledging the ways it has been mutilated. Help us feel the beauty as well as the shock of the moment of realization of what within the world is terribly wrong.

Example

From where I am standing, still in the undergrowth but not in the jungle proper, I watch iridescent eruptions, as if the clouds in the sky themselves have caught fire, blooming along the seam where the land meets the sky.

The radio had said the flamethrowing would start this morning, at 0600 hours across the jungle camps of Haiphong. Our infantry moved two miles south last night in order to clear the village of allies. Napalm—like a rubber-cement balm that explodes and sticks to everything it touches—is now igniting it.

I had never seen napalm before, and all night long I kept thinking of those capsules that come as gifts in cereal boxes. The ones you put in a cup of water, that explode open before your eyes? But those wither and fade. These blossoms I will never forget.

I have to close my eyes to the glare, and they remain, shimmering and indelible behind my eyelids.

The plumes of smoke keep pulsating, expanding and contracting gently like a jellyfish. The wind must be picking up from the water to the east, causing the puffed plumes to lengthen into a flaming field of poppies along the horizon.

Even decades later, when I close my eyes I return here over and over. Not the charred bodies, the blackened hell landscape, but the beauty of it.

Advice

We are always wanting to write in unsentimental ways about contrasts in the world, especially between beauty and its opposite. And some would even argue that everything beautiful has a dark side to it, a complexity. For every flower in a vase, there's a severed stem of a plant in the ground.

In this piece, the writer is talking about something truly horrible— the U.S. bombing of North Vietnam with napalm during the Vietnam War in the 1970s. He decides to remember it as beautiful (or so he tells us), but we have doubts because of the way he has described the experience. We see how it haunts him in all its complexity.

14.

Today, Five Years Hence

The Canadian writer Alice Munro does a lot of time traveling in her stories, moving from present day to flashbacks, to flashbacks within flashbacks, to glimpses of the future.

Juxtaposing these things helps bring perspective, and makes readers understand the repercussions of decisions a character has made, choices to do or not do things. Jumping backward or forward in time can add richness and complexity to a poem or story as well as reveal character.

Exercise

1. Think of something that has been bothering you (or a character) recently. Try to pick something small, or at least something that has been worrying you or your character that's out of proportion given the grand scheme of life.

2. Write a paragraph describing it in detail. Don't try to explain it. Just describe the thing you are worrying about. You shouldn't care if it is interesting to someone else, but provide enough details so readers can enter into the worry with you.

3. Now do the same for five years into the future from your original scene. What will you be doing? What will you be thinking? Will the worry still preoccupy you? Or will it seem quaint in retrospect? Tell us. How did it resolve itself (if it did)?

Example

When the old man behind him tells the cashier that he has forgotten his wallet, Max keeps on bagging his groceries: three boxes of Nature's Path Corn Flakes, twelve packages of Peanut M&M's, three bags of Kettle potato chips, organic with sea salt, a bunch of bananas, almond milk. He feels the curve of a banana against his palm as he hears the teenage clerk and the old man in conversation. The old man says how easy it is these days to forget the wallet when you have to remember the mask, and the house keys, and to bring your own bags. Once he forgot to change to his outdoor shoes, went out in his slippers, he says, laughing.

Later Max tells himself he was distracted by the din of people in line arguing about the latest COVID guidelines, the tempting smell of grinding coffee beans from the coffee station in the corner, the commotion over at the Amazon return station when someone's return code would not load on their phone. He was not thinking about the old man; he was thinking he should buy more vegetables; since the pandemic he's overloaded on candy, had cereal for dinner, chips afterward, while streaming old TV shows. Some mornings, he's surprised to wake up on the couch.

The old man continues the conversation as if he is chatting with a friend, extending the time he stands there, while the clerk explains she can't do anything. No, she can't hold the groceries for later pickup. It's the rules. Her boss would fire her. Her young voice has a tone, something like disgust, or pity. The man won't stop chatting; it's harder since my grandson came to live with me, he says.

Max hasn't seen the child until then. A small, doe-eyed boy, barely tall enough to see over the counter, stares hungrily at his packages of candy. The boy's Star Wars shirt has a big hole in the shoulder and he nervously pulls at the frayed cloth. As Max picks up his two bags, hearing a crunch sound and angry at himself for absently putting the chips under the milk carton, he smells something sour coming from the old man. Secondhand clothes, unwashed for a while?

On the drive home in his red Tesla SUV, he beats himself up. Why didn't he offer to pay for the man's groceries? He could have. Easily. He would hardly notice another charge on his credit card, which he paid in full every month. Why didn't he at least give the child a package of candy? Why wasn't he that man?

When he gets home, unpacking the candy, he sees the eyes of the boy. He sees the eyes of the boy when he turns on his big screen TV. He sees the eyes of the boy when he tries to sleep.

Five years later, in the hospital for heart surgery, counting backwards before the anesthetic kicks in, thinking about his life he sees the boy's begging eyes.

—JEANNE ALTHOUSE

Advice

Time gives perspective. In the long run, the meaning of the things that happen to us are viewed differently, through a different lens. This isn't to say that time heals all wounds—but it at least provides us with insight into those wounds.

A great exercise if you're stuck in your plot, or stymied as to how a character would react to a (fictional) event, try this time-traveling trick of Alice Munro's. What would your character say five years from now about this event? How would they feel? What would stick in their memory about that event? Or, alternatively, show them five years previously, to show how their life was "preparing" them for this event. You'll get lots of interesting insight that can both advance your plot and help with characterization.

15.

The Visitor

In her charming poem "Visitor," Brenda Shaughnessy talks about having the "hope" of company and "making too much pie" in expectation. But the narrator isn't sure if the person she is hoping will come has even received the invitation. So there is a strong sense of suspense, and expectations that are not resolved because the emotion of joyful expectation is the very point of the poem.

In fiction, a sense of expectation before an event of dramatic importance can be portrayed in an almost magical state—your character is excited or frightened or nervous, exhilarated, perhaps having fantasies about how things will or won't play out. You can take a character—and a plot—far on expectations. Sometimes whole novels are based on a character's expectations and how they are resolved.

Exercise

1. Place yourself (or a character) in a space where you are alone, and lonely. Those are not synonymous, but in this case, you or your character specifically wish you were not alone.

2. Set a scene—a specific place at a specific time. Where are you? Why are you alone? How is your loneliness manifested in your world? (Are you pacing? Baking (as in Shaughnessy's poem)? Reading? Watching television? Walking on the beach? Driving a car?)

3. Now make yourself (or your character) invite a visitor to your space. You can call, write, email, text the invitation, whatever is your wont to do.

4. Have the character prepare for their visitor despite

not receiving an answer of whether the invitee will come. What does the character do, exactly? Try to manifest what they are feeling by depicting actions and things in the physical world.

5. IMPORTANT CONSTRAINT: Have the character do something that surprises themselves in preparation for the visitor who may or may not come (As in Shaughnessy's case, make too much pie). It is up to you as to whether the visitor shows up or not.

Example

Stop by later, if you want to. I hesitate, then press Send.

I would love to see you, I write, then reconsider and delete.

Several minutes go by, and my phone buzzes.

I will try. I want to see you, before I go back, Shanice's message says.

I put the phone back in my pocket. It is only 3:05 p.m., early, but it is already twilight.

I long for California's endless stretches of warm days, the eternal summer, the sun that lingers until 9 p.m.

The greenhouse is like being halfway home. It is always 70 degrees Fahrenheit, with low humidity to prevent mildew spores and aphids.

Picking up the clippers, I turn back to the rows of roses and continue pruning. Large clusters of snowflakes dissolve against the warm glass ceiling of the greenhouse. I watch as rivulets flow along the panes, clinging to the heat of the windows.

I put down the clippers and go into the bathroom, I don't have to pee. In the small mirror above the sink I inspect my face. Ten years is a long time to look at yourself in the same mirror, to prune the same roses, fertilize their soil, watch them grow with greater attention than I have my own children. It is too long a time to still miss California, and her.

Will I look different to her? I am sure I will. But in this mirror, I cannot tell.

I pull off my T-shirt and look at my upper body, still firm, but no longer young, the skin less tight under my armpits, a softness to the curve of my shoulders.

Back in the rows of the greenhouse, I turn out the lights so it is almost dark. I stand watching as the roses float like sea anemones in the fading light.

If she drives by, maybe she will think I have left and not come in.

I can see the dark veins of melted snow caught on the window, dividing and racing downward. I stand like that, until I see lights in the parking lot, and the sound of a car engine turning off.

Advice

Notice how anticipation builds a scene, shows an emotional progression. It is also a great creator of suspense, which is partial knowledge (by the reader as well as the character) that something of dramatic importance is about to happen.

In this particular example, the surprising thing the character does is to turn out the lights and pretend not to be home even though they desperately want to see Shanice. We're left with a sense of mystery, and insight into the conflicts plaguing this particular character about their current location—both physical and emotional—as well as their regrets and fears.

16.

Dark Gifts

In her poem "The Uses of Sorrow," Mary Oliver writes about being given a "box full of darkness" from someone she loved, and how long it took her before she realized how valuable it was.

This exercise plays on the fact that sometimes the people we love can bestow things on us—knowledge, memories, and yes, physical objects—that we'd rather not have, only to be grateful later in our lives.

THE USES OF SORROW
BY MARY OLIVER

(In my sleep I dreamed this poem)

Someone I loved once gave me
a box full of darkness.

It took me years to understand
that this, too, was a gift.

Exercise

1. Think of a character, or just use your own personal experience if you like.
2. Write a piece that illustrates a dark gift given to you or your character by someone you loved.
3. Try to write toward a sense of gratitude for the dark gift, if possible, and manifest that gratitude with the physical senses rather than just telling us "I felt grateful."

Example

The ringing started one morning in March on the train platform in Yonkers.

I was waiting for the F train. My voice lessons were at noon, and I used the train ride to warm up my vocal cords. My voice coach, Leon, told me it would help my performance anxiety to sit close to strangers and sing.

When I finally reached the practice studio, I was holding my head between my hands, shaking it from side to side.

Tinnitus, Leon said with a thin smile. You should be wearing earplugs. Go to the infirmary. But honestly? I have seen it before. There's nothing they can do.

In fact, the tinnitus was incurable, according to the doctors. A few weeks after it started, I was put on medical leave from Juilliard, and I never heard from Leon again. I am Jamaican and on a scholarship at Juilliard, and when I couldn't return the next semester, I lost my scholarship and soon after my student visa expired.

Without a visa, I couldn't work, so I started selling pot to get by.

A few months later, I was sitting in a diner reading an article in the *Village Voice*. The author was connecting how the mostly white owners of the television and sports industries monetize Black talent. He cited how a "successful" Black comedian walked away from his career in television and millions of dollars. When asked why, the comedian declined to comment.

I was gonna be that man too. The performer, the Black man America wants me to be. I thought. I leaned back in the booth, holding the paper to my chest.

I received a letter from Jonathan Goldman in my mailbox a few weeks later. He was a lecturer and one of the few other Black people around. I met Jonathan in his office the following day.

You were the one to watch, he said to me, then: There is a better way to use that talent.

A month later, Jonathan sponsored my visa and I became the

chorus director for Music Together, a program teaching kids in Harlem.

The tinnitus is still here, ringing in my ears, but these days it is the sound of freedom that I hear.

Advice

It is just as sentimental to always slope down toward despair in writing as to write shallowly about happiness.

Yes, despair is part of the human condition, but so is joy. Just because you are trying to write serious "literary" fiction doesn't mean you can't capture some of that joy. I've found a tendency in students to steer away from happy subjects or emotions because of fears of sentimentality, yet it can be just as sentimental for a character to go through all the "expected" stages of, say, despair, or depression, or sadness, in response to something bad, or even tragic, that befalls them.

This piece of writing illustrates beautifully how a seeming curse can be transformed into a blessing.

17.

Grace Bestowed

The definition of the word *grace*, is, according to Merriam-Webster, "unmerited divine assistance given to humans for their regeneration or sanctification." The key word is *unmerited*. If we are given a moment of grace, it is a gift of help, or assistance, that we did not earn or perhaps didn't even deserve. (Who does the gift come from? For the sake of the exercise, only you can decide. God, a higher being, the universe, karma, fate . . .)

1. Think of a time you (or a character) experienced a moment of grace. In other words, you were given something of value that you did not earn.
2. Write a scene about a specific time on a specific day in a specific place dramatizing how this happened.
3. Make it occur while your character is engaged in a physical activity. You are shopping for groceries, bathing the dog, just doing something.
4. For some reason that does not have to be named, all is not well with you or your character.
5. First describe the setting (the location) you or your character are in before the moment of grace (before you are given the thing of value). Write approximately one paragraph. Be specific and detailed. Use present tense. "I am standing at my kitchen sink washing the dishes. The coffee is dripping into the pot, and the sun is hidden behind the clouds." Do not worry about whether it is boring. Describe it thoroughly.
6. Now write a short piece (poem, short-short story, prose

poem, or similar) using this paragraph as a jumping-off point and give yourself (or your character) some unde-served respite or grace.

NOTE: The grace, or thing of value that is bestowed, is usually spiri-tual—some sense of relief, or forgiveness. But you can make it any-thing you want. A pair of shoes. An extra doughnut from the waitress.

NOTE 2: You (or your character) should have some sense of awareness that what is being given is unearned—it's a true gift without strings.

Example

I have been spring cleaning, sweeping away the confetti of our old life to make way for the new. Refashioning child-shaped spaces into adult ones for third acts yet to come. Jam jars of rainbow pens are replaced with jeweled bottles of designer spirits, and an art closet becomes a bar. Origami cranes, folded by sweet childish fingers, are swapped for a fresh copy of *Bird by Bird*, and a playroom becomes a room of my own. In a drawer in the bureau, I find a packet of letters. They are tied together with my hair ribbon from our wedding thirty years ago. Ours was an arranged marriage. Our meetings chaperoned. So we wrote, putting our best selves to paper. Trying to be what we thought the other wanted.

"I'm quite sporty," I said.

"My ten favorite books," you replied. I assumed you had read them.

In the stack there is a cream card, pale yellow primroses on its front; it has been torn in half and put back together with tape. I read the words and I am taken back to that night when a woman sat in the window of her third-floor Marble Arch flat. The window is wide open and she has been there for hours. One leg rests along the ledge, the other is planted on the floor. Not safe at the best of times, tonight, it is even less so, for she has been sipping from a bottle of cheap whiskey. In the background, on repeat, plays the album she had bought last week. She belts out lines.

"All the promises we made from the cradle to the grave."

"I have kissed honey lips . . . but I still haven't found what I'm looking for."

When she is not singing, she is weeping, when she is not weeping she thinks of all the promises she has made. To her friends, that she would not have an arranged marriage. To her parents, that she would always come back. To herself, that she would follow her heart. It has been heavy, this double life. Being the daughter of more than one country. A brown body in a white land. A vessel for ancestral reckonings and secondhand dreams. She has lived her life on parallel tracks and now the trains are coming into the station and she must decide where to get off. She writes on the card and her tears smudge the ink.

Then spent and cried dry she curls on the floor and falls asleep. She awakes as the sky is brightening, the card still in her hand. She reads it one last time. "Dearest Mum and Dad—I have been away from home for too long. I cannot do this. Forgive me." Then she tears it in two.

I wonder about that other life, if I had sent the card, not gone back, but not too often for this is the life I chose and it has been a good one.

Advice

As observed elsewhere in this book, it is relatively easy to slant things to the negative to make a story interesting or to attempt to give it depth. But making a story move toward hope, redemption, or happiness is very difficult to do in an unsentimental way.

Primo Levi, the Jewish Italian chemist and author and survivor of Auschwitz who wrote deeply and movingly about the experience, produced a book called *Moments of Reprieve*, which consisted of fifteen character studies of people he met during his time in the concentration camp. But the book is really about those moments that made him determined to keep on living. To have hope. A respite from the horror.

It is a wonderful thing to occasionally give your characters (who, face it, are usually being challenged or suffering in some way—that's plot, after all) a moment of reprieve. A moment of grace. It is a great exercise in plot-building as well—throw in that moment of grace and see what happens next. As Grace Paley has said about plot, it's nothing more than, "first one thing happens, then another, then another . . ."

18.

Surviving the Plague

In his book *The Plague*, Albert Camus's narrator, a doctor tending to the ill of the town, observes this about the situation he and his fellow citizens are facing:

"Perhaps the easiest way of making a town's acquaintance is to ascertain how the people in it work, how they love, and how they die," he says.

In this exercise, you will try to characterize a town (fictional or real) the way Camus's narrator advises, and see what you come up with.

Exercise

1. Write a poem, a short piece of fiction, or a prose poem about a town, real or imagined.
2. Your writing should touch upon three themes, as Camus advises: How the inhabitants work, how they love, and how they die.
3. You don't have to be as grim as Camus—you can be funny or humanistic or optimistic. As always, give us concrete examples. Focus in and get the details.

NOTE: Think of a prose poem simply as a poem (using spare language and compressed imagery) with no line breaks.

Example

The acting troupe came to perform in the town square last summer and never left. Their brightly painted school buses came off the wheels, converted to houses exactly where they first parked, in the field behind Carlos's Mercat. Staying here means succumbing to opacity, bleeding into the vast paleness that rolls away from you in every direction until you disappear into it completely. That is the intention. The border is on the other side of the Rio Grande, and we are on the wrong side of it here.

Blood can't come from stone, but it did here. Over there beyond that hill a century ago, men burrowed underground and dug up the red cinnabar that was then turned into quicksilver. Mercury was in the air, the rain, the sand. Everyone got sick and the mine closed down. Widows put up large wooden crosses as grave markers for their deceased spouses, mourning men who had never touched them gently. The crosses somersaulted across the desert, making the locals afraid to go outside when the wind blew for fear of death by impalement.

When I was a kid my parents saved up and bought me a chemistry set full of glass tubes of brightly colored salts and a silver liquid that flowed across my hand, weighty like a marble, shining like rain. If you filled a bath with mercury and jumped in, it would break all your bones. When I opened my hand to show my mother, she put it in a glass jar and held it at arm's length from her body. Shielding me from it with the other hand. *Causa locura*, it causes madness, she said.

Advice

This exercise depicts a small Mexican town on the Texas border, and the difficult lives of the inhabitants as they loved, worked, and died. As you read this, notice how much you learn about the inhabitants despite the narrative psychic distance with which the piece is written. Perhaps Camus was right—these are very important things to know about communities. This is a good exercise for establishing the location and setting of a piece if you're in any doubt about the place you've set a character in.

When reading this piece, notice also that when looking for truths, one can focus on the setting, or location, as much as the people, to eke out meaning.

19.

Running Late

Infusing urgency into your fiction is always an imperative. Putting time pressure, in particular, on a character or situation is a good technique to use if you are at a loss as to how to get your readers riled up and engaged.

A constraint like this also adds suspense. Literary suspense is created from the reader having partial or imperfect knowledge that a matter of dramatic importance is about to happen. In the next exercise, the suspense comes from the question of whether your character will make it to an important event/meeting/occasion with high stakes to it.

Exercise

1. The setup: someone is running late to an important event/meeting/occasion.
2. The stakes if they are late are very high. (They'll lose their job, they'll be penalized financially, they'll let down people who are important to them.)
3. Something surprising happens as they are on their way (they can be using any kind of transportation—car, bus, taxi, bike, walking) that delays them even more.
4. Write a scene in which you place your character on their way to their destination right before the surprising event happens. First, set the scene: where are we? What is the time? Who is there? Remember, a scene is something that happens at a specific place at a specific time.
5. Write out the scene precisely. What happens? Describe the concrete details. What is your charac-

ter's reaction to the surprising event, given that they are already under time pressure?

Example

Romina gripped the steering wheel, the sweat on her hands seeping into the worn faux leather. The light in front of her stayed stubbornly red, and beyond the intersection she saw a long line of cars with brake lights lit up like they were part of the world's most boring Christmas parade. Why would the city schedule road work for 3 p.m. on a Friday afternoon? It didn't make sense.

She ran over the excuses she would give to Mrs. Wilder ("call me Genevieve, please") later. That there was traffic due to road work. That Romina had gotten caught up at the coffee shop when a customer dropped an entire tray of drinks right before the shift change. That she hadn't realized until she was already halfway to Highland Park Elementary School that she needed to stop at the nearest Valero because she had been hoping to make it to payday without having to fill up her tank. Although the car belonged to Genevieve, Romina was responsible for the gas.

None of it would make a difference to Mrs. Wilder, who listened to true-crime podcasts and always stressed the importance of picking up Maggie on time so an "unknown party" didn't abduct her. Never mind the fact that Highland Park was well funded enough to have dedicated staff and parent volunteers waiting with the children until their guardians pulled up in shiny new BMWs and Teslas. Or that Romina couldn't afford to lose this job, which paid as much as Java Hut for half the hours. She was trying to save up to go to the local junior college next year, but she was barely covering her expenses. America was so expensive.

"Come on," she pleaded, and let out a shaky sigh of relief when the light turned green. She inched forward into the intersection and willed the line of cars in front of her to move. "Almost there."

Fifteen minutes and counting. Maggie's first-grade class got out at 2:45 on Fridays. Romina had four—no, five—lights to get through before she pulled into the drop-off/pick-up zone outside the school. What was that, another seven minutes tops? Would Maggie have already started crying for her mommy and daddy? Would the school secretary have called the Wilders to inform them that someone needed to pick up their daughter?

At which point would Romina have to update her CV (with part-time nanny struck from the record) and begin the demoralizing job-hunting process all over again?

She made it through two green lights before another red stalled her progress. Checked the time on the dash, which read 3:04 p.m. Decided that she would take Maggie to the dog park afterwards. With any luck, seeing rambunctious terriers and drooling labs would distract the kid thoroughly enough so that she wouldn't tell her parents about how Romina was late.

The car in front of her moved forward and Romina let off the brake pedal. She saw the light—yellow when she entered the intersection—turn red the moment she cleared the crosswalk.

Romina didn't see the forest green van accelerating from the left until it was too late.

—TERESA PHAM-CARSILLO

Advice

We feel the urgency in this scene as the young babysitter/nanny tries frantically to get to the school in time to pick up her charge. Everything is nicely grounded with sensory details, and we get a sense of the financial pressure she is under—how much she needs this job, and how the whole system is against her making even a slight error—her boss, the school staff, and so on. None would have any pity for the fact that the narrator is juggling two high-pressure jobs with not enough time to get from one to the other should something go wrong. This is a good way to elicit responses from our characters—put pressure on them until they crack in some way, and, when they pick up the pieces, the story can advance.

20.

Make It Rain

Many writers get stuck when trying to advance plots. When that happens, they are usually thinking too big: plot lines that cover a broad territory or timeframe and encompass many significant dramatic events. Thinking big in such cases might not be a good idea. You might find yourself writing too generally, too distantly, and too abstractly to engage your readers.

An overall idea of where you are going with a piece is good, but you have to be able to drill down into the particular moments to get yourself there. This means plotting the small stuff. In such cases it's always best to think in the smallest increment of dramatic time possible: the moment.

This is a simple plotting exercise. You could use virtually any weather event—wind, snow, hail—to do this exercise. I happened to choose a rainstorm. Remember (I know I'm repeating myself) what Grace Paley said about plot: First one thing happens, then another thing happens. Yes, it really can be that simple.

Exercise

1. You (or a character) are in a "location" that delights you for many different reasons. (For a full definition of location see Exercise 3, but basically it means both a physical and emotional space that a character inhabits at a particular moment. So in this case, your character can be delighted by the physical things present—the setting, the furniture, the food—or for psychological or emotional reasons).

2. Now write a scene (something happens at a specific

time in a specific place) in which you are in this location and it starts to rain. It can be a light shower or heavy storm—your choice.

3. What happens? Does it ruin or enhance your day? How does it affect the things you love about the place? As always, be concrete. For example, "The waves have turned rough and angry, and the surfers are hurriedly paddling toward shore."

Example

With no buttons or zippers, the dress was a simple swath of silk that you slip around yourself until, somehow, it falls into place and you are transformed. The right clothes can do that. I bought the dress on sale that same morning at the designer's showroom. I had to get there early to get in. I spent a whole week of tips, but it was worth it to feel this expensive. Navid's party was supposedly going to be casual, but he hung out with the fashion crowd, and I knew they would recognize the dress. I looked at my watch. It was time. I'd get there somewhere between fashionable late and borderline arrogant.

I walked down the five flights of steps from my apartment with caution. The steps creaked and groaned, but I lightly stepped over the cracks and stayed away from the dusty walls. It would take just one smudge to ruin the delicate fabric of the skirt. I held the banister lightly, like a Fellini star.

Out on the street it was twilight and unusually quiet. A few cars already had switched their headlights on, as if without this illumination, they would not exist. New graffiti of large cursive letters fading from red to pink had been sprayed across a building. LOVEHER it says, sixteen stories up. The artist wrote it hanging from the roof. The risk was immense. How romantic, he must really be in love.

The guys playing dominoes turned to watch me with furrowed brows, then smiled back in recognition. Someone whistled, and I laughed, blushing. The dress's skirt floated behind me like an apparition, and I snatched it up so it didn't touch the ground.

There was a loud crack, and then a rhythmic sound and I realized it was raining, a sudden downpour to cool the sidewalks and sweep up the debris in the gutters.

I made a run for it for the closest cover, the awning of our local bodega, aware that, if wet, the dress would turn transparent, and I would be naked in the street.

Crowding in with neighbors and strangers under the awning, we watched the summer rain falling. Everyone was laughing and holding out their hands to catch raindrops. When the rain stopped, I took off my shoes and walked barefoot on the wet concrete to the train.

Advice

In this piece, the dress is exquisite, inspiring confidence in the woman and making the world around the woman—her location—beautiful. In reality, her neighborhood is the opposite of beautiful—it's gritty and urban—but being in the dress makes her see it differently, and love it. When the rain comes, she feels at one with her community, and the world.

How did the rain advance the plot? This writer had many choices. Should the character escape the rain and arrive, perfectly attired, at the perfect time, at the party? Or could something happen that would shake her up a bit, arrive at the party in an altered state (a wet dress that exposes her breasts) that would prepare her to receive whatever happens in a fresh and surprising way? As I said, you can do this exercise over and over, throwing different unexpected events (not just rain) at your characters, to see how they respond.

21.

Despair and Peace

In his poem "The Peace of Wild Things," Wendell Berry writes about what he does when he wakes in despair, afraid for his future and the future of his children.

Despair is an important word choice here, a heavy one indeed: when someone is in despair they are at the very end of their resources. When you use it to describe a character, you have put them in a very dark place. Berry describes precisely what he does when he is in such despair—he goes to nature. He watches drakes rest and herons feed. At the end of the poem he writes, For a time / I rest in the grace of the world, and am free.

Described this way, of course, the poem sounds clichéd and sentimental. It is anything but that. Look it up and read it yourself when you have a moment.

Exercise

1. Write a nighttime scene (putting yourself or a character in a specific place at a specific time) in which your character is awakened by a sound.
2. Include a detailed description of your character's imagined fears associated with this situation. Be concrete! Not "burglars" but "a man dressed in dark blue coming through my unlocked kitchen window."
3. Try to get at least three concrete images of what you/ your character fears into the scene.
4. Now (this is the difficult part) try to show how the fears deteriorate into despair. In other words, the fear triggers a deeper sense of desolation or aloneness.

5. Complete the scene by showing what you/your character does to achieve peace. Be specific! You could read a particular phrase from a particular book or poem or fix a small snack or look in on your sleeping children or take refuge in nature as Berry does. End with a sense of peace. Be careful to avoid easy sentimentality—make your images fresh and surprising.

Example

After a cold shower, Kiara lies in bed naked watching the stars come out over the mountain ridge and the sea turning silver, just beyond. *This is why I left the city.*

Getting sleepy, she slips out from under the sheet, and gets up to close and lock the wooden doors to the terrace, then shakes her head. She pushes the doors wide open again and climbs back into bed.

A few hours later, she wakes to the sound of a baby crying.

It can't be a baby. Maybe the sound is traveling in some strange echo? Maybe I am just having a nightmare. She turns over.

The real estate agent had told Kiara there were pirates up in these mountains hundreds of years ago. They climbed from the sea, eastward, over the hills. Like then, this shanty is still the only dwelling on the mountain. Kiara's mind begins to whir in a panic.

She sits up and turns on the light, then hears the noise again. It is a baby, whimpering now.

A baby. Tiny woven booties.

Maybe someone has abandoned the baby to her. She will go find it, take care of it here until someone claims it, or just claim it as hers. Yes, that is what she will do.

Climbing out of bed, Kiara pulls on her robe, tying it around her tightly. She walks out the terrace door in the direction of the cries.

Where are you? Kiara calls, and realizes she is crying too.

The stars shatter the darkness, making long shadows of the trees. An old, rusty wire fence hems in the silent fields of alfalfa. She sees something caught in the fence, writhing.

As she moves closer the cries become higher-pitched and she makes out a tiny goat with its foot tangled in the wire of the fence. She lifts the goat up, holding it tight, coarse hair against her chest. Kiara pulls the delicate hoof gently with her free hand. The goat pushes off her and she lets it go. It bleats but stays near her until, from behind, the mother goat arrives and nudges her kid into the woods. Kiara breathes deep of the earthy country air and smiles.

Advice

Association is a powerful tool in fiction. When we capture how one thought or image in a character's mind leads to another, not necessarily in a rational way, we can delve into previously unexplored layers of that character that allow us to access deeper characterizations. The way that Kiara's thoughts move from fear of pirates to babies to booties, for example, gives us a lot of information about her, as does the fact that she finds she is crying—an unexpected emotion.

Always try to see what you can do with associations—memories, half-remembered conversations, images that flashed by on a train—within your stories. That's where the richest material often comes from.

22.

Passion for Solitude

Personification is a very productive tool for getting meaning out of ordinary objects. Personification is giving human qualities to non-human things (which can include animals).

In his poem "Passion for Solitude," Cesare Pavese personifies a star alone in the sky, how it struggles and how desperately it needs its companions—the other stars. He compares it to his own state of being alone, but professes he is not lonely. "Here in the dark, alone / my body is calm, it feels it's in charge," he writes.

Exercise

1. Place yourself (or a character) in a situation, a specific physical place, where you are alone.
2. Imagine that you are satisfied, even happy, with being alone.
3. Now describe the physical place minutely—use concrete details and do not—repeat, do not—worry if it is boring. Remember, you are seeing things through the eyes of someone who is content, and that should inform the imagery. Try to avoid stereotypes like walking on the beach, being in the middle of a forest, and so forth. Try to make it fresh.
4. As an added constraint, observe a physical, non-human object in the room or landscape that is also alone: a chair or a vase or a cat, for example.
5. Using personification, describe what that object feels—is it happy? Sad? Lonely? How does its state compare to yours?

Example

I sit in my rented bedroom in Nagpur, India, eight thousand miles from all friends and family.

It feels like the inside of a dryer here. The scorching city air blows in through the open window and flaps the curtain rhythmically.

The ever-present sounds of India float in too. Three weeks ago, I couldn't differentiate these noises, but now I do. Schoolchildren laughing in the courtyard. The tangled nest of power lines buzzing beside my building. Rickshaws beeping in the street.

My room is nearly empty. There's the sleeping mat on which I sit, the wooden desk and chair, and the flimsy paper calendar in the center of the wall.

For the first time, I recognize the god depicted in this month's calendar artwork. Blue-skinned, with a tiger fur wrapped around his waist, he holds one palm facing me, one resting on his knee, and his two extra hands grasp a trident and small drum. A fingernail-thin crescent moon floats above his forehead. The calendar is weathered in the same manner as the dried-out yellow paint of the cement wall it's nailed to. My vision transitions from seeing the calendar as something separate from the wall to seeing it as a part of it. Lord Shiva is either alone against an open yellow sky, or he is one with everything: connected to the cracks along the ceiling, to the malformed cement nodules at the base of the wall, to the desk and chair, and even to me.

His face is blissful and his hands express what I imagine to be his different states of mind: open (the palm), satisfied (the hand on knee), protective (the spear), and playful (the drum). He seems to be here in this very room, feeling this hot, heavy air. The same gravity that pulls an ache into my shoulders also tugs at the paper on which he is printed. Yet despite these irritants, and despite juggling so much at once, his mind is undisturbed. He is like a mountain in the rain, or a statue in the wind—or, more apt today, a lizard in the heat: perfectly steady and content amid a violent world.

I feel familiar scratches at the top of my throat and recognize the difficulty of breathing through a nose clogged by polluted air, but I also believe, somehow truer than the tingle in my nose, that I am breathing something else. The equanimity of Shiva—this blue-skinned inventor of meditation—is filling my lungs with bliss and benediction beyond my momentary discomfort.

—JOHN DIDDAY

Advice

Personification, as poets know, can be very powerful for eliciting emotions in readers. By giving stars, or in this case, an image on a calendar, human qualities, you make the physical environment of the piece come alive in what can be an almost magical way.

Personification can also be used in a whimsical way, or humorously. It's also about engaging the reader emotionally, but unconventionally—not through empathizing with other humans but by empathizing with something not of our species. It also, as this piece represents so well, can give us insight into ourselves—or other human characters in a scene.

23.

Party Questions

Parties where we don't know many people make most of us feel uncomfortable, vulnerable. Many of us approach them with trepidation. Of course, you may be the kind of person who is excited about the prospect of meeting others, who gets energized in such situations. In that case, do this exercise with that attitude in mind—it will still work.

No matter whether you are an introvert or extravert, most of us typically enter a situation of this sort with lots of questions, whether we articulate them to ourselves or not. So this is an exercise where you *do* articulate them, as precisely as possible. It's basically an exercise in characterization. By surfacing and identifying the questions that arise in a character's (or your) mind in an uncertain situation, you learn a lot.

Exercise

1. Place yourself (or a character) in a scene where you are about to enter a party in which you don't know many (if any) people other than the host.

2. Write a piece that consists *only* of the questions you/ your character have as you walk through the door. These can be questions about people (Who is that woman in red? What is she drinking? Is Derrick going to come?); about the place (Where's the bathroom? Why would they decorate the whole house in a Winnie-the-Pooh theme?); or about the food (This is like dog food!). Try to write at least fifteen questions.

3. Try to avoid the obvious things people ask themselves like, "Will anyone talk to me?" and "Do I look
all right?" Go deeper by putting in concrete details:
Will Derrick talk to me after our fight last week?
What will that woman in red think about my new
leather jacket if I approach her?

Example

How long is this going to last? Is there somewhere I can sit? Is that
place on the blue couch empty? Is that Anna's bag there? Will she
mind if I move it? Will the other Black grad student attend? Does she
feel like she has to? Is there going to be actual food or are we going
to stand around with this cheap white wine and have nothing but this
rabbit food to nibble on?

Do I want to be drunk before I have to say hello to James? I wonder if he wants me to call him Dr. Patterson. Will anyone notice? Can
I get some water? Will I lose this seat if I look around for some? Why
is it always wine at these things?

Did James ever let the chair know about the accident at the site?
Didn't he have to file some report? Did the police talk to anyone
besides James? Why didn't they talk to me? Didn't they know I heard
them fighting? Should I tell someone? Anyone? Who would believe
me? Who would take my word against his?

Is Anna coming over here? "Hey, Anna, could you keep this seat
for me? Do you know if there's any water? In the back?"

Is that Helen? Did she see me? Is she waving me over? "Helen,
how have you been?" Does she look worried or is it my imagination?
"Why do you ask where I was doing my research? Isn't James here?
Why don't you ask *him*?"

—RENÉE PERRY

Advice

Questions, on the surface at least, are about someone (a character) seeking information they don't possess. Frequently, they can be very revealing about the character—by asking questions, they are giving away critical information about themselves.

In this piece, the questions turn into an internal monologue about the small things the character is thinking of as she attends the party—things that even the writer might otherwise not have known about her. This exercise can be helpful for those times you place your character in unfamiliar territory and are unclear of what their reactions would be. Simply have them ask all the questions, small or large, that come to mind, and you should be provided with rich material.

24.

90 Seconds
(1 of 4 "managing time" exercises)

Being able to manipulate time passing is an essential skill. As E. M. Forster says in *Aspects of the Novel*, time is like a "giant tapeworm" stretched through your piece. However long it is—and no matter how you chop it up, redistribute it, or try to keep it out of sight—readers are very conscious of the narrative clock ticking, and the order and sequence of the events involved are important no matter the structure of your piece. You can have flashbacks, flashbacks within flashbacks, flash forwards, or whatever you want, but your reader wants to be assured that you are in control of that clock.

Part of mastering time is knowing when to stop the clock—to give the reader information not possible except for directly telling her—and when to speed it up—to jump ahead in the narrative.

In this series of exercises, you will learn how to write to cover certain amounts of time. This means you will have to figure out ways to control the narrative clock, either by slowing it down (She hesitated. She could feel her heart beating. Thump. Thump. Thump); stopping it for a moment by giving us narrative or backstory (out of time); or speeding it up (later that same day).

Exercise

1. Place yourself or a character waiting either in a place that is dreadful for them (a dentist's chair) or wonderful (sitting on the beach gazing at the stars, waiting for friends to arrive).
2. They can be alone or with others.
3. Write a piece in which you describe 90 seconds (a

minute and a half) of your (or your character's) experience in that dreadful or wonderful place.

4. You will write 500 words, no more, no less.

5. Constraint: You (or your character) knows that the 90 seconds will soon end, and you/they will be faced with an opposite situation: Those that were in dreadful situations will be delighted, and those in a wonderful place will be cast down. So there is anticipation or dread involved in that minute and a half.

HINT: Control your use of time very carefully. You must dramatize the full 90 seconds while also hinting at/telling us what lies in the future.

Example

Could I have a word with you, please?

Evelyn begins politely, but I know what's coming. I take her to one side. Normally cordial, she has a fixed stare and a tightness around her mouth.

What are all these people doing in my house? Who let them in?

I can understand her confusion and annoyance. I, too, would be unhappy if I thought a group of strangers had invaded my house and were making themselves at home.

I try to distract her.

Would you like a cup of tea and we can discuss it? I invite her into the dining room.

No thanks, she replies curtly, walking into the lounge with arms folded across her chest.

It is no use saying that this is not her house, that it's a care home and all these people live here. Although it's the truth it will only make her more angry. From her perspective there is a group of people in her lounge, drinking her tea and watching her television, without her permission.

At the first sign of "sundowning" behavior, Evelyn had been given medication to ease the growing sense of agitation which is common at this time of day among dementia sufferers. I check my watch. Thirty minutes since she took her medication. Any minute now it will take effect and she will feel calm, but in the meantime . . .

What are you doing here? I want you out now. All of you!, she shouts, pointing to the door.

The lounge is full of residents snoozing, chatting, or watching TV as they wait for supper to be served. John, who is wheelchair-bound, looks over to me and shrugs, whilst Arna, always willing to oblige, gets up to leave although she has no idea what she has done wrong. Sit down Arna, I say, smiling. It's okay. She's unsteady on her feet so I assist her back into her armchair whilst Colleen, who never likes to be given orders, shouts, Sit down and shut up.

That upsets Evelyn. Don't speak to me like that. You have no right to be in my house.

Most of the time Colleen asks where she should wait for the taxi to take her home, believing us to be a restaurant and not a care home, but faced with Evelyn's outburst she replies indignantly, This isn't your house, we all live here.

Don't be ridiculous. Of course it's my house and these, Evelyn says, making a sweeping motion with her arm, are all my things. And I want you out. Now!

I can see that the situation is about to get out of hand, so I position myself between the two women to avoid the confrontation becoming physical. Later I will laugh, saying, It's all in a day's work, but at this moment my priority is to make sure that no one gets hurt.

Evelyn, could I have a word with you, please? Out here? I smile, ushering her out of the lounge and into the corridor.

—MAUREEN GALLAGHER

Advice

In this piece, a caregiver is trying to calm a dementia patient living in a group home who is confused as to where she is. You can see how the writer skillfully starts and stops the narrative clock. Whenever she gives us backstory, or explains how a particular patient acts or how the care home works, the clock measuring the time of the scene stops. What's left is the dialogue and gestures. If you actually took a stopwatch and started and stopped it at the appropriate places, allowing for natural pauses between responses, you'd see this adds up to almost exactly 1.5 minutes. Read it over again and see how the writer achieves this—and use a stopwatch yourself when writing your scene. You'll be surprised how fast (or slowly) narrative time can go, and how best to control it.

25.

One Hour
(2 of 4 "managing time" exercises)

In this exercise, you're going to dramatize one hour—you must make it seem as though (legitimately) a full hour has passed by the end of the piece. (See the introduction to Exercise 24.)

Exercise

1. Place yourself or a character in a situation where you are hungry, but it will be impossible to get food for an hour, for one reason or another.
2. You can be alone or with others.
3. Write a piece in which you describe one hour of your (or your character's) experience of being hungry.
4. Keep the piece to 500 words.
5. Constraint: Physical movement must be involved. No sitting at a table waiting for a meal.

HINT: Control your use of time very carefully. You must dramatize the full hour, no more and no less.

Example

Raven had missed the last bus to 125th Street, so she walked the ten blocks, her stomach grumbling.

She should have eaten before setting out to the church, but the decision to come to the memorial was spontaneous. Not having ever been above 116th Street, she didn't know that the blocks suddenly were much longer on the avenues in Harlem, and so she had gotten soaked to the skin on the way by the rain. Her hunger was amplified by the cold.

The church is lit at the altar with fluorescent lights, casting everything in green. Raven wriggles out of her dripping coat. She feels faint. *Why didn't I eat something? Why did I come at all?*

Raven feels the vague weight of the memorial announcement still in her pocket, announcing the memorial service of Marjorie Jenkins, with an unrecognizable photo of a smiling, brown-haired woman. The service has already started, and ends at 8 p.m., with refreshments to follow, so there isn't much time left, just forty minutes. Raven will have to wait for the preacher to finish: until they bring out the tray of stale sugar cookies and room-temperature cola. The church is nearly full, the service already started.

Raven slides into a pew at the back.

It strikes Raven now that the Birdwoman could be the name of a heroine from a comic book. A woman with supernatural powers who could sprout wings when in danger and fly.

But that was not why Marjorie was known as Birdwoman. It was because she was birdlike, with her eccentric dress, her delicate bones, and her small eyes. Raven had heard Marjorie called other names related to birds. Raven feels a tightness in her chest. She remembers how once she had been behind a group of men as they clucked and bawked as they chased Marjorie across the street. One of them threw quarters at her and sneered, That's for our date later, Chickenhead.

The preacher drones on, and Raven's mind flits to the hamburger stand on the corner. Just fifteen minutes left now.

Marjorie Jenkins was born to illiterate sharecroppers in Birmingham, Alabama. One of six siblings, she moved with her parents from Alabama to Harlem as part of the Great Migration.

Marjorie was seven when they moved. The preacher paused.

But she already could see things others couldn't. Raven thought.

Raven can envision Marjorie's face telling a story—the white hair on her head cut so short under her hat that Raven sees the sheen of her scalp beneath. Marjorie's mouth moves quickly as she speaks, lips full and poised, crooked teeth revealed when she laughed. She was the most beautiful person Raven had ever known.

The preacher continues.

During the day, Marjorie worked with her mother in a factory on Eighth Avenue sewing buttons on men's shirts. They'd lied about her age so she could work.

Now Marjorie is lying somewhere, cold, ashen, dead. How strange she is dead.

Raven's stomach makes a noise like a car grinding gears as the preacher rambles. Finally, after an interminable additional ten minutes of talk, the choir stands up to sing a final gospel hymn. Raven stands also. She feels dizzy as the voices rise and break over her. It is done.

Advice

See how the writer here controlled the narrative clock, not only by telling us directly at times how much time had passed but filling up time with actual scenes and then skipping ahead in time by giving us Raven's wandering thoughts and glossing over what is happening during those moments? Although it might take us perhaps thirty seconds to a minute to read the passage, we do get the sense that a full hour has . . . slowly . . . passed. Why introduce the theme of hunger into the exercise? Because it adds tension, and something for the character to focus on as the hour passes—probably more slowly than it would if she were satiated.

26.

One Day
(3 of 4 "managing time" exercises)

Now you are going to dramatize a full day—a waking day (twelve hours, not twenty-four hours). The goal (again) is to control time in a realistic way so as to capture the full day with verisimilitude with a limited number of words.

See Exercise 25 for a more complete explanation of what this exercise is trying to achieve.

Exercise

1. Place yourself or a character in a situation where you/ they are suffering from a lack of sleep, but sleeping is not possible until the end of the day.
2. You/they can be alone or with others.
3. Write a piece in which you describe that day of your/ your character's experience in being tired, starting in the morning and ending in the evening/night.
4. Constraint 1: You have only 500 words.
5. Constraint 2: You are/your character is responsible for completing some task that requires physical dexterity, intellectual concentration, or both, during this day.

HINT: Control your use of time very carefully. You must dramatize the full day while also having your character complete their physical or mental task.

Example

I walk in the worn path of the tractor wheel down the row toward the last of the trees. The sun is just above the horizon.

Miguel is already there, sitting on the ladder.

It will be hot within the hour, unbearably hot. Lorenzo, the foreman, will arrive soon on the truck, barking to load up and looking over the baskets to make sure the fruit is unbruised. It is easier to pick before Lorenzo comes, and today I am so tired from the heat of the past few weeks, the sleepless nights swatting at the mosquitoes.

We are almost finished with the peaches, the worst to pick. As the day progresses the fuzz covers your skin, gets in your mouth and hair. We are not supposed to eat the peaches on the trees, only from the ground, but no one does on account of the fuzz.

Lorenzo watches closely all day from the shade as we climb up the ladders, gently lifting the fruit from the limbs and placing it in the bushel baskets. The shade of the trees and the angle of the sun determines how we pick, and the timing.

Early, we pick the highest fruit, often the most ripe and also the most delicate, nearly purplish in parts. We work in pairs, one picker hands the fruit down to another, who lays the fragile fruit out on the blanket laid out under the tree.

These peaches go on the top of the full basket, so they don't get squashed and rot. When the sun rises in the sky, we move into the tree's limbs and pick the shaded, less ripe fruit.

It is sturdier, so we fill the baskets, tied to the ladder as we climb high in the trees. Fruit-tree limbs are weak, snapping easily. We only stop to drink water, and eat a few walnuts, which Miguel cracks between his palms. When the sun has disappeared beyond the horizon in the far fields, Lorenzo yells, signaling the end of the day, and we all walk back along the tire path.

Advice

Like this writer, I would pick a "marker"—an event or image—to show the start of the day (in this case, the walk to the fruit trees and the rising sun), and one to mark when it has ended (the setting sun, walking back). Use transitional phrases that evoke time ("as the day progressed," "after another two hours") to speed up the narrative clock, then slow it down again to show a scene, or an image, full of concrete detail. Remember there's a task to complete as well as a full day to render, so keep going on that front too.

27.

One Year
(4 of 4 "managing time" exercises)

In this, the last of the managing time exercises, you will dramatize *a full year* in just 500 words. It's important not to generalize to make time go faster. Keep things specific. Rather than just summarizing in a general way, dramatize individual moments to really capture the emotional essence of the twelve months.

Exercise

1. Place yourself or a character in a situation where they have experienced something huge in their life. It can be good or bad. A breakup. A wedding. A birth. A death. A move to a new city.
2. Write a piece in which you describe the year *following* the huge event—but by looking back on it. For example, a young man might be thinking back on the first year of his marriage.
3. Constraint: You must account for the full year. The clock starts ticking immediately after the huge experience is over (for example, on the wedding night).

HINT: Control your use of time very carefully. You must dramatize the full year!

Example

It is after midnight on January third, and the cake is overdone. A carrot cake, made with applesauce instead of sugar for my baby girl, Victoria, who will be a year today.

I creep down the dark hall and peek in on her, sleeping in her crib. Four stitches on her pale forehead are visible even in the dark. Frankenbaby, John calls her. She fell hard on the stone patio last Tuesday, hitting her head on a sharp corner. I heard her scream and knew it was bad. Blood gushed down her forehead, deep red, the color of fear.

I held her and ran toward the car. *You're okay, sweetie.* I said it over and over, watching her in the rearview mirror as I careened along the highway to the hospital.

I close her bedroom door and go back to frosting the cake. The cat yowls and I let her in. I can't remember holding Victoria for the first time, and truthfully, most of the last year is a smudged lens, but some moments stand out.

I was wearing blue jeans and a beige secondhand sweater when Victoria was six weeks, and I went to sit in a café, just to be alone for an hour. I felt disembodied without her. My breasts started leaking dark circles on my sweater; I rushed home without finishing my coffee.

At three months, I sat in a bar trying to sip the cold Albarino slowly, then walked home quickly. You're early? I thought you were dying for "me" time, John says. Victoria grins from her bouncy chair, slathered in mashed sweet potato.

Victoria sleeps all night at four months, I don't sleep, and my hair falls out in dark masses when I shower. She sits up at five months and I can't control my bladder, peeing in my pants in the elevator while our neighbor watches the numbers on the control panel, pretending not to notice.

Victoria crawls at seven months, wiggling across the carpet.

The past year rushes past like a fast current.

Victoria's eyes open dark brown like mine one day, and another day, tiny dark hair appears in a widow's peak, like her grandfather.

The pediatrician marvels at her tiny teeth cropping up at ten months, and I wince when I breastfeed her, my nipples raw.

When she stands up and walks at almost eleven months, John bellows, Come see this. I stand in the doorway crying with delight and terror.

Advice

You can, as this writer did, name the months as they pass, having a brief vignette dramatized in each one. That works. Or you can be more subtle, and just hint at time passing with your narrative transitions. "A little later in the year I began to feel things again, the chill of the winter wind, and even later, the traitorous betrayal of a spring snowstorm after the daffodils had already pushed their delicate shoots aboveground . . ." Use clues from the physical world to show how time is passing—the seasons, weather, holidays, and so on.

The risk of doing this exercise is to rely too much on glib summary. As in all good writing, we want concrete details, the more precise the better. So make sure to capture moments within the year. Don't try to describe the entire year with a high-level overview. It would then lack emotional impact.

28.

Nothing Personal

When you're developing plot points (things that happen in your story) sometimes it can help to force your character to try to put whatever they are going through into perspective. We want our characters to have urgent needs and intense emotions as we develop our plots (what happens next? Will the characters get what they want?). But a good generative exercise could also be to calm your characters down, to get them to see what is happening to them with perspective, or as within a larger landscape.

"The earth is always shifting, the light is always changing, the sea does not cease to grind down rock. Generations do not cease to be born," wrote James Baldwin in *Nothing Personal*.

Exercise

1. Write a list of five things that are going to stay the same in your (or a character's) world no matter what you/they are going through. Be very specific. You can choose big things like Baldwin does (the sun will always set) or personal things from within your world (The Number 10 bus will continue to be late).
2. Put yourself (or your character) into a situation where you/they are struggling with a difficult decision.
3. Write a piece in which the character ponders which choice to make. (You/they don't actually make the decision, but are just going over the options.)
4. Have your character consider all the things in their world that will go on no matter which way they decide to go. Think small, as always.

5. Keep in mind, as you write, that as Baldwin also says, you are "the only witness that these things have."

Example

The crowing started every morning about five. Becks used to hate it. I didn't much care. I could usually fall back to sleep for a couple of hours, at least until after the sun came up, but she would toss and turn and curse and finally get up to make herself some tea and do God-knows-what until I joined her in the kitchen. These last few years, she started to sleep through it and I'm the one who gets up first. It was just getting light. I patted the bedside table for my glasses. Dammit. The cats must have knocked them to the floor. I patted around by the bed, reaching as far under as I could without tipping my ass out of the bed. My fingers brushed the cool plastic and I grabbed them, put them on.

I needed to get up, make myself my one cup of coffee, but maybe not just yet. The chicken—rooster, I guess—was still letting the neighborhood know that this was his territory. I wondered if Jack and Frank would bring over some eggs. Becks liked her eggs. I looked up at the ceiling then turned on my side to look at Becks.

Strange how a face softens with sleep. When she is asleep, the frowns, the anxious grimaces disappear. I sighed, touched her cheek, then got out of bed. I needed that one cup of coffee today.

The water took forever to boil. I opened the folder that I kept in my office, under a pile of textbooks. I read it and reread it. Not that I learned anything new. Affording it wasn't a problem.

The care would be the best in the state, maybe in the country. Not like it would change anything, could change anything. That damn rooster. I made my coffee.

Beck's brother didn't make any trouble about the power of attorney. He liked me and always thought it was a shame that we couldn't get married here. The paperwork should be here sometime this afternoon. A rare day that the mail got here before three. More hours for me to think.

How should I know when it was time? She was unhappy here. She was confused here, even though we've been in this house for thirty years. She knew me, then she didn't. Sometimes she knew what year it was. Sometimes she was in 1982, when we just met and she asked me why I wanted to be a professor. She smiled and I saw that little gap between her teeth. White hair and all, this illness and all, she was still my girl. She was disappearing and I didn't know how much longer I could do this alone.

Alone, there will still be that damned rooster every morning. Alone, the mail will still come late in the day. Alone, I will still have this one cup of coffee. Alone, I will still fumble for my glasses in the morning. Alone, when she is somewhere else, with people who only know her as she is now, she will still be my girl.

—RENÉE PERRY

Advice

Our characters are always struggling to locate themselves in the world, to get perspective on what's happening to them. This is one way to force that mindset. In this piece, we see how a very important decision will not cause more than a ripple in the larger world. The fact that the world continues to spin while you are making a momentous decision has the impact of making one take responsibility for that decision. And forcing your character to feel, well, relatively inconsequential, at a critical moment in their life can reveal other interesting things about them that perhaps you didn't know before.

29.

Not Guilty

"Every snowflake in an avalanche pleads 'not guilty,'" the Polish writer Stanisław J. Lec wrote about humans' ability to try to escape culpability.

We mostly want to fit in. Standing out from what others are doing or saying can feel uncomfortable for many people. Placing your character in a situation where they could take responsibility—or not—after feeling pressure from peers to do something can result in dramatic writing. Does your character go along? Do they openly resist? Do they secretly resist?

If, as Kurt Vonnegut has advised, one way to develop plot is to pour a surprise bucket of water on our character's head as they walk through a door, then anything we can do to put our characters in positions where they feel uncomfortable or pressured is a good thing.

Exercise

Think of (or imagine) a time when you or a character were part of a group. Let's define a group as three or more people.

1. Write a scene (a specific place at a specific time) where you (or a character) "go along with the crowd" and get swept up in doing or saying something that you (or your character) don't really want to do or say.
2. In less than 500 words, render what happens precisely. Use sensory details to show us (not tell us) how this makes your character feel uncomfortable (or excited, as the case may be).

HINT: Ask yourself: How does the emotion of being part of a crowd manifest itself in the physical world?

Example

The PETA protestors are back for the third day in a row. They carry signs about the animal abuses in the circus. They shout at the people walking into the big top, little hands clasped into adult ones. The audience wants elephants. They cannot know how Ned has already put one of his trainers in the hospital at that point. I don't even know it. But I know that Ned doesn't enjoy performing, and that as an adult bull elephant, his frustration can be dangerous. My boss stations me in a folding chair next to the elephants behind the tent during our shows, where they are chained to the ground between their acts. This is to prevent any curious members of the audience from wandering back there thinking they can hug an elephant, and getting crushed under the forehead and tree-trunk legs of an angry animal that weighs as much as a bus. As I sit with Anna May, Amy, and Ned, I talk in gentle tones, telling them about my love life and the drama on the lot, and wonder what they are thinking in those big leathery heads, behind those deep eyes with the long lashes. Ned sways back and forth rapidly in agitation, swinging his trunk in a figure eight. I've seen Ned snap at one of the guys on ring crew before and get the sharp end of a bullhook thwacked under his chin as punishment. The roustabouts discuss in terms of when and not if he goes rogue and tramples the crowd one day.

The PETA protestors are beginning to upset the audience members, and management gives us fliers to hand out as a counterprotest before the show. "The elephants used in the show are well cared for, regarded as members of our circus family. They have regular veterinary checkups. Only positive-reinforcement techniques are used in the training of our elephants," the fliers read. I take the stack of fliers, but I know it's not true. The circus is a closed community, and the walls surrounding it are high for a reason. What happens in the circus stays in the circus. Years later, after I have gone, I will think of Ned, Anna May, and Amy, the youngest elephant. I will feel hot shame when I remember handing out the fliers, choosing to protect my job while in the dark crevices of night, under the tent, I see light. I see the elephant trainer's obese son swinging an iron rod with two hands to crack across Amy's hind legs. "Positive reinforcement." She trumpets in pain, then lifts them to stand on her head.

—MIEKE EERKENS

Advice

Peer and social pressure can drive our characters to behave in interesting ways. In fact, as writers, our job is to create unique characters then put them in situations that challenge them. This writer has done that in this vignette about the circus that rings painfully true.

30.

Moving Toward Beauty

Camille Rankine, in her poem "The Current Isolationism," writes evocatively of being in an emotionally bad space ("My heart betrays. I confess: I am afraid.") as represented by a physical building with closed-in passageways and walls. Through a half-open door she glimpses a beautiful, serene garden full of blooming flowers that she wants to get to.

There is a problem, however: dogs are guarding it. They are chained, luckily, but Rankine has an interesting take on that. "So they can't attack *like I know / they want to*." [emphasis mine]

So here's an interesting situation to put a character in: give them a vision of beauty that they want to pursue, but detain them with something that wants to harm them.

Exercise

1. Place yourself (or a character) in a neutral physical space. This is a scene, so make it a specific place at a specific time. Neutral here means it has no emotional significance for you or your character. In other words, you/they don't feel any particular emotion from being in that space. A classroom. Or a bathroom. Whatever.

2. Now make your character move toward an object of beauty. This can be beautiful for any number of reasons. In fact, I'd prefer it weren't about nature but about other things that could be beautiful—certain people, or urban landscapes, or even interior rooms

or things in rooms. Something you (or your character) find exceedingly attractive.

3. Put an obstacle in your/their way to getting to the
place/object of beauty. Again, the obstacle can be
anything: physical, mental, emotional. You can use
personification if you like for this one (imbuing non-
human or inanimate objects with humanlike feelings
or intentions).

Example

Nico imagines his life as a movement west, carried along on a rushing
torrent. In his dreams he is always standing in a line wearing an over-
coat and carrying a suitcase. He is about to cross through customs to
the waiting train. The anxieties of immigration have been with him
so long he is irritated by the memory of them—he has no time for the
cliché his life has become.

Until one day he dreams of turning around—out the doors of the
station, out into the street. He begins to move west to east. He is determined to make it back to where he started. At first he speeds along—
no one bars his way as he leaves the city and makes his way across
the no-man's-land. But as he approaches his destination the anxiety
returns. The border crossings have guards. Papers are checked. He
always passes but he knows at any point he might not.

When he can finally see his destination—his native land lying on
the other side of the checkpoint, the train patiently waiting for him,
he knows he will fail. He knows the guard who is checking papers
will recognize him, will tell him he does not belong, he cannot enter.
A ghost, joining the land of the living? He can hear the laughter of
bureaucrats that has echoed through his whole life. A ghost can't go
back to the land of the living. Or is he a living man trying to join the
world of the dead? This crossing should be easier. Everyone makes it
across, right? Can he?

—BEN BLACK

Advice

Notice that places of beauty can take many forms. In this case, a man who emigrated from his home country and became an immigrant by "going west" finds himself turning back toward his native land as his goal. We don't know why he left, or what he was running away from, but that it would suddenly feel attractive again after years as a wanderer without a home seems convincing.

31.

Maps

"What is a map but a useless prison?" asks Yesenia Montilla in the poem "Maps." And of course there are maps of all kinds in our worlds—boundaries between one space and another, whether physical, emotional, or intellectual. Crossing these boundaries can mean trouble, growth, or danger. Or salvation.

Maps could have affected where you went to school, where you played as a child, what laws you were subject to, what zoning your neighborhood had, where you were allowed to travel unencumbered, or any other restriction you can think of.

In this exercise, you will play with the idea of such territories to see what influence that has on character.

Exercise

1. Think of a time you were affected by a map: by a line signifying a local, state, country, or international border. This could even be an imaginary border: the wrong side of the tracks, a different neighborhood with a different cultural or racial makeup. Or an intellectual boundary: you are in one class, but there is an accelerated-learning class of "smart" kids that you long to be in.
2. Write a piece in which you (or a character) were prevented from doing something because of such a border.

Example

The sun was setting as we took the off-ramp, the last exit before the city centre. At the stop sign at the end of the off-ramp, we took the first left, drove a hundred meters, and turned left again, into a cul-de-sac. We could see the highway, with its many cars zooming past, on their way somewhere. Diesel fumes hung heavy, their smell coursing through our veins. The roads there were different, tarred. There were sidewalks. The houses were joined in a row, each with a front door and one window facing the street. We stopped halfway down the road, in front of a house painted green. Garden green. A low brick wall, with a closed steel and wire gate, protected the house from the sidewalk. This is what houses should look like, I thought. A real house has a brick wall and a gate.

I got out of the car, clutching my bag to my chest. The Quran inside felt important. The key that brought me here. I opened the gate, stepped past the boundary, closed my eyes, held my breath. I felt different, standing inside on the small square concrete stoop. What would it be like to live here? To open and close this gate anytime? To stand on the stoop and watch people go by? Yes, I'd reply, this is my house. We live here. Imagining the words filled me. I closed the gate, firmly. Our car was on the other side, its good side facing the house. On the good side, the car was one color, silver. On the bad side, the back door was black and the fuel cap was pink. If these people saw the wrong side of the car, they would know we did not belong here. I prayed my dad would not turn the car around while I was inside.

—ZURINA SABAN

Advice

The sense that this person doesn't feel she belongs in the new home is palpable from her musings as she describes the dwelling—as unappetizing as it might seem to us because of its location. That tells us more than anything that this family has sunk low in the socioeconomic ranks. Her relief at having a gate that closes, for example, is a beautiful detail that is grounded yet resonates at a much higher frequency than a mere physical gate should. She feels safe here.

32.

Love Lost

"Between what is said and not meant, and what is meant and not said, most of love is lost," wrote Kahlil Gibran.

He's talking about our inability to communicate effectively with the people we love. We do this by either (deliberately or subconsciously) saying something different from what we honestly mean, or by obscuring the truth by hiding in "subtext" what we want to say.

For example, a woman might want to express her love for a new romantic partner but be reluctant to say it directly. So she says something like "So that's the way you make your chicken soup!" and hope the true meaning (the subtext of "I love you") comes through.

This is a tricky exercise! You, the writer, have to put down words that imply things without saying them directly. The reader has to be able to discern what is true through this (false) dialogue. However, you also have the fictional tools of gesture, imagery, and association to help you express meaning that isn't directly spoken out loud.

Exercise

1. Create a scene between two characters where there is genuine affection.
2. Craft a believable conversation—using gesture and action, associations and imagery as well as words— in which the characters exchange words about some trivial disagreement. "You were late picking me up," for example. Or "You didn't do the dishes last night."
3. Within the scene, show how love is lost somehow by miscommunication—either by a character saying

something that they don't really mean, or a character not saying something directly enough to be understood by the other.

Example

Yelena pushes open the back screen door and hesitates for a minute, looking at the horizon. The sun is still high enough, and the water is flat.

Roberto sits with his back to her on the deck steps.

"You're still salty," Yelena says, kissing the back of his neck, then nestling her chin on top of his head. "Ready for our walk?"

"It is so beautiful here, isn't it?" Roberto asks, then, without waiting for an answer, says, "I think I'll leave my shoes. Easier to walk on sand." He unwraps himself from her arms and gets up. They walk side by side holding hands, close to the lip of the water. The long crescent of Stinson Beach curves ahead of them. In the far distance an enormous rock marks its northern point.

"What time is dinner?" Yelena asks.

"Mama said around seven. She's making scallops. Don't you just love it here? I am so ready to leave the city. I could surf every day if we moved here. We could start a family." Roberto gazes out at the water.

"We have plenty of time." Yelena smiles, moving closer to him and slipping her arm around his waist.

"Time?" Roberto says.

"Yes, time. To enjoy ourselves. To be alone," Yelena says.

"But I need to leave the city soon. I know you like it there, but I don't," Roberto says.

"No, I meant to take our walk before dinner. We've got an hour. We can walk to the rock and back. Just us. I love your parents, but it is nice to be just us, don't you think?"

Yelena looks up at him and pulls him closer. He resists.

"Well, it's getting to the point where I'm going to need to be with my parents more. You know, to help out." Roberto doesn't look at her, instead he makes a half circle toward the sea as he unfurls his arm and turns away from Yelena. "We don't have plenty of time. We need to decide. Soon."

She half laughs, shaking her head and looking down at her open hands. "Okay, I get it."

"No, I don't think you do," Roberto says.

Advice

Misunderstandings can start from innocuous things that are said. But what we hear when others speak, even if we are mistaken about our interpretation, can reveal truths. In this piece, despite their obvious affection for each other, the conversation and the misheard phrase "We have plenty of time" lead the couple toward an abyss in their relationship—an abyss neither was conscious of before the conversation began.

Using words rather than events to pry open characters and relationships is a very productive thing to try. Humans are always miscommunicating, misunderstanding, misinterpreting words. This can be very powerful in writing.

33.

Sorrow

Here's some wisdom from the poem "Kindness," by Naomi Shihab Nye: "Before you know kindness as the deepest thing inside / You must know sorrow as the other deepest thing."

Experiencing the world from a place of sorrow tends to make us more empathetic towards others, more careful of their feelings, and, depending on our character, perhaps more kind.

However, pushing your characters into a place where they choose to be kind to others is difficult to do without resorting to clichés and sentimentality. This exercise is structured to help you avoid those clichés.

Exercise

1. Think of an event that causes your character to experience deep sorrow. This can be the end of a life, the end of a relationship, even the end of a career (because there are people for whom their work is the most important achievement in their lives).
2. Create a scene (your specific character is in a specific place at a specific time) some years after the sorrowful event, in which your character is triggered to reexperience that deep sorrow. Try to make the trigger as indirect as possible while still making sense. For example, if your character is grieving the death of her mother, don't trigger her grief with a photo of her mother, but indirectly, such as, perhaps a woman on the bus has her mother's hands.
3. Next, in your scene, give your character the oppor-

tunity to perform an act of kindness in the midst of their rekindled sorrow. This can be helping a new mother change a diaper in the public bathroom, or overtipping a waiter.

4. Have your character make a conscious choice to be kind. Another way of thinking about this is the concept of "paying it forward."

Example

It is a gorgeous day, blue sky, not too hot. I'm sitting on our small front porch, half-hidden from the street and shaded by the century-old bougainvillea bushes that are in bloom in bright orange. It feels strange to not be in the office, not having my whole day planned out for me. Try being bored for once, Alexandra had advised. You've spent your life running around like a chicken, you know. Now is your time.

My time! I have to laugh.

The little boy from next door is drawing on the sidewalk with chalk, his mother nowhere in sight. She is very trusting. Perhaps she thinks the cat, which is winding its way through the little boy's legs, is a sufficient babysitter. I know they call the cat *gatito*. I don't know the name of the neighbors, that's what it's like here, close to the university. People move in and out all the time. Very few permanent residents such as myself on the street.

I have a pain in my chest. It's so strong I put my hands over it, and press hard. Could it be my heart? No, the heart is on the left side, and this is more center right. Yet the pain goes to the very core of me.

The fact is, I miss my life. My forties were insane, raising the twins while working full-time, I used to yearn for just one good night's sleep. My fifties, with teenagers to manage, was challenging in other ways. But I was at the top of my game then, at work, promotion after promotion came.

Then came the sixties. They started out okay, getting the twins off to college and breathing a sigh of relief, no empty-nester regrets at all.

But then, last week, the call into the CEO's office, the formal letter and severance package. With the kids graduated and working at their entry-level jobs on opposite ends of the country, and a sudden cease to a forty-year habit of getting up at six, showering, dressing appropriately, and fighting traffic to get to the office by 7:30, I am bereft. The days stretch out in front of me, to be filled—with what?

I notice the boy has stopped drawing on the pavement and is now chasing the cat, trying to catch its tail. The cat is too quick, darting here and there, and then, as I watch, springing out across the street. I jump up and run. I catch the little boy about halfway across. Luckily there are no cars. He doesn't like being accosted by a stranger, and is crying by the time we reach his door. The young woman who answers looks harried. She is wearing glasses and has a pen in her hand.

"Your little boy—what's his name?—ran into the street."

"Oh my God, I didn't even know he was outside! I'm studying for an exam. His name is Peter."

"And you're . . . ? I'm Janice. I live next door."

"Emily. Thank you so much."

"Emily, why don't you take a break and come over for a cup of coffee? Then I can watch Peter while you study."

"That's so kind of you!"

"No problem, I happen to have a free morning."

Advice

In this piece, the narrator is grieving for the loss of her familiar, busy, adult life. Having been used to feeling competent and successful—she was good at her job, and, we assume, a good single parent with kids who turned out all right—she is adrift suddenly with no job, no family. She doesn't even know her neighbors, so preoccupied has she been with her own life. By performing this act of kindness to her new neighbor, she has jolted herself out of her deep melancholy.

34.

Black Box

This exercise is based on George Saunders's definition of a short story in his book *A Swim in the Pond in the Rain*: that a story is a "black box" that a reader enters and comes out changed in some way by the experience. Each writer creates this black box with their unique combination of things in it for each story they write.

In other words, forget the "rules" of writing a story, forget conflict-crisis-resolution, forget characterization (for now). Just put together a collection of events that delights, excites, saddens, or emotionally demolishes your readers.

Exercise

Try to do this exercise without cheating. It takes some discipline. It will take a day of concentration at specific intervals.

1. Every waking hour in one day, write down something that will go into your black box. That is, something you observed, or thought of, or heard, or that you'd like to communicate, simply because it was interesting to you.
2. Do this every hour. The things you put into your black box do not have to be related to one another. In fact, they probably shouldn't obviously be too close to one another thematically. Just whatever is top of mind at that particular hour. Small, trivial things are welcome. ("A bee just buzzed too close to my face for comfort.")
3. Now write out what you've put in your box as a

numbered list. You should have at least five items, but the more the better.

4. Now consider how all the things together join up or conflict with the others. Don't judge, just observe. Are you interested in the juxtapositions? Amused? Bemused by your extremely random thoughts on this particular day?

Example

1. I find myself thinking of Dad, on his deathbed. I'd never seen anyone die before. Watching, and listening for each labored breath. Would this be the last one? Would this? He was a stubborn son of a bitch. He held on in the coma for ten days after they expected him to pass. The previous week, when he was admitted into the hospital for pneumonia (probably COVID) and the nurse asked if he had signed a DNR (do not resuscitate), he yelled, Hell no! Resuscitate! Resuscitate me! Do everything, anything, but keep me alive!

2. Being alone sometimes can be so much fun. Laze on the couch, eat junk, don't change out of your pajamas, call your friends and talk loudly without headphones on, play Bach so loud the glasses clink in the cabinet. And sometimes it can be such a drag, the empty minutes ticking away as you wait . . . and wait. . . . and wait. If and when I am widowed, I will finally get a dog. Just to get out twice a day to walk it, and let children pet it, and nod and chat to other dog owners. Not because I really want one. They're a shitload of trouble with their smelly breath and long, sticky tongues and noses that head straight for your crotch if you're not paying attention. There was Katie's and Kevin's dog that wouldn't leave me alone. I was having my period, and somehow the dog knew it and was insanely attracted to the scent of my menstrual blood. Whenever the dog came near I had to clench my thighs together and free my hands to push away its determined snout

from my private parts. I don't get my period anymore, thank God. Katie and Kevin voted for Trump. Twice. We don't speak much anymore.

3. I wonder how Susie will deal with it if James, her James, dies. She's not a very practical person. Ever since she was little, she always lived in her own dreamlike bubble. And Ricky is not an easy child. He was a biter, when small, and got kicked out the one preschool that would take him, given Susie refused to have him immunized, for gnawing at everyone who came within striking distance of his teeth, including the teacher. Now he's in high school. He was fascinated with the plague years in Europe when he was about five or six. He would ask me questions about it, as if living here I had absorbed some of the terror of the time. He kept asking, wasn't it scary? Later, he got into the Holocaust. He has a nose for the grotesque. If we have a serial killer in the family, it'll be Ricky.

4. Today was one of those deadline death-march days, actually weekends. I have to write the second half of that report on data frameworks. Thank God the research is done and put into the right order, I just have to connect the dots and actually write the damn thing. Then I have that ten-something reasons retailers are going to shit article for Mike. And then those Google emails. Those Googlers! It's no occupation for a grown person, what they have to do. They're so young, so ambitious, and so ignorant. It doesn't matter that they graduated from Stanford or Yale with straight A's, their job now is to check over copy to make sure it doesn't say anything not Googley enough. "What's the NHS?" one asked when I turned in my case study. "You never say what kind of business it is." About my lede, in which I quote an NHS doctor about his frustration at not giving his cancer patients proper care because of lost medical records, the same Googler commented, "Couldn't you write something more compelling? Like how important big data is in the digital era?"

5. Couldn't sleep last night. Weird dreams that I won't go into

here. Or maybe I will. They were about me trying to win a new client—a terrible woman, all suit and big hair and nyloned legs—do women actually still wear nylons?—but suddenly there were cannibals everywhere and we had to run for our lives. I outsmarted the cannibals by climbing up into the trees, but everyone else got torn apart and devoured, including the smarmy woman and her hair. Then suddenly I was with John in the house at 420 Fernando and he was berating me for sleeping with David, even though there was at least a decade between when things ended with John and things began with David. Even when I wake up and remind myself that I didn't do anything wrong, that I was a serial monogamist my whole life, it still takes half the morning to shake off the tawdry feeling that I'm dirty, and underhanded, and that I don't play fair by others. Especially that I owe people explanations—and apologies—for my shitty behavior and shittier thoughts.

Advice

Think of this exercise as a collection of odd items that could be called out as couples read different streams on their phones while sitting at breakfast. "Did you know that bees could tell time?" "Had you heard that X broke up with Y?"

Such things may seem—or even be—just surface happenings, simply skimming across life. But sometimes they cohere and interact with one another in interesting ways when juxtaposed and built upon.

Besides—and this is the important part—all of the observations in your black box came from you. You are the connective tissue. So even if you decide to fictionalize the real things that were put into your black box, the resulting piece will show your particular way of looking at and experiencing the world on one particular day. Which is, ultimately, what good writing is all about.

35.

Distracted by Scent

By using something perceived by one of the five senses to interrupt a train of thought, an argument, or even a daydream, you have an excellent way to nudge a scene or piece of narrative "off track." As I've said before, going off track is a good thing in a story, it encourages fresh associations and helps you avoid clichés. If a scene runs too smoothly along the track of logic, it runs the risk of being "expected," and for that, read b-o-r-i-n-g.

Here's a prompt to help you avoid predictable, clichéd scenes. You can try this with any of the five senses; it doesn't have to be scent, but our sense of smell is very powerful for eliciting memories, images, and emotions.

Exercise

1. Write a scene (something happening at a specific time in a specific place) where one character is attempting to convince another character of something. They can be discussing which restaurant to go to for dinner, for example, or what tie to wear with a particular shirt, or whether one should go out on a blind date with the other's friend. Anything goes.

2. Be careful to set the scene—where are they? What is the setting? Indoors? Outdoors? Are they surrounded by other people? Alone? What time of day is it? What season?

3. Right at the beginning of the scene, a strong smell overpowers the place—it can be pleasant or unpleas-

ant, but where it comes from or what it is exactly remains a mystery.

4. How does the smell affect the conversation? Does it make the characters uncomfortable? Does it remind them of something in their past? Do they get distracted by it? Irritated? Excited? Work the scent into the scene and make it as important as either of the two characters.

Example

Do you smell that? Mo makes a face.

No, you know my sense of smell isn't strong since I got the COVID. But listen . . . this is important . . .

It is putrid. It smells like, what, Mama, I don't even know.

I can't smell anything except dog in this apartment. Are you trying to change the subject, Mo? His mother leans her weight against the stove and turns to look at him.

No, not at all . . . Okay. I'm listening.

Mo pulls the collar of his shirt up over his nose so only his dark eyes are visible. He folds his legs up, balancing his heels on the edge of the chair, and wraps his hands around his calves. He looks like a black bug suspended in a spider web.

I am just saying that it is okay and even right to protest, but you need to be careful, and I need to know where you are at all times. Yesterday, you had me worried sick.

Mama, you really don't smell that? I got to close the window. Mo unfolds himself from the chair and moves to shut the kitchen window. Outside, the sun is shining in a blue sky. Then he turns to face his mother.

No one else's parents are tagging along. Not Rafael's. Not Kelvin's. Not even Malcolm's. He tries to say this quietly and reasonably. God, I can't stop smelling it. It is stuck in my nose. *No tengo hambre.* I can't eat with that shit.

His mother comes toward him, still holding the spatula in her hand. She is angry now.

Can you stop with this game? This is serious. Boys like you are getting shot out there. Every. Damn. Day. But as she gets closer to Mo, her face changes.

Oh my God, what is that?

See, Mama, I am telling you. Mo's speech is muffled by his arm across his nose and mouth.

Is it garbage?

His mother walks to the window and looks down at the busy street five stories down.

Is it stronger over here?

Mo's phone chirps, and Mo looks at it. He gets up. His mother is still searching outside the windows.

Diego's downstairs, Ma, I gotta go.

When will you eat? His mother moves toward the kitchen table, sniffing.

I think it is stronger here, she says, pointing to the corner, a look of disgust on her face.

Ma, I'm not hungry, I can't eat in here anyways. He grabs his hoodie and kisses her on the forehead.

She nods, holding her nose.

Maybe we should call someone? he says as he closes the door behind him, victorious.

Advice

Mo's mother is trying to have a serious conversation with him while she serves him dinner, but the smell gets in the way.

First Mo is distracted by it and his mother thinks he is diverting the conversation, but then once his mother catches a whiff, she is too. So the distraction serves to disrupt their interaction, and, inadvertently, cause Mo to "win" the argument (to go to the protest without his mother tagging along).

Any sensory disruption can do this—noise is an especially good one as well—by adding texture or even changing the course of what might otherwise be a clichéd conversation. In this case, a mother's worries about her son get sidetracked in a way that benefits Mo in his attempt to establish his independence.

36.

Toxic Touch

Being physically touched by another person can have enormous meaning.

Even a casual pat on the back can be extremely significant based upon the relationship between the characters, their history, and the relative power dynamics of their interactions.

Such a touch can feel friendly, even loving, or intrusive or dominating, depending on all these factors and more.

In this exercise, you will try to get the most effect from a slight (not overtly aggressive) touch.

Exercise

1. Place your character where they are uncomfortable. A crowded bar or restaurant. A party where they don't know anyone. A street at night.

2. Describe the scene carefully. Do not leave anything out. Try to make the character's uncomfortable feeling come out through the details. Do not say, "He felt uneasy" but "he swung around to look behind him every time he heard a noise."

3. Now introduce another character into the scene, who abruptly makes themselves known (the guy on the next barstool, a woman in an abandoned doorway).

4. Bring the scene to a point where the second character actually touches your first character Again, it doesn't have to be (perhaps shouldn't be) sexual. What does your character do? How does your character react?

Show us how their reaction is manifested in their actions, gestures, thoughts, or dialogue.

Example

It was a part of the town she didn't know, part of this strange country her parents had moved her to. But she had been to the house before and she remembered a row of white-painted houses and Pamela's was Number 36. Angelina looked at her watch; she was early. She walked along the other side of the street from the houses, next to a tall wall.

The sun was going down and it felt cooler. She was only wearing a thin blouse and she wondered if she should get her cardigan out of her bag. But she didn't; she kept on walking.

It was a quiet street. Not many people about, only the occasional car. A group of schoolkids passed her, carrying sports bags and with jackets hanging over their shoulders, dodging on and off the pavement. And then their voices, loud and excited, faded into the distance and were gone.

Angelina was alone on the street. She walked along the edge of the pavement, looking out for the row of white houses. It was a long road.

She heard a rattling sound behind her. She couldn't make out what it was. She turned around to look. An African boy was riding a bicycle along the road behind her, close to the curb. The bike was old and rusted and it squeaked and clattered as he pedaled towards her. Angelina kept on walking. He was young and lean and the setting sun glowed on his skin. He was right behind her now, cranking the bicycle up as much as it would go. As he passed her, he stretched out his hand and touched her breast.

It was so unexpected, she didn't have time to react. He half turned as he flew by and glanced at her. He didn't smile. Angelina looked straight back at him. He balanced the bike as the wheel veered awkwardly and then straightened out again. He cycled on until he reached the main road and turned left and disappeared out of sight.

She could still feel the imprint of his hand through her blouse.

Her heart was slowing down and she could see the row of white houses ahead of her and the number 36 on the wall. She glanced round to make sure no cars were coming and crossed the street. Then she pressed the bell.

Almost immediately, she could hear feet pounding down the stairs and Pamela's voice calling out, "Coming!" And then she was inside.

To her surprise, she said nothing. Angelina had imagined that it would be the first thing she would say. She thought perhaps it was the country she was living in that made her keep silent. The color of his skin, the color of hers, and the fact that he didn't smile. And she realized that she didn't want to talk about it, not to anyone.

—SHIRLEY KERBY JAMES

Advice

The tension in this piece comes, interestingly enough, from the calmness of the language. It's very matter-of-fact and unemotional. We get the feeling that much is being unsaid, left out.

Before the boy approaches the girl she sees him as an object of beauty, with the sun shining on his skin. The touching of the breast combined with his direct, serious expression doesn't feel sexual as much as perhaps a power dynamic being played out. We gather that they are of different races—he is African, and their skins are of different shades. We surmise that we are not in America but another country also being troubled with racial tensions, but perhaps these tensions are more out in the open.

All of this is rendered beautifully, with simple, clear language. After we read it, we realize that this small quiet piece about a touch holds much subtext—a good thing in our narratives.

37.

Time Travel

Moving around in narrative time is an important skill to master. Sometimes you want to tell a story linearly. But more frequently you will want to jump back (flashbacks), leap ahead, speed up the clock, stop the clock, or perform any other number of temporal tricks. Alice Munro is a master of this.

Here's an example from Munro, her short story "Post and Beam," in which she seamlessly dramatizes six (6!) different time zones in a few paragraphs (see if you can spot them all):

Lionel told them how his mother had died.

She had asked for her makeup. Lionel held the mirror.

"This will take about an hour," she said. Foundation cream, face powder, eyebrow pencil, mascara, lip-liner, lipstick, blusher. She was slow and shaky, but it wasn't a bad job.

"That didn't take you an hour," Lionel said.

She said no, she hadn't meant that.

She had meant, to die.

He had asked her if she wanted him to call his father. His father, her husband, her minister.

She said, What for.

She was only about five minutes out, in her prediction.

They were sitting behind the house—Lorna and Brendan's house—on a little terrace that looked across at Burrard Inlet and the lights of Point Grey. Brendan got up to move the sprinkler to another patch of grass.

Lorna had met Lionel's mother just a few months ago.

A pretty little white-haired woman with a valiant charm who had come down to Vancouver from a town in the Rocky Mountains to see the touring Comédie Française. Lionel had asked Lorna to go with them. After the performance, while Lionel was holding open her blue velvet cloak, the mother had said to Lorna, "I am so happy to meet my son's *belle-amie*."

"Let us not overdo it with the French," said Lionel.

Exercise

1. Like Alice Munro does, write a piece in which several characters are interacting. Put them in a specific place at a specific time (a scene).
2. Try to write three or four paragraphs where there are at least six (6) shifts in time. You can keep coming back to the present, or do flashbacks within flashbacks, as Alice Munro does.

HINT: Yes, "later that same day," or "an hour passed" are good transitions for time shifts. But don't overuse them. Try to do what Munro does: scenes within scenes and using verb tenses skillfully to make sure the audience doesn't lose sight of where we are, timewise, in the story.

Example

At 8:45 a.m., on her way to get a Hong Kong–style tea from the local Mongolian bakery, Rose spotted the run-over rat. It had not been there last week when she'd last made the same trip, purposely crossing to the side of Raul's Mexican Boxing Gym. In the very center of the street, a Subaru had made short work of the rodent, gluing hair, brains, and frothy pink insides to the cement.

When she saw the fighter at Raul's back in January, his naked torso glistening under the sign with the gym's motto—"If you can't trust yourself, how can I trust you?" in the window—she'd unconsciously committed to a weekly trip down that side of the street. Just once a week, not more. She'd learned her lesson when she accidentally locked eyes with his sparring partner. The two men clapped each other on the shoulders and laughed.

The animal control officer arrived after the sky turned pink. The expanse between Rose's and Raul's clear glass windows yawned with each passing hour, the entrance to the covert show barred by blinds, steel, and, now, decimated claws and fur. Standing directly in the center of the two sights, she could see swinging fists out of the corner of one eye, the pulpy body looming large in the corner of the other if she so much as tilted her head. Her spot was between desire and death.

Attracted to the unusual rumble of the animal control truck on their residential street, the occupants of Raul's spilled out onto the street just as Rose handed the bespectacled officer their shovel. Flash photography and loud murmuring enlivened the darkened evening. S-c-r-a-p-e went the shovel, the sound grating Rose's nerves, making the body and street separate once more. His task done, the officer called out to three sweaty men to turn on the jockey pump on the fire hydrant. His hose connected with what was left.

As the rat remains—some teeth, gray matter, otherwise unspecified—flowed down the street, Rose stuck her soiled hands into the pounding spray from the hydrant. The water wiped away the slick from having handed animal control their shovel, the insertion of her hands pushing the water out, soaking her clothes and hair. Shaking her hands out, she looked up and saw him.

Her fighter, his face a perfect mask of repulsion, watched the proverbial River Styx on its way to the gutter. Following the water back to its source, he noted her hands, the shovel's filth, and then silently traveled up her messy, soaked clothes to her face. He wiped his neck down with the towel tucked into the waistband of his shorts, blessedly free of this rodent hell. Rose jolted when their eyes connected, waiting for the disgust to disappear, for recognition, for warmth. Once a week indeed.

And yet the look of disgust remained. She did not know if it was empathy for her predicament or if he would forever associate her with run-over rat remains. Rose did know, however, that from then on, she would absolutely stay on her side of the street.

—ANNA ZAGERSON

Advice

Moving back and forth in time, if done well, can infuse your narrative with a lot of information as well as energy. A lot of times you might want to break up a sequential timeline for your story to play out. You can increase tension that way, as well as get history and backstory in.

Including flashbacks and stories within stories is also a good characterization exercise, as it can reflect more realistically how a character thinks. After all, who really thinks in a linear way? Our thoughts are usually all over the place, and capturing the seeming randomness of a character's ruminations can tell us more than all the description in the world.

Getting inside a character's brain for stream-of-consciousness writing, such as this, is also exciting for you as a writer because you can surprise yourself with what comes out.

38.

Things I Wish I Could Forget

It's important to write about things that matter. Otherwise, if we're not interested, engaged, and have substantial skin in the game, our writing will be lifeless, pallid, uninteresting. But getting to what matters can be difficult.

Often, we don't ourselves know how we think or feel until confronted with a situation that triggers intense emotions. This exercise is intended to try to help us dig into some of those things.

Yes, it's difficult. After all, you specifically want to forget these things! If it helps, write from the point of view of a character other than yourself. But make sure you get inside the character and inhabit them fully to get the right material out of them.

Exercise

1. Write down the title of a list: Things I Wish I Could Forget
2. Make a list of five things—can be incidents or images, narrative or scene—that you wish you could forget. Avoid abstractions at all costs. Make them specific things that could happen in the sensory world.
3. Describe each thing (event, incident, image, and so on) in a paragraph so we can understand why your character wants to forget it. But don't tell us *why* they want to forget it. Let that come through the imagery, dialogue, details, and context.

Example

1.

I know Nadia from the theatre program at the middle school where I'm one of the parent volunteers who paints backdrops. Last year, she was Little Red Riding Hood and the crowd gave her a standing ovation. Nadia improvised lines, improving the clichéd, familiar story into something magical. In Donahue's Bar, I tell her mother all this.

Nadia's mother is drunk, sitting on a barstool and blinking as if she can't see me clearly. Everyone knows this is where you'll find her.

I get that you want to have a big night out, I say carefully. Should I take Nadia somewhere? Does she have any relatives she can stay with?

The whole time, Nadia ignores us. She's sitting on a barstool, chewing on a straw, next to her mother, pretending to watch the TV above the bar. Some football game is on.

Her mother slides off the barstool, nearly toppling it. I step back. Then she starts to laugh.

Fuck you. You not taking my girl from me. Everyone trying, but she mine.

2.

The day after we left the hospital, I screamed at Jeremiah on the street, teeth bared. Was it a hormonal fluctuation, lack of sleep, or is this grief? I stood there, toes turned in, stomach still round, voice loud and tears falling.

Jeremiah stood, holding the car seat that should have held our sleeping infant son.

A meter maid approached to check our meter. Hearing my tirade, she skipped it and moved on to the next. Bitch, I whispered under my breath.

3.

I woke up to the sound of Meg moaning. That evening, I had chained her up so she would not chase the goats. I looked out on the terrace to see what was the matter, and she had something in her mouth.

Meg, how did you catch a rabbit chained up like that? I said.

In the dark, I could make out something slick and wet, wriggling: had she skinned the rabbit alive?

When I was just a few feet away, I realized what it was, and gasped.

It was not a rabbit at all, but a tiny puppy, eyes still closed, that she held aloft. Her eyes shone in the dark. How had I mistaken her round belly and full breasts as fat?

I unchained her and led her inside, making her a soft bed out of old towels. I boiled her eggs, which she ate ravenously between birthing eleven babies. I raised a small blue bowl of water to her mouth, to save her the effort.

By morning, a squirming mass of black-and-white mewling creatures nipped at her breasts with delicate tongues, kneading her with twenty-two pink paws, their eyes sealed shut. I could not look away.

One puppy went limp. Meg pushed it away from the rest with her nose, its tiny body shaking and foaming at the mouth. By midday, it was still and cold. Meg let out a low cry as she watched me wrap it carefully, like a China cup, in a cotton cloth.

It was no bigger than my hand and weighed less than a lemon.

4.

The woman in the nail salon is bent over my foot, scrubbing the calluses off my big toe with a pumice stone.

She rests my heel in her hand appraisingly, then places it carefully back in the tepid water.

When she pats the opposite shin lightly, I hold my other foot up to her without acknowledgment.

I flick through a *Vogue* magazine, holding it between us. What I am asking her to do, sitting below me, scrubbing my feet, painting my nails in quick, even strokes is not lost on me, but I need it. For this hour, the magazine allows me in, and I shut her out.

I respond mechanically to her nudges and taps. I do not acknowledge her, except to flinch when she pushes my cuticles too hard.

After she is finished, as I sit waiting for my nails to dry, I see her name tag. Jane, it reads. But of course her name is not Jane.

I give her a $20 tip, far too much, and she bows.

Do you want massage? On house? she asks.

No, I shake my head.

Thank you. I whisper, but she has already turned her back.

I leave in a hurry, my own head down, nails still wet.

5.

We were playing Spin the Bottle at a party in Toby's barn.

Kiss him, Laura hissed at me. I climbed up into the hayloft. Tucker followed me.

It was dark up there. I sat on a hay bale and waited. The tittering below added a chorus to the crickets humming outside.

Hey, he said.

Hi, I said.

The hay was prickly and I could feel it through my jeans. I had imagined kissing Tucker for months, written extensively about it in my journal. The tiny earring in his ear, a chip of cubic zirconia, was a fetish. His freckles and blond hair, his lanky frame I had described in excruciating detail. The Diesel T-shirt worn several consecutive days a week was a frequent topic of intrigue for my writing.

Stand up, he said.

I stood up. He stood in front of me and took my hand, I closed my eyes. Instead of soft lips and electricity I felt something akin to an eel in my mouth, wet and squirming, poking hard into the back of my throat. I stood perfectly still and erect with my hands clenched behind his back, trying not to gag.

Advice

The things we want to forget are full of possibility. They have power, the experiences so awful or sad or distressing or shameful that they trigger a visceral reaction in us.

If we do our job as writers, we should make readers feel similarly. By putting the reader there rather than simply summarizing a narrative, we can use concrete sensory details to re-create our (or our character's) experience.

The biggest takeaway from this exercise is that we should always be looking for things that have power over us. That's where the good stories are buried. A lot of times they live in the places we don't want to look. All the more reason to try.

39.

The To-Do List

One of the biggest risks when writing is that our stories come out lifeless or stagnant. That nothing happens, either in the physical or the emotional world of the characters.

One way to address this is to force them into action—make them do things and see what happens. This is a plotting exercise to help you do this: write them the classic "to-do" list.

You don't need to write about overly dramatic events. You can have "Get a gallon of skim milk" on your list. The point is to just get your characters in motion. See what happens next

Exercise

1. You can do this as yourself, or as a character.
2. Write a to-do list of things that need to be done within the next week.
3. Make it a combination of high-urgency (fix the leak in the roof) and low-urgency (don't forget the ketchup) things.
4. Now write a scene (something happening at a particular place at a particular time) when your character tries to do something on their list, but is frustrated in the attempt.
5. Either they are interrupted, or missing a tool, or don't have the change in their pockets . . . Write the scene out, and see how your character reacts.

Example

TO DO: low priority

☐ Buy a new shower curtain
☐ Clean out the hall closet
☐ Check opening hours of the new library
☐ Make an appointment to get the dog's nails clipped at PetSmart

TO DO: high priority

☐ Pick up medications
☐ Buy elbow brace
☐ Call the plumber
☐ Invite Joan to lunch

The shower curtain is gray and moldy around the bottom. It is still keeping the water in the tub, but I know when my daughter comes to visit, she will point to it, shaking her head. I imagine with a little elbow grease and some bleach I could scrub it clean, but I don't feel like doing that, so I stop at the department store on my way to the library to pick up a new one.

I volunteer on Fridays, reshelving books. I look forward to it every week, those three hours of pushing the cart from row to row, following the Dewey decimal letters and then numbers to slip the books back into their places. The perfect order of things.

In the department store, I am overwhelmed by the garish curtains. Fish in brilliant colors, polka-dot themes, curtains with shells and seahorses.

What color is your bathroom? the saleswoman asks, looking at my chest.

I look down to see what she is looking at and notice a huge glob of mustard smeared on the front of my cardigan.

Yellow, I say.

I'll be right back, she says.

I dab at the mustard and turn quickly toward the elevator in embarrassment, not bothering to wait for her to return. The elevator lets me out where my car is parked in the subterranean lower level.

Advice

In this example, see how simple entries on a to-do list can lead to full-blown scenes that, when examined, have much more meaning than the simple listed item revealed.

What's especially interesting in this piece is how this scene builds to that meaning. The search for a shower curtain becomes more than a search for a shower curtain—it takes on urgency as it progresses. This is a woman who loves order and quiet. We hear about how much she enjoys her job at the library, doing a job that might seem dull to someone else. Then we see her distaste of the brightly colored shower curtains on display. Finally, we feel her shame when she realizes she has a stain on her blouse—to someone like her, this is an awful moment—hence her escape from the store before the saleswoman can come back.

40.

Suspense

This is an exercise in suspense—an essential tool for writers. If you can't build suspense, you won't get your reader to turn the page and continue reading—the ultimate test of a piece of writing.

> Suspense must be achieved in a piece of fiction just before the discovery of a body, for example. You might perhaps describe the character's approach to the body he will find, or the location, or both. The purpose of the exercise is to develop the technique of at once attracting the reader toward the paragraph to follow—making him want to skip ahead, and holding him on this paragraph by virtue of its interest. Without the ability to write such "foreplay" paragraphs, *one can never achieve real suspense.* [emphasis mine]
>
> —*The Art of Fiction*, JOHN GARDNER

So what tools do we have to write these important "foreplay" suspense paragraphs?

1. Language/imagery: The sky was low and brooding, and the fog was creeping darkly into the punishing terrain.
2. Backstory/History: They'd heard on the radio that the madman Captain Hook had escaped from the local insane asylum.
3. What characters say: "Did you hear that noise?" she asked.
4. What characters do: She tripped and fell onto her knees, jarring her whole body, and as she tried to recover, something soft brushed her hand.

5. What characters see/don't see: She suddenly had a clear view under the bed. She couldn't believe what she saw there.

6. Sounds: They could hear a muffled noise, like heavy breathing, coming from the other room.

7. What characters think/how they make associations: She remembered the last time she had been alone with Jack. It had not been a good time.

Exercise

1. First, imagine a moment (or moments) of drama. A baby is being born. Someone is unwrapping a special present. If you want to really go for it (it's risky, but try it) do what Gardner suggests: discovering a body. Or perhaps the moment before a riot begins. Or if you like, think small. Small things can lead to big drama.

2. Now write a scene (something that happens at a specific time in a specific place) that *leads up* to that moment. In other words, everything that happens *before* the dramatic event.

3. Make sure to end the scene before the dramatic moment occurs.

4. Keep in mind that suspense is achieved by your reader *having partial or imperfect knowledge that something of dramatic significance is about to occur.*

Example

It was dark when I saw Matias's car pull into the white expanse of the empty parking lot. The snow muffled the engine's noise, so it moved silently, like a creature navigating the sandy bottom of the sea.

Matias used to work here, so he knew Suzy and the guys would all be gone by now and the lights would be off for the night after 9 p.m.

Suzy never liked me, better not be seen with me, he said on the phone.

He told me he would pick me up behind the rink, near the garage where the Zamboni was kept. Matias had been the maintenance guy at the rink, and drove the Zamboni to smooth the rink in between skate sessions. This was my third winter working in the booth handing out skates after school. When skaters returned their skates I tucked the laces back inside and sometimes found a dirty sock. Once I found a twenty-dollar bill.

I often have a nick or two on my fingers from sharpening the skate blades. The week before Matias was fired, a blade hit the rotating wheel and skidded, cutting my hand. I nicked the bone on my wrist pretty badly. Matias had seen it happen and wrapped it up for me, putting betadine in the cut from the first aid in the storage room. The day after, he came to check on it.

It's fine, really. I said.

Let me just see, sweetheart, I think I should be the judge here, he said.

In the storage room, he held my wrist in his hand tenderly, stroking my fingers, his dark face so close to mine I could feel his breath on my cheek.

The next day, it was slow and I had no skates to sharpen. I stood beside the rink watching the lessons through the scratched Plexiglas. The girls were younger than me, all of them white, of course, dressed in flimsy skirts, shivering in the cold until it was their turn to perform for the coach. Then they would circle and fly across the ice, every muscle visible beneath their white tights, like skinned rabbits.

Matias came and stood next to me, but looked at me instead of them.

I'll pick you up after work tonight, he said. It wasn't a question.

Advice

This piece shows how to build suspense with implications rising mostly from the imagery.

We know very little about these characters, but sharp objects always imply danger. The sharpness of the skate blades, and the fact that the character had already been not-insignificantly injured by them foreshadows that something not good is coming.

The narrator's youth and naïveté shine through the details. The way she describes the skaters as resembling "skinned rabbits" indicates that she knows she is in the position of a helpless victim. That Matias didn't ask her for a date but told her they would have one is another foreshadowing. This piece is full of tension because we know from the "frame" in the beginning (before going into a flashback for the backstory) that a clandestine meeting is about to happen, and that there's an uneven power dynamic at play.

41.

Survival

We can learn a lot about writing stories from other genres. Take the time-honored fairy tale. There are wonderful opportunities for borrowing plot devices and developments from them. Take this observation by the writer Rebecca Solnit:

> In [fairy tales], power is rarely the right tool for survival anyway. Rather the powerless thrive on alliances, often in the form of reciprocated acts of kindness—from beehives that were not raided, birds that were not killed but set free or fed, old women who were saluted with respect. Kindness sown among the meek is harvested in crisis in fairy tales, and sometimes in actuality.
>
> —REBECCA SOLNIT, "Apricots"

Exercise

1. Pick a situation in which your character is in a position of powerlessness. Perhaps they are a younger sister with bullying siblings. Perhaps they are an underling dealing with an obnoxious employer.
2. Write a scene (something happening at a specific time in a specific place) in which your character performs an act of kindness, or makes an alliance, with someone with even less power than they have.
3. Now write a scene in which that kindness "sown among the meek is harvested in crisis." In other words, it pays off. Try to avoid simplistic scenarios

where someone "comes to the rescue" in an obvious way.

Example

The view from in here is exactly the same every day. Like being adrift in the ocean. Each time you think you see land, it slips out of sight. Every day is the same. Fear keeps you alive, and when all you want is to die, you can't even do that.

Neil is new, and he is small, five-three at most. They put him in my bunk for a few nights because Jerome just got out.

At intake, they make you choose your race. Neil identified himself as Black instead of Mexican, but he looks more Mexican to me. Like my brother.

Hombre, eres Negrito? I say.

I'm from Minnesota, I don't speak Spanish, Neil says.

I know better than to try to help him. There is no sense in helping anyone in here.

He cried that night. His muffled sobs infiltrated my dreams.

Stop that shit right now, or I will come down there and stop you, I said.

The next morning I take pity on him on the way to the canteen.

Stand up tall, and look straight ahead, don't look down. Do not accept gifts from anyone. Not a cigarette, not a slice of bread, nothing.

Neil gets transferred to another cell, and I don't see him for a few weeks, until today, when he is behind me in line for breakfast.

I nod at him and he nods back. He looks fine, and I am surprised.

Jose is serving up oatmeal that tastes like dirty water.

Fuck you, Francis, he says to me, spitting in my serving.

I used to fight, and I cut him years ago. His scar is long, running from his ear to his mouth. I am sorry I did it, but it was necessary at the time. Now it means I skip breakfast when Jose is working the line.

Hola pequenito, Jose says to Neil, looking him over.

Give Francis another helping, with extra brown sugar. Or I am going to give you this, Neil says, straightening up and flashing a smile. His tongue comes out. A razorblade sits on the pink flesh.

Jose obeys.

Advice

Alliances between characters can be just as interesting as conflicts.

When someone offers kindness in the form of help with no expectation of reciprocity, complicated relationships can develop.

In this case, the narrator takes pity on Neil and gives him some advice on his first day in prison. Later, Francis reaps benefits that he had no expectations of. What might happen next? Who knows? That's the fun thing about writing stories . . . there are always surprises.

42.

Story Within a Story

Writing a story within a story is a very common fictional technique. *The Arabian Nights* provides a wonderful example, in which Scheherazade prevents her cruel husband from killing her by telling him a cliffhanger story every night—stopping when the sun rises. So eager is he to hear the rest that he postpones her execution until the next morning. And the next. And the next.

Juxtaposing one story against another can have wonderful dramatic and emotional effects in a piece—especially when the embedded story bounces off what's "real" (in the main story) in surprising and insightful ways.

Exercise

1. Think of (or make up) a time when someone close to you, or to a character you have in mind, was down in the dumps for good reason—that is, they were in a difficult situation because of real, not imaginary, events.
2. You will write a piece in which you or your character tries to cheer them up.
3. First, make it clear specifically how the first character is in a bad place.
4. Then, your other character tells them a story (real or made up) as a way of distracting them.
5. *Do not* use language like "cheer up," or "things aren't that bad!" And *do not* make the story-within-a-story too sweet or nice—make it complicated. It doesn't even need to be particularly related to the character's

specific situation—but it should have resonance with what's going on all the same.

Example

Brendan is in Golden Gate Park. He has no shoes on, and can't remember where they had gone, so he's just sitting on a bench looking at his bare feet when the big guy, Calian, appears. Brendan has been staying put there, in the sun, all morning. You can't really go anywhere if you have *no shoes*. He laughs to himself about that. When he wants to stop thinking, he concentrates on trying to wiggle each toe individually.

Shit, dude. Where's the party? Calian sits down on the bench. Good to see you, little brother. You ain't looking so tight.

Brendan laughs, hugging him. Good to see you, bro! When did you get out? I lost my shoes! He lifts his dirty feet off the ground. Legs splayed wide.

I see that. Must have been good? Calian asks.

I dunno, man. I am down and out, Brendan says, trying to rub the dirt off his heel with his hand.

Listen, let's go get some breakfast and some shoes, Calian says.

I got some heat on me, Brendan says. He leans his face into his hands on his lap, open like a prayer book.

Nothing that a bacon, egg, and cheese can't fix? Calian punches him lightly on the arm.

Listen, I ran into Jesse yesterday. He is all cleaned up, wearing a suit! He has a job in the Valley at a start-up; he got his act together. Remember how cashed he was? He went through some kind of training program, got his shit together.

That's not exactly what I've been up to, Brendan says.

You're young. You have time. Calian stands up. Let's get out of here.

Jesse? Whoa. He was a real mess, Brendan says. He tries to stand up, too, but his feet are badly blistered on the bottom and he winces.

But I have to say, Jesse always had shoes, he says. So I guess he wasn't as big a mess as me.

I got you, Calian says, putting his arm under Brendan's.

Advice

Stories within stories can play off each other, contrasting what's happening in one with what's happening in others, either in parallel or going in opposite directions. Even here, where the story is supposed to be a morality tale to inspire Brendan to clean up his act, we get insight into how far Brendan has fallen, and how long he's been in the mess he's in, from the story Calian tells.

43.

Sins of Commission/Omission (Part I)

In the Catholic theology, sins aren't just what you do that are wrong—you can also commit sins of omission, where you sin by *not* doing something. In Catholicism, for example, it is a sin of omission to not go to Sunday Mass.

We're going to play on this concept. For the idea of sin, substitute simply something you did (or didn't) do that you knew was wrong.

This is a two-parter: First, write two lists, either from your own point of view or from a character's. Then, in the next part of the exercise, you will do something with your lists. This is both a character study (how does your character evaluate their own morality?) and a plotting device (you will have a lot of material to play with to develop scenes or even whole stories).

Exercise

1. Think of a character, real or imagined (it can be you, and you don't have to tell us).

2. First, write ten "sins of commission"—things that your character considers wrong that they have done in their life. No murders or large-scale robberies please. Keep it something your character would do in the normal course of their life. It can be an emotional sin; I hate my cousin Jackson, for example. Keep it small and detailed. Just a one- or two-sentence description of each sin.

3. Next, write ten "sins of omission"—bad things about your character that are the result of *not* doing some-

thing, for example—not loving their mother as much as they should. Again, keep it small, concrete, and *specific* . . .

Sins of Commission

1. Joyce found out who Alison was from her sister Jane and pursued her friendship because she was fascinated by Sahar's fortune.
2. Joyce asked Chris at the beach to rub sunscreen on her back when Alison was swimming.
3. Joyce lied about the dent in the car door.
4. Joyce knew people felt sorry for her loss of a limb, and used it to her advantage.
5. Joyce was happy to see Jane had gained weight and her clothes didn't fit anymore.
6. Joyce stole small items: underwear, a black cashmere sweater, a thin gold chain from Jane.
7. Joyce did not return the extra $20 to the cashier.
8. Joyce wanted Alison and Chris's marriage to fail.
9. Joyce lied about smoking to her doctor.
10. Joyce said she mailed the package and pretended it had gotten lost in the post.

Sins of Omission

1. Joyce walked out and did not tip the waiter.
2. Joyce did not tell Lee she had an abortion.
3. Joyce did not intervene when the professor reprimanded Edna.
4. Joyce did not give Jane the letter from Sam. She threw it away.
5. Joyce did not help the woman who was lost, even though she heard her say where she needed to go and Joyce knew the directions.

6. Joyce did not return the library book when she knew others were waiting to read it.

7. Joyce did not put on her bio she was missing an arm for fear it would influence her candidacy.

8. Joyce did not raise her hand in her women's studies class when the professor asked about affirmative action.

9. Joyce did not reveal to Jane what Eddie told her about Sam, their younger brother.

10. Joyce did not speak up when Eddie threatened the young kid.

Advice

From these two lists—from the things Joyce does that she knows are wrong to the things Joyce *omits* to do that she also knows are not right, we get a fairly strong sense of Joyce's character—not just what is "sinful" about her behavior but her knowledge of her own shortcomings.

44.

Sins of Commission/Omission (Part II)

Exercise

Now you'll write a piece in which your character is made to feel guilty about one—just one—of the sins (either omission or commission). Do *not* directly reference the sin itself. Have the characters in your piece move "around" the subject by way of subtext.

NOTE: This writer worked from an item of her "sins of omission" list about not being kind to the odd girl out in school.

Example

The cafeteria, which doubled as the middle school auditorium, was filled with round, blue tables with six seats each and two long, white tables with twelve seats each. The white tables were at the front of the room near the stage. The round, blue tables were where friends sat together. The long, white tables were where lonely sixth graders sat quietly. Marcella had sat at the end of the left of these tables with a turkey sandwich and two Oreos every day since she had moved six weeks earlier.

But she had been working on Marie from her French class for three days now, ever since they partnered on performing a scene in a grocery store. Marie sat with Janet, Vicky, Vivian, Carolina, and Janet's red backpack. The backpack didn't contribute much to the conversation, but it did prevent any undesirables from sitting in the sixth seat. Marcella just needed to be cooler than Janet's backpack and she wouldn't need to sit at the white table anymore in front of the whole school.

The grocery store scene had been a coup, and since proving her skills with vegetable-related vocabulary, Marie had been quite friendly and even once implied that she would be willing to walk together to the library after school one day in the future. For three days now, Marcella had walked directly past Marie and her table on the way to the front and Marie had smiled, and once Janet had made eye contact, but no one had moved the backpack to the floor.

Today, though, Marie had left French class saying, "See you at lunch!" and this had filled Marcella with hope. Sure enough, as Marcella slowly walked by the table, the most magical thing she had ever seen happened. Janet lifted her backpack and moved it gently to the crumb-covered checkered floor.

"You can sit here," Janet said, and Marie eagerly nodded. Marcella could not believe her change in fortune. It felt amazing to sit in a circle, as a part of something, a feeling she hadn't experienced since before the move. She sat at the round table every day that week.

On Monday, Vicky was out sick, and her chair sat empty. As the lunch line thinned out and the last sixth graders took their seats, Colleen from the white table passed by. "Can I sit here?" she asked quietly. Marcella wanted to say, "Sure," but instead she looked at Janet. She couldn't risk losing her place.

Janet pulled her backpack from the floor and placed it on the chair. "It's taken," she said.

Colleen nodded. She had known the answer. She continued with her tray to the long, white table at the front of the room. Marcella watched her as she sat and bent over her pizza.

"Ew," said Janet.

"Ew," agreed Marie.

Marcella nodded. Conversation continued as she watched Colleen twirl her straw.

—DANIELLE STONEHIRSCH

Advice

Sins, even small ones, can be like pebbles that are thrown into a pond, where the water ripples out in widening circles, causing disruptions. They have consequences. Delving into those sins and the resulting consequences is excellent fictional territory. In this case, this young girl does something very understandable—having just made it into a valued group, she then denies another girl membership.

45.

Clothes Make the (Wo)man

The point of this exercise is to dramatize the magic that can happen by putting on a particular piece of clothing.

It doesn't have to be shoes (as in the following example); it can be any garment. True, not every character might be sensitive to such an action. But in surprising ways, most people are (men as well as women). It has to do with self-image, how people want to appear in the world. You can get a lot of mileage out of a piece of clothing when it comes to building character.

Exercise

1. Name your character's favorite piece of clothing.
2. Make a list of all the qualities that make it their favorite.
3. Then, describe the item precisely and exactly. Don't worry about whether it's boring.
4. Now write three vignettes of three times when your character was wearing the item and something happens that could only have happened because they were wearing it.

Example

Booker loves his navy patent leather stacked-heel pumps because:
- ☐ The pumps make him four inches taller and elongate his legs.
- ☐ When he walks in the pumps he feels himself—powerful and feminine.

☐ The wingtip detail is masculine and dandy.
☐ They are Christian Louboutin, an expensive designer
brand.

Vignette 1

Booker's pumps have never been worn before; the inside of the
shoes are pristine brown leather, the soles bright red. Made in Italy is
stamped in tiny silver letters on the insole.

The dark-blue patent shimmers slightly when the light catches it.
The toe is neither pointed nor rounded—exactly the shape of a man's
brogue, with hand-tooled wingtip-style serrated edges.

The stacked heel is four inches, made of wood, and surprisingly
easy to walk in, despite the height.

Booker had found the shoes at the Episcopal Church thrift store
on a sweltering Friday night after work. His feet were swollen from
standing at the checkout line all day, and from the heat, but the high
heels slipped on his narrow feet as if they were made for him.

My Cinderella slipper, he laughed to himself.

The woman at the checkout smiled at him as he placed them on
the counter.

I wish these came in my size. They are expensive, Louboutins.

I am worth it, Booker said, handing her his credit card.

At home, he hurries into his room. He opens the box. He slips
a shoe onto his right foot, not bothering to take off his food service
uniform. He stands up and gazes at himself in the mirror.

Suddenly, Booker's legs are elongated, his small frame elevated to
almost the hanging light. Booker feels like he has been turned inside
out, and seeing himself like this for the first time. Herself.

Vignette 2

It is Friday, and Booker is meeting his cousin, Keisha, downtown.
He puts his pumps in his backpack and wears sneakers to walk to the
train. The train car is empty; it is still early. He pulls his pumps out of

his bag and slips them on, putting her sneakers in her backpack. When the train stops at Marcy Ave, she gets off. The elevator is broken, and so she takes the stairs. There are three sets of endless long, narrow stairs just to get aboveground. Normally, in sneakers, she would bound up the stairs, but now her left foot is throbbing after the first twenty steps. The heels of her pumps are getting scuffed on the metal treads of the stairs. Man, is this worth it? she asks herself.

Vignette 3

Booker is wearing the pumps with a long, wide-legged pair of trousers that graze the floor. The toes peek out when she walks, but without looking closely, they appear to be normal men's brogues. She first tries walking quickly through the train station, but because her feet are hurting, finds a bench to sit down on. She hikes her pant legs up to her thighs to get a closer look at her feet, which are blistering. A little boy sitting next to Booker sees the shoes and points.

Momma, that man is wearing girls' shoes.

At first Booker feels panic. Then she smiles at the boy. Yes, I am, she says.

Advice

In this story, Booker is transitioning gender. The shifts in pronoun are meant to show how the shoes help with the transitioning, and how she is experiencing the highs and lows of the transition. And all this comes from putting on a pair of shoes. As I said, you can do this with any piece of clothing, or even accessories, like a bracelet or a ring. Your fictional world can bounce off such things in many interesting, fresh ways.

46.

Sheltering in Place

The pandemic affected us all very deeply. No matter where we were living, or what restrictions had been imposed on us, it was a strange time for everyone. Emerging from it, we all had different reactions to being out in the world again. This exercise tries to explore reactions to being in public after more than a year sheltering in place.

Exercise

1. You are in the place that you (or a character) lived in during the pandemic, sheltering in place. Finally, comes the day you can finally go out to do more than go to the food shop, exercise, or visit the doctor.
2. Describe the place you have been sheltering in in detail (don't worry about whether it is boring—just describe).

IMPORTANT: Write this description from the perspective that you are now free to leave this place. Does it feel confining? Dark? Dingy? Or is it suddenly friendly again now that you can leave? Let the description tell us how it feels.

3. Then continue by writing a scene that dramatizes what your character chooses to do on their first day of freedom. Do they drive their car to the beach? Play basketball with friends? Eat in a restaurant? Build a scene that shows how they reenter the world. Is it easy or difficult?

Example

For fifty-one weeks, Ramon has not left the confines of his apartment. The morning the lockdown lifted he woke up later than usual and spent most of the morning in bed reading, with his cats kneading their claws into his old blankets. The sun streamed into the bedroom through the yellowing curtains, the dust and cat hair floating on the light's beams.

Ramon had no urge to get up and go out. What would he do?

After all the weeks of staying inside and DoorDash and Amazon deliveries, he had adapted and found the limitations oddly comforting.

I really am just an old Communist, he mused.

His apartment is a small one-bedroom place, the kind of apartment a graduate student might live in. The dimly lit living room has become a nest: an archeological excavation of his last year. Stacks of books and newspapers surrounding the cheap gray couch. His desk piled high with papers. A dead lightbulb that he replaced lies tenuously close to the edge of his desk. He did not know whether it could be recycled, so he has left it there for more than two months.

Each Monday for the past year a delivery of necessities is left in a box on his doorstep organized by his daughter, Rosella. Five cans of cat food, a bag of kitty litter, milk, six eggs, coffee, a loaf of sandwich bread, four cans of soup, apples, lettuce, cheese, pecan sandies, and butter. Rosie also calls him to check in almost every morning.

Papa, are you okay? Depressed? Need anything? she always asks.

I am fine, sweetie, really.

And it is true; he is surprised how relieved he is to not have anything to do.

Other than Rosie, he has spoken to no one. He can hear the young couple arguing through the walls. Sometimes the arguments were really just strained voices bickering, but sometimes he heard the baby crying and things crashing.

Stop, please. For the baby, he wanted to yell, but instead he stood there with his head against the wall, listening and waiting.

This morning the noise is different. The baby is quiet and he hears

the woman laughing, her husband's low baritone broken occasionally by her quick, excited talk. Ramon goes to the window in his
underwear and watches as the couple leave the building. The view
is obscured by the new leaves budding on the maple tree. The father
pushes the stroller, his arm around his wife.

Tomorrow I will go out, Ramon says, and climbs back into bed.

Advice

Sometimes when we are prevented from doing something, there can
be relief in it. Being confined might seem like a punishment for many,
but it turned out to be a welcome event for others. We've heard many
stories of how, during the pandemic, many people got used to not
going out or seeing anyone, and that it became an entrenched habit.
The people who came out said they found the world altered from
when they first retreated. Rendering exactly what a character went
through during the shelter-in-place period is an excellent exercise in
characterization.

Note how much can be depicted by the images and the details. We
don't need to be told Ramon's state of mind directly—it comes out in
the way he sees his apartment, how he views the outside world, even
the food he eats.

47.

Self-Sabotage

This is a plotting exercise. Remember, we are always thinking of things we can "do" to our characters to get them to reveal themselves and surprise themselves—and us. What better way than having them do something to undermine themselves?

Exercise

1. Make a list of five ways that you (or a character, of course) can self-sabotage.
2. Be as specific as possible. Not, "I put myself down," but "When someone says I look nice, I always say, No I don't."
3. Next, write a list of five successes that your character has achieved, despite these self-sabotages. They can be small successes, but successes nonetheless.
4. Now write a scene (something happening in a specific place at a specific time) in which your character is tempted to sabotage something that could possibly be a good thing.

HINT: Whether your character succumbs to the temptation to self-sabotage is up to you.

Example

He thought of himself, when he thought of himself, as just a schlub from Nowhereville. He was a nothing and nobody from nowhere who just had a way with words. Words that had garnered him a small bit of fame; he was still waiting on the fortune. But, just perhaps he thought, after his third book and two National Book Award nominations, one win, and now a long-shot Pulitzer nomination, he figured he could start earning some money so he could pay his landlord on time. Ugh, he thought. One day I will be a real writer.

Last year he was flown to four different foreign countries to read and pontificate on all things writerly and poetic. All he knew was how to raise a pen and pour out his Nowhereville anguish. He always felt so awkward and out of place at these talks. Once, in NYC, some famous writer asked for his opinion on the state of modern African American literature in Obama's post-racial America. He feigned nausea from the shrimp or bad mayonnaise in the Waldorf salad and hustled off to the restroom.

He knew he was an imposter, a hack with a golden pen, nothing more. Even though he loved his writings, he knew there were better writers out there; he knew he was just lucky and once his style of in-your-face journalistic prose and poetry died, so would his career. Once America grew tired of reveling in the pain and death of Black Americans, he'd fade away into the dark nothingness he had come from.

There in the bathroom, instead of going into a stall to get away, he stood in front of a urinal, pants unzipped, pretending to urinate. Ughh! Such a dork-loser, he thought. I can't even run away and hide like a real writer. Instead of a dramatic scene where I'm found in a stall regurgitating my dinner, here I am fake-peeing.

So, he went to writers' conferences and fake-peed—a lot. Attended literary festivals where he would sit onstage and fake-pee while in his folding chair. In front of hundreds and hundreds of watching eyes, he would read and then act like a man with a bladder problem and spew junk phrases all over the audience.

Tonight, while writing, he remembered that he has an award show next week where he will be receiving some prize. He wonders if his impostor outfit—black sleek dress pants, a black, Elizabeth Holmes–style knit turtleneck, and a black tux jacket—is fancy enough. He doesn't own a tux.

He is already worrying about what he will say on the dais. He thinks about how he almost declined the invitation, his fear of being found out as an impostor almost had him write back to the prestigious award board members and say, "Nah, y'all got the wrong writer."

Satisfied and happy with his time writing, he turns off the lights and crawls into bed. He'll dread the awards ceremony when he wakes up.

—S. Shaw

Advice

This piece is about a writer who has a big problem with imposter syndrome. He recognizes that he has a true talent for putting the words on paper, but fears that he will be caught and labeled a fraud because he can't replicate his (obviously successful) creative process unless he's tapping at a keyboard. When he tries to conjure up something to be said aloud, he fails miserably. So he sabotages himself by his fake trips to the bathroom at critical moments rather than dealing with his challenge in a more constructive way.

48.

Second-Person Reflexive
(1 of 3 second-person POV exercises)

Second-person point of view (POV) is when the narrator speaks to a "you" rather than as an "I" or about a "she" or "he." It's fun to play with. You get totally different results than when using first-person or third-person points of view.

Second person is actually a complex POV. There are three different kinds of second-person POVs. Which one you choose depends on the effect you're after.

This exercise asks you to try the most common second-person POV: second-person reflexive. This is a direct inverse of first-person POV. Instead of saying "I," you say "you." The you refers to yourself (the narrator). For example: You're not the kind of woman who would normally shoplift a pair of shoes. But in fact you just did it, and are breathless with excitement as you leave the store. You could substitute "I" for "you" and it would have the same meaning (although not the same tone—more on this later).

Exercise

1. Imagine your character in a position where they have done something that they know is not right.
2. They do not intend to apologize, but instead to make excuses.
3. Use second-person reflexive point of view, in which "you" really means "I." "You are not the kind of person who would . . ." is always a good place to start.
4. Write a piece where your character makes excuses

for what they have done in an interior dialogue with themselves.

Example

You have spent so much time worrying about what other people think, you don't even know your own mind, do you? It is apparent. Even when you are in the health-food store standing for too long in the dairy section, perusing the yogurt. You reach for the low-fat yogurt that Marie has in her refrigerator when what you really want is the thick, rich, creamy full-fat Greek yogurt. Eating low-fat yogurt will not make you petite and articulate like Marie, nor will buying the same brown suede loafer you can't afford make you willowy with a posh accent like Kate.

But still, when you are standing in front of the mirror and you slip on the dress that you borrowed from Rosanne, you feel somehow better than yourself. As if wearing her dress will put you inside her skin, so smooth and tan. Laughing, it occurs to you that you are not unlike the serial killer in *The Silence of the Lambs*, wanting to slip inside someone else's skin.

Sleeping with Mark when Jeanette was away was the last straw. Lying on your back on their bed, you looked at the ceiling as you imagine she does, pretending to be her. Afterward, you dressed quickly, smiling at Mark but not meeting his eyes.

Sitting in the Datsun outside their house afterwards, a kaleidoscope of other people's lives overwhelms you. Images flash of Rob and Amy laughing with their kids at the beach, Jane smiling on Instagram from the Hollywood Hills, and Lauren sitting at her desk, typing intently, wearing her Gloria Steinem–inspired glasses.

I just want to be more like them, you whisper to yourself as you burst into tears of frustration, and the keys in the ignition jingle as you start the car engine.

You never see Jeanette again, never apologize. You hear they are moving to Tucson, and you breathe a sigh of relief.

It will take years for you to realize that your mind is a light-filled chapel without a roof. You kneel in your garden, knees of your jeans sinking in the damp soil.

Advice

Second person is an interesting POV to play with. If this had been written in first person, it might have seemed like navel-gazing or whining, and if in third person, perhaps you'd have struggled with psychic distance.

But with second-person POV, this piece works—perhaps because of the distance the "you" puts between the narrator and what is going on. We understand that the narrator (whatever her name is) is lacking some sense of self. Her inability to say "I" reflects that—that she is constantly looking outward, to others, to see who she is, or what she might be capable of.

49

Second-Person Complicit
(2 of 3 second-person POV exercises)

In this exercise, we're going to try a second kind of second person ("you") point of view: second-person complicit. This time, the "you" referred to is the reader, and you are putting them into the story. This is done often in journalism, and in nonfiction essays. For example: You are driving to Tahoe to go skiing for the first time this season. You are almost past Sacramento when it happens. A huge truck is on your tail . . .

By keeping the focus relentlessly on what the "you" in the story is doing, you draw the reader into the narrative, making them part of it, and making them complicit in whatever is happening.

Exercise

1. Imagine yourself (or a character) in a position where you/they undergo an incredibly tension-filled experience in which the outcome had been uncertain. A potential car crash. A house fire starting. Taking a chance and asking someone new out on a date.
2. Write a story in which you use second-person complicit. This means the "you" is the reader, and you are putting them into the story.

Example

At three p.m., you've just woken up and gotten out of the shower. This night-delivery business is a bitch. You were riding your bike at one a.m. in the dark to get some Kentucky Fried Chicken to some stoned students over in Professorville. And no tip. Which means you made $3 that last hour of pumping through streets deserted except for the occasional drunk driver.

You don't want to bother with breakfast. You lose your appetite real fast toting all that food around. At first, it's enticing: hot Chinese noodles, full meat-loaded pizzas, garlic bread. Then you just get sick of it. I mean, really sick. You picked up an order from the Indian place on El Camino and Oxford and had to vomit into a bush, the curry smell was so overpowering.

So, you're sitting on the couch in your living room. The place needs dusting, but you're too lazy to do it. You leave it for one of your roommates. Then you smell it. Is that smoke? It's something. You get up and go to the kitchen. Holy shit! The dryer stacked in the corner on top of the washer is in flames! You instinctively go for the fire extinguisher under the sink but hesitate. Do you use this on an electrical fire?

While you wait, the tongues of fire coming now from both the washer and the dryer make a spectacular leap to the curtains. They flare up as though they're soaked with gasoline. Now the window frames are bright with flame. You catch yourself, and start spraying, but it's too late. The fire is now in the living room, with all the wooden upholstered furniture. You fumble for your cell. You dial 911 and try to remember if you were able to pay your renters' insurance bill when it was due last month.

Advice

In this piece, the "you" is the reader—the author is trying to put them into the story so that they feel what the author wants them to feel— and to be complicit with the things that are happening—in this case, a fire. Angela Carter is the master of this point of view. If you read her short stories, you'll often find her beguiling the reader into being part of the story. "The Erl-King will do you grievous harm" is one such famous sentence in her story "The Erl-King" that forces the reader to confront some evil in the heart of the wood a character is entering.

50.

Second-Person Direct Address
of Character
(3 of 3 second-person POV exercises)

In this exercise, you are going to write a piece in which you use second-person direct address of character.

This means "you" is another person/character who is part of the story. Not the uninvolved reader but someone who is engaged with what's happening.

For example: I know how much you trust me, you always have. But I have something to tell you that might surprise you.

Yes, this involves some (implied) first-person POV (of course). But focus on the other person (the "you") and their responses and reactions as you write this scene. If you can manage to use dialogue ("What are you talking about?" you ask) so much the better.

Exercise

1. Imagine yourself (or a character) in a position where you're trying to convince someone to do something they're not inclined to do. Assume you have a close relationship with this person.
2. Address that person as "you."
3. Keep the piece focused on the conversation with the "you," the character whom you are trying to convince.
4. Constraint: Make this a mix of scene (something happening at a certain place in a certain time) and narrative (telling), not just narrative.

Example

Randy!

What? you ask.

You know you're not allowed to smoke in here! Put it out!

Aw, no one will ever know, you say. The place is empty, you reply.

But it's a church! This is a sacrosanct place. You should put that out immediately.

You are standing too close to the altar of the quaint little church we found on the outskirts of Campanet, in Spain. To our surprise, it was unlocked and unattended. You immediately strode in; I followed, a little hesitant. I'm always afraid of breaking the rules, whereas you delight in flouting them. Right now, you're ignoring what I'm saying, examining the waist-high statues that are scattered throughout the church. They look very old but are not chipped or damaged in any way. You actually reach out and stroke the gold crown of a statue that I assume is Mary.

Don't drop ash on this floor. It's marble, I tell you.

You don't say anything, but make a kind of a face at me. I know that face. It's what you must have looked like when you were two years old, your you-can't-make-me expression. I've been thinking for three years that this expression would eventually fade from your repertoire if I just pointed out how infantile it made you look. Instead, your propensity to use it has gotten stronger.

Hey, you know how easy it would be to take one of these things? you ask. They're not secured in any way.

There are probably cameras, I tell you, but you're not listening, you've stubbed out your cigarette on the edge of a column, and have picked up a statue of a male saint with both arms.

Wouldn't you love this for our porch? you ask.

Advice

In this piece, you see that the interaction is between two people. The "you" is a character in the story, someone who is acting badly and knows it. The important thing to keep in mind if you want to use this particular version of second person, is that the "you" has to play a major role in the story. It's like you're telling the story directly to them, to get a reaction.

Stories or novels that consist of letters between two persons often fall into this category, as do monologues where the narrator is speaking specifically to a person, instead of to the audience (or readers). The end goal of the piece, in those cases, is to build to a point (or several points) of drama between the narrator and the "you." In other words, the relationship is front and center thematically in the story.

51.

Point of View and Truth

Everyone has their own unique perspective on the world. No two people will witness the same accident or crime (that's why firsthand witnesses are so unreliable), or otherwise perceive anything that happens in the world in the exact same way. We're going to play with this concept in this exercise.

You will write three pieces. They are all about the same thing: an incident in which two people have a (slightly) unpleasant interaction. To get the two characters interacting, thinking, and feeling, have something happen that both of them see or experience. For example, they observe a car accident. Or one trips on the pavement and the other helps her up. You'll show the incident from both points of view. And then you'll give us the omniscient, Godlike view of what actually transpired.

HINT: It's really important to let yourself go within each point of view. One character may notice things the other doesn't—which can completely distort their telling of the incident. One character may make a big deal of the weather. Another of the smell of a nearby bakery. These sensory details may evoke others relevant to each character. See where your thoughts take you.

Exercise: Part 1

1. First write about the event from the point of view of one character (first person point of view). Think about the "limitations" your character has. There are the obvious ones (geographic, temporal, and so on) but what about emotional limitations? Intelligence?

Moral? What biases does this character have (political, social, or otherwise)? From this POV you should be able to ascertain three things:

a. What happened (according to this one character).

b. Something about the narrator's personality.

c. Something about the other character's personality (as observed by the narrator).

Example: Part 1 (Alice's POV)

When Marlo approached the front desk, holding a dripping pool net, I sighed and looked up from the reservations book.

What are you doing? That's dripping all over the floor. Someone could slip. I pointed to the water gathering on the marble tiles.

Alice, I need your help, Marlo said. Out by the pool.

He seemed calm but he was just frozen there with his net, dripping. He caught my glance and said, I was cleaning the pool.

He led me to a chaise longue with a naked woman lying on it. At seven a.m. I could feel him trembling next to me. He was not as calm as he appeared. It was Mrs. Lewis. She and her husband were regulars at the hotel in the winter, and she was different than the other guests who visit. Quiet. She didn't drink, didn't play golf or gamble with her husband. She would order cobb salads from room service every day at two, but only ate the bacon, Lewis in the kitchen had told me.

Ma'am, I said. Then: Mrs. Lewis?

I picked up a towel from the edge of the chair, still neatly folded, and tried to cover her gently. She didn't notice. As odd as it seemed given her character, she must have been really drunk. I pulled the towel up to her neck, and that's when I realized she wasn't breathing.

Call an ambulance. I yelled to Marlo, although he was standing right next to me.

Exercise: Part 2 (Marlo's close third-person POV)

Now do the same thing from the POV of the other character, but use close third-person POV. (She saw the wasp coming. It was right on her arm. Why couldn't she move or scream . . .)

Example: Part 2

What are you doing? Alice asked when he ran up to her desk in the lobby, dripping water everywhere.

That's dripping all over the floor. Someone could slip, Alice said, pointing to the water gathering on the marble tiles.

Alice, I need your help, Marlo said. Out by the pool. I was cleaning it. Marlo held up the net full of leaves he was still holding, but faltered. What was he going to say about the naked lady? He blushed again thinking of it.

This better be good, Alice said. But after Marlo told her, she moved fast.

Alice first tried to cover Mrs. Lewis, then tried to wake her, shaking her gently, then firmly, but the woman was floppy, as if all her bones had been removed. She was lying on the chaise just the way she came into the world. Marlo looked away.

She must be drunk. Go call an ambulance. The number is in the book on my desk, Alice said.

Okay, okay. Should we find her husband first? Marlo said.

No, Marlo, *go*, Alice said.

Marlo began walking across the grassy lawn, the first light of dawn making everything appear slightly out of focus. The grass, wet from the sprinkler, glistened. His shoe tips darkened as they dampened.

RUN. Alice called after him. RUN.

Marlo ran to the front desk and pressed 9 for an outside line. Then he hung up. He needed the number first. He flipped through the concierge directory for the private ambulance number. It took several minutes for him to work out that Ambulance was before Airport Transit Bus; the listings were alphabetized.

Mierdamierdamierda. Shitshit shit, he muttered. Shit.

Hello, I need an ambulance. Hotel Miranda. Yes, immediately. She's dead. He wanted to breathe the words back in and then fly into reverse through the morning, undoing what had happened.

Exercise: Part 3 (Omniscient POV)

Now write it from the POV of an omniscient (knows all, sees all) narrator. Your Godlike narrator can: see the past, see the future, understand what it all means (put it in context), make judgments, have opinions, see into the characters down to the bottom of their souls. So what your omniscient narrator says is capital-T Truth. In this piece, you establish what the truth is about the encounter.

HINT: It shouldn't match either of the two previous versions, but should speak to something larger, more complicated.

Example: Part 3

Marlo had seen dead people before, but had never been there when they were dying. He knew Mrs. Lewis died while he was fishing leaves out of the pool, just a few feet away. Mrs. Lewis had been lying there the whole two hours before he noticed her, as he put out the towels, cleaned the pool, and checked the chlorine levels. She died while he was plunging the net in the pool, singing to himself. He knew it when he saw her, her skin so translucent, her mouth open in a way that was familiar.

When he went to tell Alice, he wanted to say the word *dead*, but decided against it.

Alice didn't realize that Mrs. Lewis was dead right away. Guests got drunk and passed out at the hotel often, so Alice just assumed this was the same kind of thing. She felt uneasy that Mrs. Lewis would pass out there by the pool, of all places, but if there is one thing that

Alice knows from working in this hotel for six years it is that nothing is what it seems. The gardenia are replaced every week on the veranda, and men come with their families one week and with a female escort the next.

At that moment, Alice was more worried that the pool would not be ready for the morning crowd and her manager would be upset about the incident. The body must be moved.

She must be drunk. Go call an ambulance. The number is in the book on my desk, Alice said to Marlo.

Advice

You can see from these examples that changing POV is different from just searching and replacing pronouns. Each point of view will reveal different things about character, situation, and theme.

Knowledge comes into play, but so does distance. How close do you want your readers to feel to the action? You might think you would always want to be very close, but that is not the case. There are times—particularly in times of dramatic action—that you might want to distance your audience. It all depends on your intent.

Character also drives the point of view. Alice has her own concerns (What about the other guests? What will her manager think?), Marlo his own preoccupations (Did she die when I was singing?), but only the omniscient narrator has the true story—which she may or may not reveal to readers. In other words, just because an omniscient narrator knows everything, she doesn't have to tell it all.

52.

Life's Losses

In his poem "What We Have Lost," Michael Ondaatje writes a list of the things that he (and other Sri Lankans) have lost over the years. The things range from the practical, from instructions on how to approach a forest or make an arrow to the fanciful, such as testing the limits of betrayal or how we understand those who have departed. All this, he concludes, "was burnt / or traded for power and wealth."

This is a two-part exercise. First you make a list of what you've lost, and then you riff on it in a free write.

Exercise: Part 1

This is an easy one! You will simply make a list of what you have lost since childhood. Try for ten things—but go for more if you can. They can be physical objects, but much better if you can pull off what Ondaatje has by homing in on the subtler losses that are abstract but still rendered precisely. As always, be as specific and concrete as possible.

Examples

- ☐ The ability to yell *yes* without hesitation
- ☐ My grandmother's tarnished silver locket
- ☐ Being a moral authority on adultery
- ☐ A preference for high heels
- ☐ Corroboration of childhood memories
- ☐ The ability to declare myself a resident of a particular place
- ☐ My country, may it make a comeback
- ☐ The firmness of youth: in both thighs and opinions

☐ A scarf my mother knit that I refused to wear
☐ My firstborn
☐ My sixth birthday
☐ Patience
☐ Continence
☐ Dreaming while asleep
☐ My father's signed copy of Hemingway
☐ Running, for pleasure
☐ Opportunities for infamy
☐ A love of butterscotch pudding
☐ Desire
☐ The names of many things in other languages

Exercise: Part 2

Now take what you've written and do a free write where you try to weave the different losses together into a coherent narrative or prose poem.

Example

I did not know when you died that there would be other
    things gone forever.
The sea, not that it's lost, but without you, the conversa-
    tions are silenced.
No walks along the shore, musing of clouds and terns,
of the seagull that flies low and grabs the sandwich out of
    my hand,
another one posing for us on the roof of our camper.
Finding a quarter, the silver worn away by sand and waves
    to its copper core.
The shifting tides. We stay long enough to hear the pause
    between ebb

and flow, wade through the leading bubbles swooshing
  around our feet.
If I return now, time is truncated, uncomfortable. I cannot find my place
in this vastness of sand and sky; the nip of salty tang drifts
  aimlessly.
I want to return to what was and I do, in memories of the
  rocky beach
dotted with dying jellyfish that wash away with the next
  high tide.
Of how the sea floats in a sawed two-by-four, a
  wrenched-loose lobster buoy.
The water's edge ebbing and flowing. I never know how
  far the tide has moved until
I've walked farther along the shore and looked back. We
  hike up the rocky
trail to the overlook where we've parked, the golden sun
  setting behind us,
the sea tugged or pushed by a gravitational pull I cannot
  explain.
Cormorants stand on ancient fish weir posts and hang
  their wings to dry,
hesitating to fly inland until the silvering seawater reaches
  their feet.
And under the darkening sky, the sea turns slate, the
  breaking waves
flicker white, their whispers bidding us goodnight, and
  now goodbye.

—BRIGITTE WHITING

Advice

Loss is always worth exploring creatively. It implies that you had a
connection with something of value to you—an idea, a person, an
object—that is now gone.

Just articulating what, exactly, you have lost that is of value is an enormously helpful exercise for generating ideas for both fiction and nonfiction. This writer could take any of the items in her list/poem and do a free write, and probably come up with interesting writing.

The second example, the meditation on loss as seen through the different images and moods of the sea, helps us understand the loneliness of this person left without her partner, when "conversations have ceased."

53.

Last Letter

Last things always carry weight. The last time you saw a loved one. The last time you shut the door on your childhood home. You can use this weight to generate terrific writing. You have to be careful to avoid sentimentality, of course. But if you focus on small, concrete things, you will succeed. In this exercise you will write a last letter to a loved one.

Exercise

1. Create a character (or imagine yourself in the situation) who is writing a last letter (an email or text is okay) to a loved one.
2. This does *not* have to be before a death. It could be a letter to a teacher when you leave school, or a letter to a friend you are cutting ties with (for whatever reason).
3. Constraint #1: You have something very specific to thank the receiver of the letter for. Make it concrete! Not "thank you for loving me" but "thank you for letting me use your toothbrush when I forgot mine."
4. Constraint #2: You weave in a memory of something that happened to the two of you—an experience you either suffered through (traumatic), or got great joy from (exhilarating).

Example

October 1947, India

My beloved son,

Destiny decreed that my hands wield ploughs, not pens, and so it is that a kind stranger is putting these words to paper. Do you remember when you used to try and teach me English? You, patient tutor, and I, slow learner. All by design, for those evenings by your side made ambrosia of my days. I would tease you as you put away your English workbooks that Urdu was the sweetest language of all and you would shake your head in that serious way of yours. "But Bapuji, there are so many languages in the world, I am sure they are beautiful too," and then shyly, "I would like to learn as many as I can."

But enough of the past. Of times and places that are no more. Our motherland has been cleft by red lines spat from the pens of the retreating British devils. They took a civilized country and ripped it apart, and left us to piece together a map with no legend. Our joy for our hard-won independence is dimmed by this final atrocity as we are left homeless in our homeland.

My son, I had believed there would be a whole lifetime for me to tell you all that I wished you to know. That you are the descendant of warriors. Bearer of the name lion. That I saw all you did as our feet were forced on this terrible march, as we traverse lines that should never have been drawn. How, instead of rushing off with the other children to play one last game of pitthu, you stayed behind to help your mother and me load the oxcart with bundle after bundle of all we owned. How, just as we were about to leave, you hurried back to the courtyard to untether the buffalo, for in our haste we had forgotten about them and you were worried they might starve.

That I heard the songs you sang to your little sister as you carried her on your back. That I saw you help your mother keep the cooking fires alight even while the smoke brought tears to your eyes. I will never forget how after I had told you to hide under the cart when the fighting was at its worst, you came and stood by my side with no weapon but your magnificent brave heart. A better man that day than most men are in a lifetime. The pain in your eyes as you watched us become savages, make enemies of our brothers and sisters, and cross lines that should never have been drawn.

Time runs short, my sickness has the better of me. Forgive your foolish father this last indulgence. This letter you will never read. For you left your father behind, crossed uncharted territories that no child should cross before a parent, alone. To the ticking of galloping clocks my beloved boy I am hastening to your side.

Your Bapuji
—Nirmy Kang

Advice

In this last letter to a beloved son, an old man on his deathbed thinks about the momentous social, political, and religious events that shaped his lifetime. Because this is a last letter, these moments he recalls are presumably the ones he gives the most weight to in his long life. We don't find out until the end of the piece that the reason he hasn't been able to say these things to his son directly is not due to physical distance but because the son himself died long ago. This gives what the old man says even more emotional weight.

54.

A Fall in Slow Motion

Surprising our characters is always a good thing. Whether it's with a plot twist, an unanticipated development, or unexpected interaction with another character, it's always good to throw curveballs to see how our characters react.

We've tried to do this numerous times in this book. This is another such exercise: an unexpected physical fall.

If you slow down the action, and focus on the details, you'll learn two things: how to choreograph physical action (it's counterintuitive, but you often want to slow down fast-moving scenes to get the physical movements just right and increase drama), and how to coordinate that with appropriate (surprising, yet convincing) emotional responses.

Exercise

1. Think of a time when you (or a character) fell. You could have tripped over a crack in the sidewalk, fallen off the bed, or perhaps just been clumsy going down some stairs. If you've never fallen, you will have to use your imagination. It doesn't have to be a dangerous fall. You might not have been hurt at all.

2. Write a scene (something happening at a specific time at a specific place) in which a character takes a fall.

3. First, write a paragraph setting the scene: where the character was; what the character was doing, thinking, saying.

4. Now choreograph the fall in slow motion. That is,

   a fall usually happens quickly. I want you to slow it
   down and describe every millisecond—what is happening physically, what is happening to your character's body, what people around them are doing or
   saying, what is going through your character's mind.
5. Next, describe the physical end result after the fall
   was completed. Use only short, declarative sentences:
   "Her knee was bleeding. A bruise would eventually
   appear on her thigh. Her leg was broken."
6. Now describe the emotional sensations after the fall.
   Put it in context of what is happening. Are people helping your character up? Has an ambulance
   appeared? How does all this make your character
   feel? As always, try to manifest those feelings with
   concrete details.

Example

In the shower I felt nausea first, then as the water pelted down on my
head, a pricking sensation, like I had walked directly into a thicket of
thistles. I vaguely took note of the florid pattern of the plastic shower
curtain that had been here when I moved in. I need to replace that, I
remember thinking, feeling the slick surface slip through my fingers
and the orange-and-green pattern blurring in front of my eyes. A
lightness came into my legs and then the lightness crept up my body
in a wave. When I looked around, a thousand tiny beads of light first
illuminated the shower tiles, replaced by a soft darkness. I heard a
thump and thought that must be me, as I slid to the tub's smooth floor.

When I woke up my first thought was that the hot water had run
out because I was shivering, crumpled under a frigid falling stream. I
reached up to the faucet and shut it off.

Staying low, I pulled myself on my elbows to the back of the claw-
foot tub. Holding the curved edges in a firm grip, I pulled myself into
a seated position, balancing on the cool porcelain lip with my legs at a
right angle. Water trickled down my front, catching on my chest and

pubic hair and scrotum and gathering there before falling in rivulets. I exhaled and inhaled slowly, my breath tasting sweet. There was a noise I could not quite place, a rhythmic thumping. My heart in my temples? No, it was the door. Someone was pounding on the door.

Honey, you okay? Answer me if you can. I can't open the door. It was my husband.

Then, louder: The ambulance is here, Kevin.

Advice

By paying attention to minutiae and concrete details, the narrator slows down the scene so we can see every physical action and sensation. Fainting in reality happens in just an instant, but if you wrote it like that—"I fell"— it would have no drama or tension in it. Through the details we gather that this narrator does not like losing control and was taken unawares by the physical illness or condition that caused him to fall. That his husband is concerned and calling for help means he's in a committed relationship where people care for each other. And the scene is set up to continue—in the ambulance, hospital, or doctor's office.

55.

Sister Ship

I'll never know and neither will you of the life you don't choose. We'll only know that whatever that sister life was, it was important and beautiful and not ours. It was the ghost ship that didn't carry us. There's nothing to do but salute it from the shore.

—CHERYL STRAYED,
"The Ghost Ship That Didn't Carry Us"

Many of us wonder about the "road not taken." What would our lives have been like if we hadn't made a certain decision, gone to a certain party, accepted a particular job, married a certain partner? It's interesting terrain to explore.

Exercise

1. Write a sentence or two about a character's "sister life" fantasies. What was one of the roads not taken in their life? How would their life be different if they *had* taken it?
2. Write a scene (something happening at a specific time in a specific place) in which the character is startled by an association that tells them what their life could have been.
3. Make it concrete! And always think smaller if you are having trouble.

Example

It was spring, but this early in the morning the night chill still hovered over the silent street. It was once a dirt road to the northern farms, now paved and subdivided in the ubiquitous American manner. Anina was completely alone at this hour, her sturdy shoes striking a staccato rhythm on the concrete sidewalk. There were not even lights yet in the windows of the houses.

The faint scent of manure off the few remaining farmed fields to the east touched her trained nostrils, but this time of year the way to the church also treated her with varied floral fragrances—the houses had gardens with roses, lavender, and jasmine. Anina sometimes wondered whether, if old age would cause her to go blind, she might be able to walk the route by the scent of the flowers alone.

The first new sound startled her—a bird's innocent song as it flitted and rose in front of her, drawing her eyes to the heavens at the cusp of dawn. The sky was at that exact moment changing its garments from night into day, and the vivid blue of it made Anina stop so quickly that she had to grab a rough fencepost, driving a small sliver into her palm. It was strangely not painful, yet the memory arose as shockingly as the bird, and as sharply as the shard of wood.

Suddenly she was looking down from the upper reaches of Genoa at the jeweled blue of the Ligurian Sea near the harbor. She was on her way to the port. It was the day she left on the steamer. She had been alone that day as well, her papers tucked safely into the lining of her coat, a basket of fruit and nuts from her family on her arm. The prospect of a new life, a salvaged life, a life useful to her family, perhaps colored her judgment—then she had been so naïve as to think it would be easy to return.

Here, a Catholic church had been built among the little houses to accommodate the many families like hers. The earliest weekday Mass was only for the nuns, but they had invited her to join them. It was a small gift from God, this place of solace in her second country. But for that day of the bright-blue sea and the steamer, she might have been one of them—though half a world away—one of these women who had devoted herself solely to God. This church, this rectangular country, this entire life of husband, children, and grandchildren would have been just in her imagination.

It was not a thought to dwell on; Mass always started promptly at six. Anina extricated her wounded hand and with the other felt for the comforting beads of the rosary in her pocket. Soon the harbor and the sea receded, along with the night sky, and were overtaken by the sound of her footsteps as she continued on her way.

—Cynthia Cima-Ivy

Advice

An elderly immigrant woman, on her way to early Mass, gets sidetracked by a memory of what it was like leaving her home country decades earlier. Her "sister life," she thinks, would have been one devoted to God as a nun. We have no way of knowing, of course, how realistic this was—why would she have chosen church work in her own country yet not in her new one? This could be well worth exploring further if this writer wanted to . . . perhaps a life uncomplicated by marriage and family seems attractive to her now, having chosen the other path? This small passage could well have legs.

56.

Think Big, Write Small

Let a man get up and say, Behold, this is the truth, and
instantly I perceive a sandy cat filching a piece of fish in
the background. Look, you have forgotten the cat, I say.

—Virginia Woolf

Usually, for very good reasons, we should think small when we write.
It helps us to avoid abstractions and clichés. But sometimes we want
to write about the big things that are happening around us—politics,
climate change, wars, economic issues . . . The challenge is how to
do this without preaching or abstraction.

For centuries, writers have addressed this issue by making the
Big Things very, very personal to a character or group of characters.
By dramatizing a small bit, they capture the whole. Think: Daniel
Defoe's *Journal of a Plague Year*, or Barbara Kingsolver's *The Poisonwood
Bible*. Both manage to capture *huge* events (the plague in London,
Africa in political turmoil) by focusing on the personal dilemmas of
a few characters.

With this exercise we're going to try this: To think big and write
small.

Exercise

1. Think of a major event that occurred (or is occur-
ring) in the world.
2. Pick a character, or a group of characters.
3. Have your character(s) set out to do something physi-

cal: taking a walk, working in the garden, preparing
or eating a meal, or what-have-you.

4. Make sure they are affected in some way by this
   major event. How do they react? What can they do?

NOTE: What your character does physically doesn't have to be
directly related to the big event. For example, they do not necessarily
have to be donating blood for victims of a disaster or packing meals
for hungry children. They *can* be, but they don't have to be.

YOUR CHALLENGE IS GOING TO BE TWOFOLD:

1. It is much, much, harder to write about big things without
   getting preachy or abstract. So try to avoid those two hob-
   goblins of bad writing: abstraction and generalization.
2. It can be difficult to bring big events down to a personal level without trivializing them. You don't want
   it to be that you (or your character) doesn't grasp the
   immenseness of the big event, or can only think of it
   in relation to yourself (themselves). But their personal
   thoughts and their personal emotional engagement
   with the big event *do* have to be an integral part of
   the writing.

Difficult! Give it a try!

Example

The diced sweet potatoes roasting in the oven were perfect, golden
brown spots blistering, crispy skins beginning to caramelize. I baste
the chicken, removing the pan from the oven so I can coat it evenly
with the sizzling juices. On the BBC, Radio 4 is playing a speech
from the Queen. I am half listening, preparing lunch for my English
in-laws who will be arriving within the hour, even though John,

their son and (unbeknownst to them) my soon-to-be ex-husband, is away on business in New York.

The house is a mess, James's toys strewn across the living room. I step on a small red LEGO. Goddammit. Jojo is whining at the back door and I let her in, wiping off her feet with a rag so she doesn't tread mud across the yellow rug.

Not today, I shake a finger at her.

Back in the kitchen, the Queen's crisp, even monologue has been replaced by an excited reporter with an American accent.

One of the World Trade towers has been hit by an airplane. It is burning. Oh, oh, it appears the second of the towers has just been hit by another airplane, this is unbelievable. Unbelievable. They are both in flames. It appears, oh, oh, the first tower is falling, people are running. There is so much smoke. *We need to go, we need to go,* he is yelling now.

Then the reporter is cut off and there is quiet. I go into the living room and turn on the television. I see the plane circling around, the towers crumbling, over and over again. Tiny figures plunge from high windows down to the ground. Some are holding hands. I cannot move.

From the kitchen, as if in a strange solidarity, suddenly billows of smoke. The sweet potatoes have charred. They are now black and shrunken on the sheet. I rush to take the potatoes and chicken out of the oven, both now inedible.

John. John is in New York. He had a meeting today.

The doorbell is ringing. I wipe my hands on my apron and walk toward the door, I start to step over the LEGOs, then, leaning down, I pick them up, one by one.

Advice

It's difficult to capture the enormity of an event like 9/11. The only way to do it justice is to reflect it off the experiences of individuals. John Hersey did something similar in *The Wall*, his book about the Warsaw Ghetto, in which he dramatized an important chapter of the Holocaust through specific personalities, and portrayed what happened when those characters met extreme adversity. It's an extraordinarily complicated thing to do well. But if you manage it, then you've really done something important for the world. This particular scene as written could be the beginning of exploration of the enormity of 9/11 as affecting one family but extending out to the world.

57.

Bad Advice

This is a generative plotting exercise. It's a useful narrative trick: if your character is debating a decision, large or small, have another character proffer an opinion—an unwise one, if possible. It might not determine your character's actual choice, but it should affect them in some way as they make a decision and take action.

Exercise

1. Think about a time when someone gave you some bad advice. They told you to marry someone you didn't love. They told you to turn down a job you really wanted.

2. You decide for your character whether the bad advice is taken—or not. Try to free write with a loose mind and full imagination—moving intuitively from line to line about the repercussions, good and bad, that flowed from that advice, and that decision (whatever they were).

3. Don't worry about staying on topic. If an idea or image suggests itself to you, even if it doesn't make logical sense, go for it.

Example

That morning, Laura and I walked to Kyle's together. We are friends mostly outside of school these days, because she is a junior and I am a freshman.

This is going to be amazing, she says.

Who's coming?

Well, Daryl, Kyle, Rich, Ian. Joel and Sarah, oh, and Kim. They are all cool. You should hook up with Kyle.

When we arrive, Kyle and Daryl are taking the seat out of the back of the van to make more room.

The den of inequity, Laura giggles.

Laura piles pillows in the back of the van and hangs a purple block-print tapestry across the back window. In the window, she puts a hand-painted sign with a large green peace symbol and rainbow-colored block letters RICH OR BUST in reference to the stadium where we are going to see the Grateful Dead with Crosby, Stills & Nash.

When we get into the van, she climbs in the back with Rich and motions for me to sit in the only space left, next to Kyle. She presses a tablet into my hand. Take it. We'll have a fantastic trip, she says.

A few miles from the stadium, traffic comes to a standstill. I lean on the window, eyes closed, perspiring. I feel Kyle lean over me, his chest pressed against the width of my back, to look over my head out the car window.

Can you see the colors of the sky ahead? or is that the color of the music? he says in my ear. He is certainly tripping. One of his hands strays to my left breast.

I don't see them, I say, nudging him away.

But Daryl, the driver, hears something, too, and turns off the boombox so we can all listen. The sky is just a pale blue to me, but I can now hear the low strains of the concert, broken by an occasional howl and whoop from the cars ahead. Everyone is quiet as the car starts to move, and the music becomes clearer.

I look around. Everyone in the car is tripping. Having a collective hallucination that I am not part of, my tab still enclosed in my sweaty palm.

Doors are opening in the cars ahead of us on the road and women with flying hair in long dresses, men in shorts and sandals, are stumbling down into the fields toward the sun, running toward the stadium, abandoning their cars on the highway.

I grab my backpack and pull the sweatshirt out of it, tying it around my waist.

Hey, why are you leaving? Kyle asks.

I gotta go, I say, jumping out of the van. I don't bother to look back.

Advice

In this case, the character decides not to take the acid, which is an interesting decision on the part of the writer, as a more common one would be to take the acid and describe the changed world. However, that would run the risk of being a cliché. Drug experiences, like dreams, have to be handled very carefully in both fiction and nonfiction. (Read Denis Johnson's *Jesus' Son* for a wonderful example of how to do it right.) In this case, the character deciding not to take the acid allowed her to protect herself against a sexual advance, and to take a bold (and surprising) action when she wanted to.

58.

Comfortable

"I'm Pretty Comfortable, But I Could Be a Little More Comfortable" is a very funny poem by Lydia Davis in which she complains about so-called first-world problems of the sort that plague privileged people:

> *The people in front of us are taking a long time choosing their ice*
> *cream.*
> *My thumb hurts.*
> *A man is coughing during the concert.*
> *The shower is a little too cold.*

The point, of course, is that many of us are wanting to be "a little more comfortable" when others in the world are truly suffering. It shocks us from our complacency with humor.

Exercise

1. Make a list (like Lydia Davis) of first-world problems that plague a character. As always, think small! Make a list of at least ten items.
2. Now take just one of these complaints and do a free write on it. Anything goes!
3. The writing can be fiction or nonfiction. Let your unconscious have free rein. See where it takes you.

Example

The apple tastes like onions from the knife I used to cut it.
The sheets are pilling
The car doesn't have AC
I gained ten pounds from eating ice cream on vacation
My son is home from school with a cold
I cannot go to the gym because I hurt my back
I can't go swimming because I need a bikini wax
My roots are showing
My flight was canceled
I burned my tongue on my latte

Somehow, the reason I get out of bed these days has become coffee. Not to read the news or kiss my children. Not to run in the park or hear the birds sing. But not for a simple black coffee: it must be a latte, which requires a machine I don't own, and for rich creamy froth sweetened with brown sugar (and it must be brown). It is the difference between a good day and a bad one. If the coffee is perfect, I sigh in relief, sipping it greedily. If something is off, say the café is out of brown sugar, the coffee is too weak, or the temperature tepid, I get in a mood.

I don't know how it happened; I was always a dignified tea drinker. English Breakfast with whole milk and a dollop of honey in a porcelain cup. I kept teabags in my wallet, in case they only had Lipton when I was out. I drank green jasmine tea in the afternoon, when feeling parsimonious—I love to watch the flowers open up, then sip sharp bitterness, inhaling the fragrant steam.

But this woman of refined tastes is gone.

This morning I waited in the café for my takeaway paper cup with the plastic top as usual.

The woman smiled at me and made my latte with a lovely heart in the foam, to prove she poured the espresso in after the milk, a trademark of barista savvy. Impatient to take a sip, I put it to my lips and slurped the foam as I fumbled in my wallet to pay. The coffee hit my tongue, and I made a gurgling noise, swashing it around in my mouth, then sealing my lips so as not to spit it all over.

Hot! I stammered, furious, my tongue numb and scalded.

Advice

This is a great plotting device if you are trying to write a story without being melodramatic. It can be the smallest incidents that can crack open our characters and get them to reveal things about themselves. In this case, we learn that the "woman of refined tastes" is gone— somehow she has gone through a life change that causes her to gulp down hot coffee without waiting—which opens up opportunities to explore exactly what has changed in this woman's life and what the overall effect has been for her.

59.

Looking at Pictures

In his poem "Looking at Pictures to Be Put Away," Gary Snyder starts by describing a particular photo that stirs no memories: "Who was this girl / In her white night gown / Clutching a pair of jeans / On a foggy redwood deck."

The poem ends with a question: "What will we remember? / Bodies thick with food and lovers / After twenty years."

In this exercise, we will play off photographs—not the ones to be cherished but the ones we'd rather forget—for any reason.

Exercise

1. Take out a photo that you have ambiguous feelings about. (This can be for any reason—your hair is frizzy, it includes your ex, or it was a terrible day that you'd rather forget.)
2. Write a piece in which you first try to describe the photo objectively.
3. Now describe your (or a character's) associations with the photo. What comes to mind as you look at this photo? What about the period of time, even day, that it was taken? About the people in the photo? If you don't remember, write that down, as well as your feelings about not remembering.

HINT: The associations might wander far from the actual people/ events depicted in the photo. That's a good thing! As usual, this can be either fiction or nonfiction.

Example

In the photo they look like the perfect family. Cute kids, handsome parents, big smiles, dressed to the nines. She had thought, I'll put on a smile for this moment, though inside she was fuming. The photographer had positioned the whole family and instructed them to be still and stand tall, to tilt their heads just-so and of course to smile. Her smile did not reach her eyes. Later, every time she viewed the photo she felt the same anger and fury and relived the whole thing over again. She thought how skilled she was at hiding her feelings. After all, this was how she was raised.

Never being permitted to freely show too much emotion, especially anger. Not sure exactly how much damage that does, but that is another story perhaps. So what anger was she hiding? Something that ate her up, and almost twenty years on she still remembers the humiliation and events leading up to walking into that studio for that family photo shoot. What was her anger about? A careless comment by a stranger. A comment the stranger may not have spent much time thinking about. Many would say "Ah, don't care about it so much, she's just stupid. Yeah, and she's probably a racist too." Fits the description of a racist, white, old, rich . . . she muttered five words that changed everything. Five words being "Get them off of me."

Not sure how she meant it, but it was interpreted as get your dirty brown kids who are running around away from me. No, they didn't touch her or frankly get that close to her. Her immediate reaction was to scream something back at the woman. Very uncharacteristic of her to do, the way she was raised (make no trouble, be invisible, stay quiet, don't make a fuss). Her words back were "Were you ever a kid or just born an old woman?" Not sure how effective it was, but though short-lived it certainly felt good.

That said, in other circumstances these two women, the old, rich white woman and this young brown mother of three could have had much in common. They could have had a similar love of books, travel, baking, who knows? But what remains is an ugly memory and a captured image that still sits on the piano for all to see. After all, who doesn't display a paid-for studio photograph? Never trust a photo.

—SURINDER DOSANJH KANG

Advice

By ruminating on this photo, a woman remembers the story behind the "perfect" image of the photograph, and the ugly story behind it: having her children treated badly in the studio by a rich white woman who made assumptions based on the color of her family's skin. And how she did something uncharacteristic—to speak up and actually yell something at the woman. So the photo sits on her piano, reminding her of ugliness and shame instead of pride in her family.

60.

Ducks

Ducks, Newburyport, is Lucy Ellmann's brilliant, nearly 1,000-page novel that reads as though it is made up of a single sentence (you can find a few periods in there if you look hard). Read the following excerpt and notice how many phrases begin with the words "The fact is . . ." followed by a concrete detail or fact, followed by a free association about that fact or detail. Despite this seemingly endless list of nonsense, a riveting story gets told by Ellmann.

> . . . the fact that there's nothing for breakfast around here except raw cinnamon roll dough, the fact that I'm hungry but not that hungry, the fact that Gillian would eat any amount of raw cinnamon roll dough if I let her, no problem, eggs, pantry, diamond-paned windows, "pained" windows, the fact that cats can eat all kinds of stuff and not get salmonella, the fact that chicken cacciatore was one of Mommy's buffet party specialties, peaches and cream, beaches and cream, cardamom, cinnamon, Margaret Wise Brown, Laura Ingalls Wilder, Robert Louis Stevenson, Wolfgang Amadeus Mozart, shoofly pie, whoopie pie, chess pie, Chesapeake Bay, the fact that I could have an egg, I guess, but I need them for other things, the fact that despite having fourteen chickens out there in the yard, we still run out of eggs . . .

Exercise

1. Write a 500-word piece consisting of one long sentence.

2. Begin each new thought with "The fact is," followed
   by a fact, observation, or concrete detail, which then
   leads to a string of free associations.
3. Try to get at least five (5) "the fact is" statements in.
4. See where this takes you. Don't try to control the
   flow.

HINT: Make sure that the facts are facts—not abstractions.

Example

The fact is that there were nearly 2,100 cars in the line of cars ahead
of us, as we learn later on the NY1 news, and it is a sweltering 100
degrees without AC. The fact is that the driver, a bearded teenager
named Ronald whom I do not know but who wears a spiral tie-dye
T-shirt, is afraid playing the car stereo or running the AC will run
down the van's battery, but if we turn the engine on, we may run
out of gas, which means we are listening to homemade mix tapes on
a boombox someone brought to record the concert, and the beat is
too loud of the drum, the feedback being purposeful but not effectively amplified on a tape. The fact is that I would rather have silence
anyway, and I am not even into the Grateful Dead; I paid $100 of my
babysitting money that I have been saving for a new Raleigh Alyeska
eighteen-speed bicycle to buy a shitty bleacher seat in hopes that the
music wouldn't be too loud. The fact is that now that I have been sitting in the hot car for the better part of eight hours for the sole pur-
pose that on Monday I can say I was in Rich Stadium in Buffalo on
this day. The fact is that I have my period for maybe the tenth time in
my life, and have no OB slim tampons or Always Wings maxi pads to
speak of and I have not asked anyone else in the car if they do, which
makes me afraid to move in case someone in the car might notice the
trickle of blood that is spreading out into a large red splotch aided by
sweat and gravity on the back of my shorts, thank God they are dark
blue denim, and that the seat is vinyl. I close my eyes.
    The fact that Gerry is sitting so close to me in the back of the van,

so close I can feel his upper arm sticking to mine and I can smell his deodorant—Men's Speed Stick Fresh Scent, just like my brother uses when he remembers and which he steals from my dad—means somehow my entire family is present, squashed in the car between Gerry and me. The fact is I want to lean my head on Gerry's shoulder and have him put his arm around me, but I am not sure if that is because of the familial deodorant or if I am starting to have a crush on Gerry. The fact is if I can smell his deodorant, he may be able to smell my period, and that makes me lean away from him instead toward the window, which is down, and I stick my head out like a dog.

The fact is I am amazed how the road is not moving at all right now, it is not flying underneath in the usual way that nauseates me if I watch for too long out of the side window—which I often do anyway because it reminds me that the Earth is round and that far-off places like Japan and Istanbul are waiting for me on the other side if I can just make it through this car ride without dying. The fact is today the highway stretches out long and gray and slim as an eel; miles of the flat gray rippling with heat in either direction and the long white line a primordial spine leading to the horizon alongside the shimmering lengths of cars that appear to be molting in the afternoon heat.

The fact is that everyone is going to start tripping in this car any minute, in fact they may have already, and that may be why no one is talking. Everyone ate several hits of acid half an hour ago before the traffic jam, carefully timing to peak after we had the car parked and just as Crosby, Stills & Nash started to play their second set. The fact that we made a wrong turn in Watkins Glen and were waylaid for forty-five minutes according to the map meant we would not make it there for the eight p.m. start of the concert.

But no concert like this starts on time, Gerry had said.

I nodded in agreement, but I have never been to a concert. The fact is instead of eating the acid, I still had it in the sweaty palm of my hand, and was wondering at this point if it had dissolved—absorbed into my bloodstream and that soon I would have four hits of acid wreaking havoc on my brain's synapses—which are already misfiring due to my epilepsy. The fact is I had no way to hide them. If I reach for my pocket to stick them in there I will have to sit forward and the crime scene of the seat will be revealed. The fact is I planned to sell the acid at the show so I can recoup the forty bucks I gave Daryl at school on Monday for the acid I never intended to take, and maybe even make a profit, so I am hoping it will not dissolve.

Out of the window I think I can see the line of cars slowly beginning to undulate toward the horizon.

We're moving, someone yells from another car; hollering and cheering breaks out.

The fact is at this point, when the engines thrum alive in unison, our car lurches ahead eagerly, then falls to a wistful creep, too slow to blow my hair back.

I close my eyes, imagining the other side of the world: what if you burrowed directly through the molten core the layers and layers of rock and sand and sea, where would you be?

Gerry says, I can feel it, and everyone in the car starts to laugh.

Advice

You might notice that this is the same writer writing about the same situation as in Exercise 57: Bad Advice, but with a different approach due to the exercise, a whole bunch of new, interesting details come out.

See how in this example the writer sticks to facts with each "the fact is," observation, which grounds the stream of consciousness (and helps us, the readers, understand what exactly is going on in the physical world of the story), but from that fact the writer rambles on about seemingly random things. And these things ultimately tell us a good deal about her. What do you know about this woman just by reading her ramblings, other than that she's on her way to a concert? What do bicycles and Istanbul have to do with the narrative? Knowing how to decide which seemingly obscure details belong and which are superfluous is an essential writing skill.

61.

Bitch Is a Word

"Bitch Is a Word I Hear a Lot," a poem by Kim Parko, starts with the lines: "I hate the word, and I guess that's why it is said? / People love to hurt one another. / It is what makes us human."

Then she goes into an exploration of the word *bitch* by talking about dogs she's had or encountered. The poem ends with the lines:

> *I had a dog who once kept me from walking into the arroyo.*
> *She blocked my path and wouldn't move.*
> *I'll never know what, or who, she saved me from.*

This is both a character exercise and a generative plotting exercise. It illustrates how you can start with one idea—the idea of being called a nasty name—and segue into another theme altogether, quite naturally that of dogs, in this case, and in the end, how she's been protected by a bitch from an unknown danger.

Exercise

1. Write a brief piece that begins with "X is a word I hear a lot," using a descriptive word, complimentary or not, that people can use to make a point. You can use words like *pretty* or *fat* or *dark*—whatever you like. As always, you can do this from your own point of view, or from a character's.
2. See where it takes you. Don't worry if you seem to go off topic. In fact, consider that a good thing!
3. But keep it concrete and (mostly) in the sensory world.

Example

Black is a word I hear a lot. A man who has dark skin is defined by it. It comes before man, before name. That Black man there. On the news the anchor says: a Black man has been arrested. In the paper I read: a Black man is in custody, a Black girl has been suspended, a Black baby has been found.

Black magic, black humor, Black market.

Black is the opposite of light.

Black is the color of mourning, of death.

A white man is just a man. In the news he is just a man who won the election, who discovered the vaccine. In the paper, other colors are not defined. First a name is written out, and then they are differentiated by age, where they live, or their work. What would it be like to just be? Undefined, free?

Advice

Like Kim Parko's poem, this writer plays with a particular word and its associations. By commenting on how the word is used to describe him, and others of different races, he begins to riff on the associations with the word, and only gradually leads us to the climax of the poem, which is how he longs to be a free human being.

This is a lovely example of free association that both defines character and provides opportunities for plot development.

62.

Nonsense of Summer

This exercise is just for the love of language, just for fun.
First, read the following fourteenth-century English song:

SUMER IS I-CUMIN IN

Sing, cuccu, nu. Sing, cuccu.
Sing, cuccu. Sing, cuccu, nu.

Sumer is i-cumin in—
Lhude sing, cuccu!
Groweth sed and bloweth med
And springth the wude nu.
Sing, cuccu!

Awe bleteth after lomb,
Lhouth after calve cu,
Bulluc sterteth, bucke verteth—
Murie sing, cuccu!
Cuccu, cuccu,
Wel singes thu, cuccu.
Ne swik thu naver nu!

SOURCE: *The Norton Anthology of Poetry* (Fifth Edition)
(W. W. Norton and Company Inc., 2005)

Exercise

1. Read the poem, which is written in Old English. Read it out loud. Don't try and figure it out.
   Although some words and phrases are intelligible,
   much will sound like nonsense to your ears. Good.
2. Think about summer. How do you feel when it is
   almost over? Try to pin down your emotions about
   the ending of summer (they may well be mixed
   emotions—which is good).
3. Write a paragraph or two of nonsense. You can use
   real words but also make up new ones. If you like,
   you can try to write a poem. Rhyme it! Or just do it
   in prose.
4. Try to capture the emotion you feel in the rhythm
   and sound of the language. Use different-length sentences, sentences with different constructions, and
   use punctuation to bring out nonsense language that
   captures the meaning of the end of summer for you.

Example

Psht Psht Psht Cricket
Say Brrrr be fall-lowin

Shh blowerin
Sh Sh lighterin
Sh Sh is waterwaryin

Lo lo lo in the co co co

Psht Psht Psht Cricket
Say Brrrr be fall-lowin

Peep a peep Sing a day
Peep a peep fly away
Pom a sweeter sweetay

Lo lo lo in the co co co

Psht Psht Cricket
Say Brr be fall-lowin

Advice

Although some of these words (or the way that they are used) are not recognizable, they convey meaning by their sounds and associations. Here a sense of melancholy permeates the poem, despite the fact that the words are nonsense. See if you can achieve something similar.

63.

Brevity and Intensity

In this exercise, you will combine brevity with intense emotion. Writing succinctly is always something to strive for. We want every word to count. Forcing yourself to write within character or word limits is a wonderful way to train yourself.

In this exercise, you will try to capture an emotionally intense experience or image in just a few words. As always, you can do this as a character (or persona), if you wish.

Exercise

1. Scan the last three months of your (or your character's) life.
2. Capture three (3) intense moments (vignettes, really) of only 100 words each.
3. Do this by using sensory images (what you can see, hear, smell, taste, and feel) rather than abstractions like "I felt sad."
4. Describe the things around you and see how they contain emotion when viewed through the lens of the narrator's emotions.

This exercise is great for character development and also for figuring out possible plot points when you're stuck.

Example

#1

My young son and I have been sleeping in my mother's bed. Her bed is narrow and we don't sleep well. We wake up stuck together, hot and hungover from our dreams.

Her sheets are soft and worn—they still smell like her, and now like us, too.

The rug is from Tibet and pale blue like the walls, with a large dark red and golden yellow rose—not my colors, she said when I gave it to her as a present, but it is the first thing and last thing she has seen every day for the last twenty years.

#2

It is raining again.

My father is standing on the porch, watching us pack the car, keeping dry.

Sorry we will miss your birthday, Dad.

He turns his attention to his dog, who is peeing, again.

He smells like Irish Spring and his own urine when I hug him.

I will be seventy-seven this year. He brushes some crumbs off his shirt.

I haul a huge duffel bag down the stairs and lay it in the wet grass next to the car.

Yes, I know, Dad. Do you have trouble stepping up into the bathtub?

No, why?

#3

For my father's birthday, I am putting together a photo album.

I go through old boxes, separating photos into envelopes, trying to make sense of them.

On envelopes I write Kids, Iowa Family, Veterans for Peace, etc.

There is one envelope full of people I don't recognize. I write a "?" on it.

Blurry graduation photos, photos of babies and old women in horn-rimmed glasses. Dad comes in, looking suspicious.

Do you know who these people are?

He holds one up.

No, I'm not sure.

Can I throw them out?

No! They might be someone important, he says, snatching the envelope away.

Advice

Notice how these three vignettes reveal emotional hot spots just by describing sensory details.

In the first story, the narrator is slanting at the fact that her mother is no longer there using circumstantial evidence. They are sleeping in her bed, and the sheets still smell like her. The loss of a parent is this intimate.

In the second vignette, the narrator is struggling to address the fact that her father's smell has changed and her father's aging and mortality are implicit in his incontinence.

In the third vignette, the old box of photos is universally a nostalgic symbol of loss: people, places, and events that only matter if someone knows what they are. There is also the implication that the father has something to hide, something he doesn't want his daughter to know.

Each of these could be developed further into a new story, or perhaps could find a home in an existing piece.

64.

Precious

Rachel McKibbens's "Poem for Three Dead Girls of Last Summer" talks about what she would do to protect her precious daughters:

> *When there is a knock at my door, I hide my darlings inside a*
>   *cupboard*
> *like bowls of sugar. When they sleep, I wrap them in kites*
>   *strings,*
> *line them up like ants so no one can take them and carry them*
>   *home.*

The poem ends with the line, "My sweetheart says I can no longer watch the news."

The lengths we will go to protect what is precious to us can be extreme, as McKibbens illustrates. This is a wonderful characterization as well as plotting exercise.

Exercise

1. Think about one of the most precious persons or things in your life. The most precious thing or person in your life must be concrete—that is, discernible by the senses. It cannot be an abstraction like "love" or "safety."
2. Let's leave the kids and romantic partners out of it. (Both are too easy a choice and too difficult to do well.) Besides, Rachel McKibbens has already nailed it.

3. Write a short piece in which you dramatize what lengths you would go to protect your precious person or thing.

4. Don't hesitate to go into a mode beyond realism to make your point, as the persona of the poem does (no one believes she actually wraps her daughters up in kite strings).

Example

When John calls me to wish me a Merry Christmas, he slips in that he'd heard Deirdre was getting married.

You still there? he says.

Yeah, so good to hear from you, man. Let's talk again soon, okay?

Hey, are you upset?

Naw, not at all. Merry-Merry. Look I gotta go, there's an electrical pole down on the eastern ridge.

I put on my boots and gear, and walk out of the station, up along the station road to the mountain pass.

Deirdre, with delicate collarbones that quivered when she laughed. She had wanted me to stand in front of our families to exchange shiny bands and vows, and then make babies. Lots of babies.

They will have your eyes. I know they will, she'd said.

I can still see her face, the way she stood, bent like a willow branch when she left me at the station.

Up near where the pass splits, I sit down on a mossy stump and look at the clouds thickening around the mountain peaks. They hang gently, delicate as a lace veil.

I have lived alone in the station now for years, eaten alone, slept alone, but never felt lonely. The yearning for a warm body or a voice in the silence is subducted by this view. I am wed to these trees and this mountain, for better or worse. I laugh at this and pick a round circle of soft moss off the root of the stump. I hold it in my hand, stroking the velvety sporophytes.

I missed my father's funeral. When June called, I was sleeping in a lean-to. Instead of putting on a tie and carrying his body down the church steps, I was deep in the woods, tracking diseased saplings and planting tiny seedlings on the other side of the ridge.

Three weeks later I arrived back at the station and found the letter from June saying come home, Dad's sick. I still have it, unable to throw it away. It is a memento, a keepsake from another life.

Advice

The narrator works in forest management and has given up marriage, family, and human contact and connection for his work. His first loves are the woods and mountains. He will do anything to protect them. Notice this is dramatized by his actions (or memories of his actions), not by telling us directly. That is what makes the piece so powerful.

A similar exercise that I've heard other teachers use is: if your house is on fire, what do you choose to take with you? It can be very instructive what characters grab as they run out the door.

65.

Acting "Out of Character"

This is another character-based exercise. As we've said before, characters are complex. Making sure a character is always acting "in character" can be dull and predictable if you don't have a sense of the whole person—both the good and the bad they are capable of. Often it is interesting to get characters to surprise themselves by doing something unexpected.

As a guide, here are some of the literary tools you have for revealing character:

1. What the character looks like (description of appearance).
2. What the character says (dialogue).
3. What the character does (how they behave or interact with others).
4. What the character thinks or feels (thoughts or emotions).
5. How the character experiences the world (through sensory imagery that shows their perception).

Exercise

1. Think of a character. (Or this can be autobiographical, if you like).
2. Make a list of five things that your character always does. They can be small: She bites her fingernails. She practices piano two hours a day.
3. Make a list of another five things that your character rarely does.
4. Now, make a list of five things your character *never* does.

5. Write a short piece in which your character does something on the "never" list. Write *how* the surprising thing happened, not why. In other words, don't try to explain the so-called out-of-character thing in psychological terms. Use the five literary tools to show how it plays out.

6. And try, as always, to make it surprising, yet convincing.

Example

Ezekia always:

☐ Eats oatmeal with almond butter for breakfast
☐ Goes to bed at 8 p.m.
☐ Rides his bike on the sidewalk
☐ Sings when he is excited, hums, is always making a noise
☐ Is the first to get in the sea, last to get out

Ezekia rarely:

☐ Goes to sleep alone
☐ Sits down to eat
☐ Brushes his hair
☐ Feels irritable
☐ Is content to sit still

Ezekia never:

☐ Is alone
☐ Uses sharp objects
☐ Drinks cow's milk
☐ Desires anything for himself
☐ Disobeys his father

Ezekia's dad gets into the shower and yells to him, Be right out, sweetie. Ezekia hears a dull, even noise, the sound of water on flesh. Ezekia is working on a LEGO project, sitting at his small table. He holds up each small piece and inspects it, then connects it to another in a symmetrical colored space-ship shape, his dark head bent over intently.

He sings: *LEGO, LEGO, LEGO.*

After a moment or two, he goes into his parents' bedroom. His dad's watch sits, silver and gleaming, on the bedside table. Ezekia picks it up, admiring the cool, smooth crystal. He holds it to his ear, imitating a gesture he has seen his father do, to make sure it's ticking. He puts the watch onto his wrist. The steel bracelet slips up to his forearm. He wears it like that for a moment, then holds it in his palm.

He goes out onto the small balcony in the bedroom that looks over the street. It is narrow, and he can hear the traffic honking and see the tiny cars speeding below. The wrought-iron balcony is painted gray, and has filigree separating the narrowly spaced bars. Ezekia hangs the watch on one of the *s* shapes. The watch glitters in the sun, its black face more blue in the bright light, a circle of tiny Roman numerals.

Ezekia picks it up again, holds it out, and then lets go. His eyes follow it down to the sidewalk. It is so far down, he doesn't hear anything as it lands.

He stands there, hands on the bars, looking down.

Ezekia, there you are! You should not be out here, his father says, coming out onto the balcony, but he is smiling.

Advice

In this scene we see Ezekia, a child, being left alone, something he is unaccustomed to. We know from the list that in general he is a well-behaved child, but in this piece he does something surprising—enters his father's private bedroom and takes his watch. The engaging imagery that describes how the watch looks to Ezekia gives us insight into how he sees his father, and the world. That he decides to drop the watch off the balcony is surprising, yet convincing—we are convinced by all the details leading up to the act that Ezekia would be capable of something like this. He is acting "out of character," but because of the moments and images leading up to it, it is believable.

66.

On Animal Friends

This is a rather whimsical exercise, playing off a character's self-image and connection to the natural world.

In it, you will conjure up your character's "spirit animal," the species of animal that embodies most of the same characteristics that your character possesses. Make it a real animal, not a unicorn or other fabulous beast. In this exercise, we will explore how your character responds to being face-to-face with themselves as embodied by that animal.

Exercise

1. First, decide what animal is the so-called spirit animal. Deer? Fox? Robin?
2. Write a list of the character traits that make this particular animal the chosen spirit animal. (A cat is independent, strong-willed, and aloof, for example.)
3. Now write a scene (something happening in a specific place at a specific time) when your character encounters their spirit animal. To keep this in realistic mode, they don't have to meet it in person—it can be via television, or a photograph, or in a zoo.
4. What did they see? What was their reaction? Did they feel a kinship? Or revulsion? Fear? Make sure to describe the real, not ideal, animal they encounter.

Example

Spirit Animal: THE BEAR

Introverted
Vicious
Forest-dwelling
Hungry
Sleepy
Deviant
Loyal
Intelligent
Fast

It's a bear, a brown bear! Holy shit. Holy shit, Mom! It just walked right by my window, a foot away from me. No, I am not kidding. No, I am not stoned! Hold on! I put the phone down.

I see the bear framed in the window, head high. The sun falls on its long snout and black nose. Its perfectly pointed ears are erect. The fur around the upturned curve of the bear's closed mouth is slightly paler; a few silky whiskers glisten and then it moves and the frame goes dark, filled with the fur of the bear's thick brown coat.

This is an image I return to over and over. They say memories morph every time we retrieve them, but this one is always exactly the same.

I see Laura scrambling to the front deck of our tiny cabin and closing the glass sliding doors. Not that it will keep out an animal of that size. Brown bears are far more dangerous than their black cousins, and if they are in close proximity to humans it usually means they are hungry or rabid, or both. Introverted, they keep to themselves unless provoked.

The creature lopes across the sunny grass patch that is our lawn, and we watch it disappear into the woods. To see a brown bear up so close is like seeing a ghost; no one will believe us.

I can't get it out of my head, the size and beauty of it.

Laura and I are at a dinner party years later and she is telling the story to our hosts, an older lesbian couple. Just like us in ten years. She takes a toke of the joint they pass her, pausing the story as she holds in the smoke and then slowly exhales.

It was amazing, I say, to fill the silence.

I pick up my wineglass to take a sip. Slightly stoned all night, I have been unable to make small talk with our hosts, Marsha and Gail. My mind has wandered as it often does when I am in these situations, and I would rather be home in our own cabin.

Laura turns to me, her voice rising. You weren't there!

What do you mean? I say, folding and unfolding my napkin.

You were in Mexico! We were talking on the phone, on the land-line for chrissake! It was before we had cell service out there. I remember because I was so pissed that you left me alone out in the woods with all those bears. She shakes her head at me, laughing.

Of course I was there. I remember it clear as day, I say.

Advice

A brown bear so close to their house made such an impression on the narrator that she is remembering being there, although it is unclear as to whether she actually was.

Her description of the bear up close—how it appeared physically—plus the fact that the bears are usually loners, and very, very dangerous—give us insight into how she views herself. One gets the sense of how in awe she was at the image of the bear, as she still expressed her astonishment and delight years later.

67.

Not Guilty

According to the Cambridge English Dictionary, the word *guilt* means a "feeling of worry or unhappiness that you have because you have done something wrong, such as causing harm to another person."

We have all felt guilt. What's more, you've (probably) suffered from false guilt—when accused of something you didn't do, feeling uneasy and unsettled despite your innocence, perhaps even protesting so much that people would suspect you. In this exercise, you'll generate a scene to explore this psychological phenomenon.

Exercise

1. Write down five things you (or a character) are guilty of in a relationship (it doesn't have to be a romantic relationship).

2. These can (should) be small things. Not cheating on a partner, but perhaps sniffing deeply of a coworker's perfume at an office party. Not being overtly cruel but leaving your dirty socks on the floor for your partner to pick up.

3. Write a scene in which your character is being accused of something, but it happens to be not something they're truly guilty of.

4. How does the scene progress? Dramatize what your character does, thinks, and feels using concrete descriptions, dialogue, associations, imagery. Do they feel angry to be accused of something they didn't do? Or do they still feel guilty, knowing that they *are* guilty of other things?

Example

What the narrator is guilty of:

1. Joining in with the other girls to make fun of Mitali for her less-than-acceptable hygiene
2. Not giving Mitali some of her chow mein when asked
3. Running off to another part of the playground to leave Mitali behind
4. Pretending to Mitali that her lunch was not just adequate, but "delicious"
5. Lying to Mitali about playing with her after she, Mitali, finished her lunch

Mitali offered me a dirty cheese ball at lunchtime. She'd rolled a part of the cheese from her sandwich into a ball between her thumb and forefinger.

Her jagged nails were gray with grime underneath. Unlike the rest of us, Mrs. Sen never scolded her for her dirty nails or unpolished shoes.

"Here, take this." Mitali held it under my nose.

My friends snickered.

"Yuck, chhi!" I exaggerated my disgust and made them laugh.

Mitali wore braces; her plump lips were always pulled downward. Her speech slurred.

"Can I have your chow mein?" Drool collected in her mouth.

I looked at the contents of my lunchbox and then at my friends, who seemed amused by the interaction.

We'd later discuss how those cheese balls, a shade of beige mixed with the dirt from her fingers, looked like nose boogers.

In class, we'd caught Mitali tasting the contents of her nose. Sometimes, she'd flick them in the air. No one sat beside her.

"Tell you what, why don't you try some of Dimple's lunch? Mine is boring. Her mother makes the best chole bhature."

She turned to Dimple. I did a little gesture of relief by swiping the imaginary sweat off my forehead.

Dimple shut her lunchbox and pointed towards Sinjini. "Go to her. She has yummy poha."

And like this, each of my friends kept sending her to someone else till she came back to me again.

"Why don't you go to that banyan tree over there and eat your delicious cheese and bread? After you're done, we can play together."

We quickly decided to slink to the other playground behind the primary section to finish our lunch in peace.

Turning back, I noticed she was still staring at the dirty cheese ball in her palm. Her steel tiffin box lay open on the grass beside her, untouched. Her plaits tied with blue ribbons stood at odd angles over her ears.

When she caught my eyes, I felt accused. She quickly lowered her gaze. Then she threw the cheese ball into the grass.

—KASTURI PATRA

Advice

This piece gives an interesting example of how our consciences work—how we can feel guilty even without any words directly accusing us. The specificity of the response of Mitali when the narrator catches her eye—to throw her cheese ball into the grass—is an expression of her hurt and anger, something she probably couldn't articulate directly, given that all the aggression against her by the other girls was done with great politeness and propriety.

68.

Meet the "In-Laws"

The goal of this plotting exercise is to put your narrator in an uncomfortable situation, and then to exacerbate that discomfort.

In this particular case, we will first set up a typically anxiety-causing scenario: meeting your partner's parents for the first time. Then we will cause further disruption.

Think of it as a science experiment: what happens when you mix these particular ingredients with your character?

Exercise

1. Your character is on the way to meet their partner's parents for the first time. This is a big deal, as the parents really liked the partner's ex, and your character is worried they won't measure up.

2. Start the scene at the point where the character is standing on the doorstep of the parents' home.

3. When they enter, they immediately see three (3) things that disconcert them. Describe them exactly. Don't tell us why they are disconcerting. Show us through the description.

4. Then write a short scene about what happens when the introduction is made. Try to avoid all the clichés about this kind of scenario. This should be a fun one—use humor and exaggeration if you feel like it.

Example

Karen was late; she took a deep breath and rang the bell.

The address James had written down for her had somehow gotten smudged in her perspiring hand. She was sure it said 375 Saint Nicholas, but when she rang the bell of the brownstone, an elderly balding man came to the door in a bathrobe.

Mr. Robinson? she asked.

He shook his head, peering at her over his glasses.

You at the wrong address, little lady.

By the time Karen figured out that the 3 was actually an 8, she was twenty-five minutes late. She hailed a cab and sped uptown the thirty blocks between 375 and 875.

A well-dressed woman opened the door.

Hello there, you must be Karen. I am James's mother, Susan. We have heard so much about you.

Oh hi, gosh, I am so sorry I am so late. Karen laughed nervously, handing Susan a box from Zabar's.

Oh, what's this? Susan immediately tore off the ribbon and began prying it open. She didn't look at Karen.

Chocolate babka, Karen said, but she wasn't sure that Susan heard her. The hall table was so dusty, you could write your initials in it.

Susan lifted the fluffy loaf from the box with both hands. She admired the bread, holding it aloft. Then, cradling it with both hands, she quickly opened her mouth wide. Karen could see she'd had a lot of dental work. Then Susan pushed the loaf into her mouth. A dark chocolate streak appeared on each of her cheeks, and bits of babka fell all over the hall floor.

Delicious! she said with her mouth full, holding up what was left of the mutilated loaf. Then, Come in, come in.

Karen nodded and took off her coat, handing it to Susan.

Susan tossed Karen's coat onto a chair but missed, and it slid to the floor. Susan ignored it and kept chewing.

Karen reached down to pick up the coat—she'd bought it for this occasion—and folded it over her arm, fingering the crimson velvet of the collar.

Susan, wobbling slightly, motioned for Karen to follow her through enormous wooden doors.

In the large foyer was a life-size portrait of Jim dressed as a Confederate soldier in a period landscape, a plantation burning in the background. The portrait was so large it touched both the ceiling and floor.

Is Jim here? Karen asked, motioning to the portrait.

No, he's running late. His father is eager to meet you, though. Stephen! Karen's here! Susan yelled.

A moment later, a middle-aged man appeared, wearing nothing but a towel around his waist and with toothpaste at the corners of his mouth.

Hi, Karen! he cried. He took hold of her arm and jerked her toward him, pulling hard until she was pressed against his hairy bare chest.

Advice

This writer played the exercise to comic effect, which works nicely. The mother stuffing cake in her mouth, the missing partner (Jim) dressed as a Confederate soldier, and the father in a towel make what would ordinarily already be a very anxiety-producing meeting into a bizarre vignette.

We have no idea where the writer is going with this, but it is almost certain to surprise and delight us.

69.

Invisibility

In his poem "Black Matters," Keith S. Wilson describes what it is like to not be seen.

> dark matter is invisible.
> we infer it: how light bends around a black body,
> and still you do not see black halos

The poem continues with commentary on how his race condemns him to invisibility, and that even praiseworthy acts or characters are simply not visible in today's society, with its engrained systematic racism.

In this exercise, you're going to try to imagine yourself in a situation in which you feel overlooked, that makes you feel like an outsider. Explore what that means to you (or a character).

Exercise

1. Imagine yourself (or a character) in a situation in which you feel uncomfortable. Can be for any reason, physical or emotional.
2. Now, imagine that you (or a character) are being treated as though you don't exist—as if you are invisible—by the other people (or perhaps even the things, if you incline to go in the direction of personification) who are also in the situation.
3. Write the scene out in detail. What are the other people doing or saying to enforce the feeling of invisibility? What are they not saying? What do you (or

your character) do in response? Stay silent? Act out aggressively? Act passive-aggressively?

HINT: Try to manifest your feelings in physical sensations, not just thoughts or "told" emotions.

Example

I don't know why I remember quail hunting with my dad that late-winter day in the woods near our Missouri home. I was probably twelve years old and didn't carry a gun, didn't know how to shoot. Dad worked all the time and when he wasn't at work, he was out hunting. I wasn't allowed to talk because it might scare off the birds. I can still see the spaniels skip, Molly and Blackie, their tongues lapping, their noses sniffing the crisp morning air. Crows cawed. Snow-melt dripped from trees and puddled on the soft ground. Off in the distance was the call of the quail. "Bob White!" they cried as if missing someone.

The dogs were frantic as they caught the scent of the quail. Dad went after them in a trot. I tried to keep up, but a branch tangled in my hair. I tripped over a log and fell. "Dad, wait up," I said. I imagined myself lost in the woods for eternity and no one would miss me.

"Quiet!" he said. "You shouldn't have come if you wanted to talk."

He lumbered ahead. His back faded in the distance and the ground was too lumpy for me to run after him. If I didn't behave, he'd never take me hunting again and moments with Dad were rare. I walked alone in the direction of the dogs' yapping. At last, there was Dad's brown coat and Molly and Blackie were both standing still, Molly's paw lifted in mid-step like a marionette. I stopped too. Blackie sniffed the ground. Molly pointed at a pile of brush partially covered with new-fallen snow, a perfect hiding place.

Suddenly, there was a flapping of wings and the sound of a hundred tiny helicopters all taking off at the same time. Dad's gun fired once, twice, and tiny feathered bodies fell. Dad smiled, but I swallowed a lump in my throat.

Each of the dogs picked up a crumpled heap of bird and stood before Dad like soldiers.

Dad reached down and gently took the birds. It was as if he might hurt the birds, but I knew they were dead. I wanted to cry, but I wanted Dad to be proud of me.

The woods were quiet again except for the wind whispering maybe a eulogy or a prayer.

I looked down and scuffed my boot in the snow, pretending to clean ice from the bottom. With a gloved finger, I swiped at a rogue tear.

"Good girl," Dad said, his voice electrified.

I looked up just as he was stuffing birds into his pocket, thinking I'd done well after all.

He reached down and patted Molly on the head. She licked his hands and wagged her tail and he stooped and gave her a big hug.

—SHIRLEY JO EAVES

Advice

In this piece, a young girl is treated negligently by her father, to the point when he says, "good girl" to the dog, she is overjoyed to hear it, thinking it is meant for her. It dramatizes how eagerly she seeks his approval, and, likewise, how unlikely she is to ever get it.

70.

His Terror

In her poem "His Terror" by Sharon Olds, she talks about how her father is behaving in the hospital as he is dying—clearly holding on to life, as if he is afraid of something. He's not necessarily afraid of death, but of something else.

"Maybe his terror is not of dying / Or even of death, but of some cry / He has kept inside him all his life / And there are weeks left."

This is a terrific plotting exercise, to conjure up an emotionally resonant scene about someone in pain, who is for some reason unable to alleviate it by herself. By slanting at it instead of addressing it directly, you can reveal deeper, previously unknown things about your character.

Exercise

1. Imagine that your character has just weeks left to live.
2. Now imagine something unsaid or undone in your character's life, despite it being something of great urgency.
3. Write a scene in which your character considers revealing this unsaid/undone thing. It could be revealed via conversation, via letter, via text, any way you want.
4. Whether they actually *do* reveal it is up to you.

Example

Before the doctor tells me the bad news, my lungs do, creaking like an old barn.

Twelve weeks at most, I can't believe you are still walking around, Larry, the doctor said when he delivered the prognosis.

The next afternoon, I am repairing a fence behind the chicken coop and I cut my finger pretty bad on a bit of barbed wire. I sit down in the grass, watching it bleed into the snow. It is time.

I get up and head back into the house to call my sister Anne. I am composing what I want to say as I dial her number when my wife, Jeannie, pulls up into the driveway and I put my hand on the black lever, cutting off the call.

Tomorrow, I will call Anne and tell her. Really, I will. I watch Jeannie get out of the car and pop the trunk.

Still holding the dead phone to my ear, listening to the dial tone, I whisper into the receiver:

Anne, this is Jason. Please, hear me out. I need to tell you a few things.

I did take cash from our brother Harry's wallet; he still doesn't speak to me. I did steal prescription drugs from our neighbors in Highland when Jeannie and I lived there. And you were right, it was me who took the rent money from your dresser that New Year's Eve party.

I know you heard Jeannie's side of things. She complained righteously over brunch how everyone was accusing me. She chose not to see it, and to stay with me. But you came to the logical conclusion. You never confronted me, and you never called again. Jeannie said it was because of our politics, but I knew why.

This will all mend once I am gone. Please forgive me, for Jeannie's sake. She'll be needing you soon.

I take a deep breath, and, still holding the phone, continue.

I was a fireman with FDNY Ladder #3 during 9/11. That is not a lie, I was there. Those weeks of losing everybody drove me crazy,

I guess. I was not as heroic as the rest. And then afterward, I started using again; it made everything easier for a time.

Jeannie understood this and still saw the good in me. Imagine, someone who can see your light when there is so little of it. She knew you were right about me, that everyone was, but she chose to stay with me, even if it meant losing you.

Jeannie was your best friend; that's how I met her of course. So I know how traumatic the loss of her must have been. I found photos in the box under the bed of the two of you smiling and laughing together—so young, so beautiful, so long ago.

I put the receiver down, and sit at the kitchen table for a minute, before I slip out the back door and walk back out to the field.

I have not told Jeannie my prognosis, I wish Anne could be here to help me tell her. I can see Jeannie out the kitchen window taking groceries out of the car, her long braids swinging, laughing at our dog, who is leaping around her in the snow.

Advice

In this piece, the narrator wants to make amends with his estranged sister, who also happened to have been his wife's best friend, so they had both lost her, due to his behavior. He wants to do this not only for his own sake but for the sake of his wife, who will be needing support soon.

We know from the details in this piece, however, that the narrator will never do such a thing, just like he won't tell his wife about his diagnosis. We suspect that he will keep everything to himself until the end.

71.

Caring

Exploring the times that we have cared for others—or have been cared for by others—can be good fodder for both fiction and nonfiction.

Caring is such a complicated act. It can be altruistic, yes, but can also come with extreme sacrifice on the part of the carer, and resentment and anger as well.

Also, some people don't like to be cared for. They are used to being independent, and if now forced to accept the help of others, might not act gracefully.

Exercise

1. Write a brief piece (500 words) about a time when you were cared for, or when you cared for someone else. This can be a memory, or something happening in the present. It can also (of course) be about a character.
2. Show us how the complex emotions involved in caring are manifested in the world of the senses on both sides of the care relationship.

HINT: Give us the details. Don't worry about whether it is boring (it won't be). So don't say "She was impatient when he asked for water for the umpteenth time" but "She sighed as she picked up the glass and splashed it half full of tepid water from the faucet."

Example

When at two a.m. your mother, in a lucid moment, asks if she is dying, don't say yes. Don't talk about the cancer, give that hideous word no sway, let it choke off her breath with sorrow. Don't speak of the sepulchral rented hospital bed that now carries her through her days, a mahout on the back of a stalled elephant once charging loudly through, now still giving her time to see her life in memories before it is gone. She already knows the answer, so just hold her hand, perhaps ask her if she is ready to see her family members that have already passed on. Remind her about better days, digging in the back-yard garden when she was strong, her vein-crisscrossed hands sturdy enough to carry tools that helped nurture cucumbers, the tall corn, green beans, the eight kids that she fed from her hard labor. Remind her about her mind sharp enough to know when to till or plow or how to not overwater. Remind her of resting the soil between seasons, of the potatoes she would leave in the ground all year to go to seed, anticipating the next year's crops. Tell her she is Yukon, Idaho, in a field and place of her own waiting for spring. Remind her of how she guided your tiny hands through soil both rocky and loamy rich, how she bathed you after, her long fingers cradling your head and body. Go to the kitchen of her one-bedroom senior-living apartment and get her a glass of water. Perhaps some juice to soften her throat, ease her hoarse and husky words, no longer familiar with being uttered, out.

Then
slowly with parental acuity wash
Her body
For she is the child now. Smile at her.

Dying is such an irreversible Word, so don't say yes,
Remind her of living. Caress her long, thin, brown and
    age-spotted

nicotine-stained fingers that
as a child you would sit
and wonder over their
dexterity, marvel at the many
ways they could conjure
A meal up from out of
Bare cupboards, bare necessity. Tell
Her you loved the way her
Fingers smelled
All warm and tobacco calming
As you laid your mama's-boy head
in her lap and inhaled her
essence.

Now her hands carry no weight, curl into themselves her fingers wrinkled and becoming arthritic, look to bury themselves into her palms—just six months ago they were free-flying birds; now they are nesting in the bowl of her palms. At times they release their tension and lie flat beside her on the bed, but they never fly or dance anymore.

If
She still trying to croak and caw out words, cool her burning and
    inquisitive
mother tongue with honeyed wine, maybe a mimosa, liquid
    meds for the pain that you have been told by the doctor to
    administer
to her whenever needed—"She is dying," he says, "give her what
    she needs you to ease her pain"
At moments like these, you must hold
room for yourself, push the tears inside of your green space where
    you go to cry silently
When alone, when you are ready to burn
off your day's rage with tears
and think of plants and gardens and growing things—breathe.

When the doctor says four weeks
Do not listen.
Do not tell her. Let your mother
believe that life is stronger than the vessel she has called home
> *for ninety years. That her blood lives within her eight chil-*
> *dren who come daily to take their turn at watching over their*
> *mother. So, she will live on in and with you and your siblings.*

When she asks at two a.m. if she is dying, when she, in her lucid, moment looks you in the eye like a child needing comfort, maybe say yes. Say, "I am here with you, Mama, we are all here." Maybe curl up around her on the bed, or in her reclining chair where she sits for hours and days, and rub her temples, that cancerous spot on her spine that aches. Maybe just smile. She already knows the answer.

—S. SHAW

Advice

This hybrid piece (half poetry, half prose) speaks tenderly of caring for a loved one who is dying, and all the complex emotions that arise in such a situation: love, anger, frustration, grief. Having to make decisions that one doesn't want to make. What makes this so powerful is the specificity of the language and imagery that this writer uses.

72.

Controlling Chaos

We can't control chaos unless we have some chaos in the first place.

—FRANK O'HARA

The definition of *chaos* we will use for this assignment (the definition physicists use): the property of a complex system whose behavior is so unpredictable as to appear random, owing to great sensitivity to small changes in conditions.

For this exercise, you will be creating chaos—building a "complex system"—a family or group of people, friends or otherwise—that appears unpredictable yet makes logical sense given the personalities of the characters.

Exercise

1. Remember (or make up) a road trip you took with friends or family. (It can be an airplane or even a walking trip.) You must have at least two characters participate. Three (or more) is optimal to get the most out of this exercise.
2. You will write about one stretch of the trip in which the moods/thoughts of the characters are especially at odds.
3. Make something happen to disrupt the trip in some way. It can be anything: roadworks, someone need-

ing to use the bathroom, anything at all. Make it chaotic.

4. Note that although everyone is in the same physical space, they can (and should) be in radically different mental or emotional spaces.

Example

I think we can make it to the next exit, it is right there.

My brother and I sit quietly in the backseat. The car is jerking backward and forward as it inches toward the exit ramp. There is a sign with a gas pump and an arrow pointing left. The exit ramp goes straight up.

We have run out of gas enough times to know that when it gets to this stage, you need to coast, downhill.

The car chortles and then stops, and goes quiet. My mother rolls it to the side of the road where it turns to gravel. She puts her head on the fraying plastic steering wheel and sighs.

She looks back at us.

You guys can stay here in the car, I'll just walk up the ramp and get the gas and bring it back. Lock your doors. No fighting! She gets out of the car, waving, and walks up the road, disappearing around the curve.

We are on the highway, still several hours away from the tiny island in Northern Maine where my mother's brother has a house. My brother and I talk all year about going to eat lobster and riding our bikes to the sleepy cove to swim and collect periwinkles.

My brother kicks his dirty sneaker against the front seat, looking out the window. He gets anxious without our mother around.

A car slows down, pulling off the highway next to ours. A woman with big sunglasses rolls down her window, her brow furrowed in concern.

Are you kids okay?

Oh yeah, we're fine, I yell to her. I push my hair back from my face and lean down to roll up the window and lock the door, but the window is stuck.

Where are your parents? the woman says, getting out of the car. She eyes ours. I know it's not a pretty sight.

Our car is rusted out around the bottom, and when you sit in the backseat you can see the road passing below where it has deteriorated completely. My brother and I make a game of throwing pretzels down when the car is moving and watching them disappear.

My mom is coming right back, she just had to get something, I say through the crack of the window.

We have no gas, my brother says. I glare at him. Could you give us some? Please?

The woman circles our car, inspecting it. We have the back of the car filled with bags and books, and the car smells like the ripe peaches my mother bought at a farmstand. Avocados ripen on the dashboard for our lunch.

Don't do anything until I get back, okay? I'm just going to get the police, the woman says, shaking her head. She gets back in her car and drives off.

A few minutes later, my mom appears in a pickup truck.

The man driving the truck fills the gas tank with a red plastic jug.

My mom thanks him, and he smiles.

Have a good trip!

Thanks! my mom says.

Some people are so nice, she says to us, handing us each an ice-cream sandwich.

Let's go, Mom. I say. Now.

Advice

In this piece, you have movement in four different directions. You have the mother, who treats running out of gas in a matter-of-fact manner and takes decisive, calm action; the narrator, who is protective of the car and her family, and suspicious of the world; the brother, who is anxious at being left; and the lady who stops to "help," who appears judgmental. Although they are all in the same situation, they each react differently to it, so we get a slice of characterizations in the midst of the chaotic situation.

This is a nice effect to pull off. Virginia Woolf does it in the amazing party scene at the end of *The Years*, where she weaves in and out of the minds of many different characters, each of whom is thinking their own thoughts and reacting in their own way to the party's goings-on. I recommend that book highly to anyone interested in writing about complex familial relationships.

73.

Surprised by Joy

Expectation is a terrific emotion to play with. We have expectations of all sorts of things: how our food will taste, what our day will be like, what our life partnership will bring us. Sometimes those expectations are fulfilled, sometimes exceeded, sometimes completely wrong. This generative character exercise will explore what happens when negative expectations are unexpectedly turned upside down.

Exercise

1. Put yourself or a character in a situation where you were dreading an event. It could be a letter, a phone call, a meeting, a doctor appointment, a visit, anything.
2. Write a scene (something happening in a specific place at a specific time) where your character is expecting this negative thing to happen.
3. Make sure your character is doing something physical while they wait: gardening, riding a bike, working on a spreadsheet on their laptop as they wait in the doctor's office, for example.
4. Now, dramatize the event itself in a scene, only instead of having the scene's events have negative consequences, make them extremely positive, even joyful, if you can pull it off.

IMPORTANT: Avoid pregnancy/childbirth, death, divorce, and other "big" topics as the anticipated event. Think small, as usual.

NOTE: Happiness and joy are difficult to write about. That's why we shouldn't take the easy way out. For example, *never* use any of the following expressions (and avoid all references to the "heart" if possible).

- ☐ Her heart leaped for joy.
- ☐ Her mood lifted.
- ☐ She was bursting with joy.
- ☐ She could hardly contain her happiness.
- ☐ Her face brightened.
- ☐ She glowed with happiness.
- ☐ She felt a surge of joy.

Make sure your scene depicts this surprising joy, but avoid abstractions like the above. Show how the joy is manifested in the physical world (gestures, imagery, dialogue).

Example

I hate this town, Luciana said. The sky was overcast as usual as they drove down the straight streets with large, once-loved but now-aging houses on either side. She wished she were back in the apartment, alone. She had nothing to say to anybody.

Her mother stopped the car in front of a yellow Italianate house with peeling white shutters. Yellow roses bloomed along the front walk. Luciana's mother opened the trunk and gathered piles of papers and reams of glossy labels and envelopes out of it. She handed a stack to Luciana, and, patting her daughter's head, bent to kiss her cheek.

Rita asked me to help with some work for the school summer fundraiser. Her daughter is your age. She'll be in your class in the fall, Luce. You need to make some friends, we're living here now, baby.

On the front porch, her mother rang the bell. A woman opened the door. She had on a checked apron and gave Luciana's mother a hug. Someone was playing the piano upstairs.

Come in! I'm Rita and you must be Luciana. Noaa's in the back. Go ahead. I think she's planting cucumbers.

They were standing in a living room on a thick rug. The house was filled with plants, and sunlight streamed in through open windows. It was everything that Luciana's mother's tiny, grim apartment was not.

Luciana hesitated, then she walked down the hall. The kitchen door was open and Luciana could see Noaa kneeling in some dirt, next to a raised platform.

Hi! said Noaa.

Luciana was quiet.

I'm planting some seeds, Noaa said, smiling, she pushed her glasses back with a gloved hand. The sun had come out, and the garden was full of flowers and bright shrubs and potted plants that Luciana did not recognize. There was a slight breeze. It smelled calm.

Noaa handed Luciana a trowel and some gloves, and showed her how to dig a trench in the damp soil, then place the seeds one by one an inch apart from each other. Luciana then patted the soil over each seed gently. Noaa worked beside her.

Luciana liked the smell of the dark soil. A worm got caught in her trowel and she carefully picked it up and put it back in the hole.

That's right, said Noaa. Worms are good. We like them.

The two girls grinned at each other.

This is fun, said Luciana.

Noaa nodded, smiling.

When they finished the row, they moved to another bed, and Noaa showed Luciana how to remove the small tomato plants from the plastic trays and repeat the process of embedding them in the earth.

Noaa rubbed a green leaf on Luciana's hand, then took hold of her hand and squeezed it lightly before raising the leaf up to Luciana's nose.

Doesn't it smell good?

Luciana nodded, closing her eyes and drinking in the sharp scent.

That's next. The basil.

Oh, I could do this all day! Luciana spontaneously cried.

Don't worry. My mother will be happy to let you! said Noaa.

Advice

In this piece, we see Luciana moving from a very glum place to one of joy. Notice how the transition of her mood is reflected in how she perceives the world.

In the car, the sky is overcast and the houses are aging, but once she is inside and greeted by Rita, Luciana starts having different emotions. Although not much is said between Luciana and Noaa, their camaraderie as they plant the seedlings lifts Luciana up to a different emotional plane. Notice how gradually this happened—and how the emotional changes were reflected in the imagery of how Luciana was viewing the world around her.

74.

Sad Steps

The aging persona in Philip Larkin's poem "Sad Steps" gets out of bed at four a.m. and, "after a piss," is startled by the sight of "the moon's cleanliness" as it moves swiftly through clouds on a windy night. He finds it preposterous that it was once a symbol of love and art to him, and shivers at "the reminder of that strength and pain / Of being young; that it can't come again, / But is for others undiminished somewhere."

Comparing ourselves to who we were in a different, younger, stage of life from the one we currently are in can raise complex longings and frustrations, along with gratitude. It depends on the individual, of course. That's what you will play with in this exercise.

Exercise

1. Imagine getting up in the middle of the night to use the bathroom.
2. Don't turn on the lights.
3. As your character walks back to bed, pick an object (either inside or outside the window) that resonates in some way for them. The mirror on the nightstand. A photograph. A tree glimpsed through the window. Yes, even the moon, like Larkin does.
4. Write a piece that begins "Groping back to bed at three a.m. . . . ." that focuses on the object and "names" its meaning: all the associations that it has for your narrator. Don't think too hard about it, use memories, associations, fantasies, anything, to make the journey back to bed resonate.

Example

Groping back to bed at three a.m. I stop on the stairs. The moonlight comes in through the small window on the stairwell and creates a path of light directly in front of me—a moon ladder, I have heard it called. The window is old and has a crack in it that simply appeared one morning. I was somehow sure that the weird kid, Andy, who makes loud screeching noises down the street had tried to break in, but the window is too small for even a child to crawl through.

Normally, I do not walk around naked. I have no curtains up, and the Jensens next door can easily see in here at night. No one deserves to see me naked, not even me. I always sleep in the nude, but throw on my underpants or a towel when I get up to relieve myself. I loathe my fleshy reflection in the bathroom mirror when I flick on the lights.

But we are in the middle of an Iowa heatwave, and over the past two nights, even at midnight, it has been nearly 100 degrees. Turning on the lights feels like it intensifies the heat, so I turn them off again. I feel my way to the toilet to relieve myself, naked and half-asleep.

The moon ladder is like one of those old portraits that have eyes that follow you around the room. From each step I take on the stairs, it shines directly at my feet, illuminating my entire body, then disappearing behind me. My naked silhouette casts no shadow, and everything behind me is lost in the darkness. I stand there in amazement as my entire body is illuminated, beautiful, a silver fish in a dark pond. When a cloud comes and obscures the moon, I remain standing there, smiling in the dark.

Advice

In this piece, the narrator, who is clearly not comfortable with their body, gets up in the middle of the night. The moon gives the room an altered look, and gives the narrator a vision of themselves that is beautiful—something we somehow know they rarely feel.

So instead of being a melancholy moment, as the Philip Larkin poem is, it captures a joyous one.

This is a good exercise to use to develop moments of realization (I hate to use the word *epiphany*, but that is possible) or a plot point that indicates a change. Or perhaps just a disruption in a character's ordinary way of looking at things.

75.

Regrets

Regrets are awful in life, but wonderful in creative writing. Thinking about the things that you wish you had done, or hadn't done, or had done differently are terrific to explore, because they reach into the very heart of characters, how they see themselves and how they want to see themselves.

This exercise plays off the idea of regrets. It's a great plotting exercise if you're stuck.

Exercise

1. Think of regrets you have (or a character has).
   Things you did in the past that you *now* regret.
2. Think small and particular. Avoid the abstract and general. Not "I regret not being a better father" but "I regret yanking the brush through Annabelle's hair this morning because I was in a hurry."
3. Now write a 500-word short piece in which you turn that regret into a scene or section of narrative.

Example

Back then, it rained. Rained for weeks on end, so when Dana and David and I moved into our new apartment in San Francisco on Divis near Haight, we were high on light. Me, with a stiff-sprayed and blow-dried wall of dark bangs lugging furniture from a U-Haul with a pair of gorgeous gingers. Dana enhanced her red tones with dye, but David was a real strawberry blonde with eyelashes so long and translucent, he looked as if from the pages of an insect encyclopedia. We didn't have enough stuff to break a sweat, even if the sun beat down on move-in day. The place still smelled of the must of humid hardwood and damp trapped in the welcome mat the previous tenant left behind. And jasmine. It grew wildly in the backyard. We didn't get access privileges, but who cared if perfume wafted up to the rickety porch. We'd scored a three-bedroom with a sunroom and view of the Transamerica Building for $900 a month. We were lucky. Lucky our strategy worked. I'll call him Michael, the landlord, because I can't remember his name as much as his laugh and the bulge of his crotch in his faded jeans. Back then, a landlord could get away with trying to fuck his gay tenants. Back then, a nineteen-year-old femme, like me, could lead with his youth, and butch it up just enough to flirt for a signed lease. I'm not proud, but I'm not ashamed. By then, the three of us, queer teenage runaways, had done worse for less. Dana served as our protector as David and I decided which of us appealed to Michael, a gym bunny and drunk who wore tight T-shirts with faded iron-ons under a thick yarn cardigan. The look on his face that meant "I want to fuck you" was exactly like the one that meant "Die, faggot!" It was still new to David and me that someone with power could trade it rather than take it, then spit on you or kick your head. Dana watched the verbal negotiation as she reapplied her copper lipstick. Dana had enough of old men by her mom's fifth or sixth marriage, so she carried a gun along with a murderous rage. David and I felt safe doing what needed to be done. Prior to meeting each other, we'd each slept in cars and shitholes, and we'd paid so much to find each other, the city, waitress jobs with family meals and decent tips. We wanted someplace nicer than we could afford. We were smart enough to know that AIDS was the reason for vacancies, gay landlords, and welcome mats left behind. Eventually we moved, and even with all we knew, I was still shocked to see Michael's picture in the *Bay Area Reporter* a few years later. Dead of AIDS too. I say Michael, but here's what I am ashamed of: I can't remember his name, never asked if his mom had knitted that cardigan or if the tiny blond hairs on his T-shirt and jeans belonged to a cat or dog. He seemed more like a dog person, as I recall. I think of him now as rain, however temporarily, breaks drought.

—MATTHEW DAVISON

Advice

In this powerful vignette, a gay man thinks back to his youth in San Francisco at the height of the AIDS epidemic, and although he never says the word *regret*, the emotion echoes throughout all the images and thoughts. He does mention the word *ashamed* for not knowing the man's name who had rented to him and his friends, who had helped them get out of the cycle of homelessness and shame they had been inhabiting for months or years.

76.

Heartbreak

Life will break you. Nobody can protect you from that, and being alone won't either, for solitude will also break you with its yearning. You have to love. You have to feel. It is the reason you are here on earth. You have to risk your heart. You are here to be swallowed up. And when it happens that you are broken, or betrayed, or left, or hurt, or death brushes too near, let yourself sit by an apple tree and listen to the apples falling all around you in heaps, wasting their sweetness. Tell yourself that you tasted as many as you could.

This is from Louise Erdrich's *The Painted Drum*, and she is correct—we get our hopes disappointed, and our hearts broken all the time (well, more than we'd like) and in many ways that are not associated with romantic love, although that is what we generally think of as heartbreak.

This exercise is based upon the premise that most people have been badly disappointed by events or people numerous times in their life. You'll be surprised at how many good scenes you can get out of this.

Exercise

1. Write a list of ten things/events/people that broke your (or your character's) heart.

NOTE: *None* of these things can be about romance or romantic relationships. They must be about things other than romantic love.

2. Pick the one that resonates the most with you.

3. Write a scene (a specific place at a specific time) in which something happens that reminds you of this heartbreak. Not the heartbreak itself—keep that in the background.

4. Try to "slant" at it as much as you can. In other words, don't be too direct. Not "I saw my friend sharing a joke with her father, which reminded me that I had lost mine." Be more subtle than that.

Example

The day the dogs came was hot like this. This same sort of hot that turns the air heavy, makes it too thick to inhale. The kind of heat you can see, seeping up from the earth in blurry waves. I wade through such an ocean of refractions now, back across the grocery-store lot to my truck. It's a race against time to rescue the ice cream. The plums are sweating in their waxed paper sack. But grief is impolite. It strikes quickly and without convenience. It leaves you weeping in the front seat of your Toyota, a pint of mint chip liquifying on the bench seat beside you.

The day the dogs came, I'd been out in the yard, squinting at my phone, the deck above me offering little respite from the mountain sun. A bit closer to the edge of the foundation and I'd hit that sweet spot for cellular reception. I shifted, now only half in shade, and my parents' voices buzzed once again through the phone's speaker. Mom was working on a coastal mural for Trafalgar Funeral Home. "An entire wall of waves and clouds," she said, while my father mumbled through a list of recent funerals around town, the ones he'd gone to, the ones he'd missed. "So much blue paint," she said.

The Suppino reception had served lobster rolls and cannoli, but yeesh those Catholic services with all the kneeling and all the incense and that mumbo-jumbo. "I might need to add a bird. Something other than blue." Their voices overlapped in that familiar discordant harmony achieved only by decades of sturdy marriage. I could feel the tickle of sweat running between my breasts, soaking into my sundress. It ran further still from my thighs down along the inside of my calves, pooling in my snip-toe boots. "I see ocean every time I close my eyes."

I hung up the phone and dropped it into my boot. I felt the screen sticking to my calf in what was a poor substitution for pockets. The dry, yellow yard in front of me looked haggard, beaten down nearly to dirt. My best goat, Lucy, was nosing through a disappointing corner by the scrub oak and grunting into the dry red clay atop its roots. Lucy, my misguided housewarming gift when I'd first moved to the farm, had become my constant companion. She looked up at me then, just once, chewing on air and wagging her little tail. I remember thinking that I should go pick some plums for her.

I wavered there in the half shade. It was too hot to move, so I wavered. The moments just before a tragedy have a way of freezing in perpetuity. That phone conversation. Those seconds after. All the moments when I could have been doing a million little things that may have turned everything around. If I'd been by the plum tree, I might have stopped the dogs from bursting through the split-rail fence.

If I'd been feeding her the tart, yellow flesh of the wild plums, fingers sticky with juice, I may have shielded her instead of standing a bit too far away as one dog shoved her down the hill like a battering ram, instead of standing there as the second dog tore at her trachea, stifling a garbled bleat. I'd have something other than these memories of doing nothing. Something other than a stain on the dry yellow grass. "Something sweet for my sweet girl," I'd thought.

—LORI SAVAGEAU

Advice

This powerful episode evokes the heartbreak of a pet owner who is not able to save their pet goat from some wild dogs. The focus on the plums she had wanted to feed her goat is a lovely device that captures the futility of what the person feels, having failed to protect something they loved.

77.

Eating the Stars

In her poem "Antidotes to Fear of Death," Rebecca Elson talks about "eating the stars":

"Those nights, lying on my back / I suck them from the quenching dark / Til they are all, all inside me, / Pepper hot and sharp," she writes.

It's a lovely, whimsical poem in which she talks about her terror of not existing, and how she finally deals with it. You're going to try to do the same with this exercise.

Exercise

1. Write a piece in which you first name a fear. (It can be real or abstract. Fear of the black dog around the block, or fear of the dark, for example.)
2. Then write a 500-word story about how your character copes with this fear. What kind of antidote they need. If you like, you can make it something that is not realistic (like "eat the stars").

Example

When I was ten, I found the skeleton of a pike on the smooth stones of the lake's shore.

A body, flat with decay, attached to an open jaw of jagged teeth. After that, I stopped swimming, sitting instead on the shore, scratching names of crushes on water-worn stones and flinging them across the water's flat surface while swimmers floated and dove into the dark waters.

Adam 2 skips, Tim 3 skips, Corey 5 skips.

Corey must be the one.

I went to Inverness, in Scotland, and walked around the perimeter of Loch Ness, branches snapping underfoot. I counted steps, 573. I watched for shadows under the glassy surface, taking pictures. To capture fear and examine it, like a butterfly, before letting it go.

Water ripples away, cold and sweet, moving toward the shore.

I count strokes.

Nothing lives in here, Nothing bigger than my fist.

Frogs, minnows, A silver trout or bass.

Nothing bigger than my forearm.

When I go under I can hear my heart in my ears, irregularly keeping time.

I count twelve beats before I come up, gasping.

Advice

Here, the narrator ties finding a skeleton of a fish on the beach to her fear of going into the water, because of what is unknown that could be lurking there. She does some very specific things to alleviate her fear—skips rocks, thinks of boys she has crushes on, and then, finally, goes to Loch Ness, in Scotland, where one of the most famous underwater monsters is supposed to live. There she goes into the water, and conquers her fear. This is a prose poem, but could easily be turned into a story, or even a chapter in a novel; there is much rich material here to be delved into.

78.

Dramatizing Love

Writing about love is always difficult without resorting to clichéd or sentimental language or imagery.

Typically, falling in love is described as a sort of vision—seeing someone in a new light, or differently because of something they do or say, or perhaps something in the environment that sets them apart. The trick is to do this in a fresh and surprising way.

Anything is fair game in this exercise. Just make it concrete and avoid smarmy language if possible. See how you do.

Exercise

1. Think about (or imagine) a time when you (or a character) falls in or out of love (take your pick).
2. Write a scene capturing that exact moment. (Line written by a friend of mine: "Oh, that's the way you brush your teeth!")
3. Constraint: This has to happen in an unlikely place—not a fancy restaurant or a party or on the beach under the stars or the like, but somewhere where romantic love is not necessarily nurtured.

Example

On Saturdays, I closed early and the girls, Lee and Sang, stayed to sew while I worked on the books. I'd asked Tom, a recent vet from Vietnam to join us. He'd fitted the main room with shelves and proper windows turning my '40s-era bungalow into the shop of my dreams. He sat with the girls in the tiny sewing room brainstorming ideas for taming the growing mess. It was going to be a late night for me, and I got up to tell them it was after seven; they should go home.

Tom was sitting on the floor cross-legged mirroring Sang, who preferred the floor when hand sewing. Lee sat at the machine. Even though Tom had told me his Vietnamese was basic, the chatting among the three was fluid and lively.

I leaned on the doorjamb. Sang and Lee were uncharacteristically animated; their voices high and bright. Smiles accentuated their cheekbones, transforming them into beauties; the beauties they were meant to be. It struck me how Tom, as quiet as he was, seemed to know just how to make people relax and smile, even me.

He patted the floor for me to join them. I sat cross-legged, too, my knee close to Tom's. "Ladies, shall we tell Benni our ideas?"

"Yes," they said together. The three of them spoke, the girls hesitant as always with their English, he coaxing them like a proud father showing off his brilliant children.

Something shifted in me. I couldn't say just what, not then. But it was as if everything I had been was moving over to make room for something I could be, would be. I had no doubt that this shift was necessary and true and oh so welcome.

—CHARLOTTE PREGNOLATO

Advice

In this lovely piece, we see the unnamed narrator falling in love with Tom, the Vietnam vet, by watching how he interacts with (and charms) the narrator's employees. The writer successfully captures the exact moment that "something shifted," and although that goes into the abstract, everything else is grounded so thoroughly in the concrete that it works.

79.

Capturing an Experience
in Three Stages

Philip Larkin writes in his essay "The Pleasure Principle":

> It is sometimes useful to remind ourselves of the simpler
> aspects or things normally regarded as complicated. Take,
> for instance, the writing of a poem.

He goes on to say that it consists of three stages. To paraphrase
Larkin:

1. A person is obsessed by an image or event or experience until
   she is compelled to do something about it.
2. What she does: use language to reproduce this experience in
   whoever reads it.
3. When people read about the experience, they re-create in
   themselves what the poet felt when she wrote it. Larkin writes:

> The stages are interdependent and all necessary. If there
> has been no preliminary feeling, the device has nothing
> to reproduce and the reader will experience nothing. If
> the second stage has not been well done, the device will
> not deliver the goods, or will deliver only a few goods
> to a few people, or will stop delivering them after an
> absurdly short while. And if there is no third stage, no
> successful reading, the poem can hardly be said to exist in
> a practical sense at all.

Exercise

1. Think about what Philip Larkin advises and identify something in your or a character's life (the smaller the better) about which you/they became obsessed to such a degree that you/they were compelled to do something about it. (You had to buy that purse, you had to get that job, you had to have that baby.)
2. Write about it in such a way as to reproduce the emotion in whoever reads it. Think of all the "devices" you can use to do this: imagery, dialogue, associations, description, narration, scene, metaphor, language . . . all the techniques in your writing toolkit.
3. Give it to someone to read, and ask if the experience has been re-created.

Example

Running on the treadmill and I'm thinking about how
    my knees became self-definition.
Strange, how time does not mean I have learned.
Time is a serum of honesty, an act of holding the mirror.
And I need to be someone worth attention and warmth,
    breath.

        I wish I had paper towels
        to put on the counter, so I could
        say "They're right there,

                            next to the toaster," then
    someone
                        would be grateful for me.

Do I want the cave of my knees to collapse? I can no lon-
    ger run
without fear that I will no longer be able to. But I do not
    care
as much as I should. I am waiting for someone
who will want this body, no matter how much pain it is in.

                    The couch cushions have been indented
                    and indebted by two bodies. Mine, wanting
                    to make this last longer, maybe forever. Theirs,
                        kneading bread and feeding the cushions.
    Mouthfuls.

The idea of pain has cocooned itself in my mind
and has metamorphosed into what could be—if I just kept
    eating it.
I could be everything to someone.

                    When I build a garden, I will be happy.
                        Gardens are meant for sharing,
                            and being close to love.
                    My legs through cotton
    underwear,
                            my knees sunkissed.

To sit across the oak table and know that sacrifice was
    worth it.
The crops are growing. The illness has been cured. There
    are clouds in the sky once more.
I can smile deeply and feel it in my chest, and the
    moment is still.
A true stillness that holds two people instead of me alone
    again.
                                        —MARISA VITO

Advice

This writer took an "experience"—running on the treadmill—and
the images, thoughts, and especially associations that flashed through
her head, re-created the experience so we also could go through her
longing and pain and sadness to emerge into a place where she didn't
feel quite as alone—or at least, where she can tolerate her aloneness
until she finds a partner worthy of her. It follows Larkin's formula
exactly. Read it out loud to get the full effect.

80.

Misalignment

I still remember my junior high teacher telling us the three kinds of conflict in literature: Man against man, man against nature, man against himself. Although I suppose you could squeeze most fictional conflicts into these categories (or perhaps combinations of these categories), it's not a very inspiring way to think about conflict. You run the risk of setting up clichéd situations that play out in expected ways.

In this exercise you're going to play with the idea of a slight misalignment, not a full-blown conflict, between two characters who mostly agree with each other. Yet (as I always say, I know) it's the small things that can be the richest material for exploring character.

This exercise is also excellent for plotting stories by spinning out the disagreement to its full conclusion.

Exercise

1. Imagine a character in a situation where they are doing something active with a beloved companion. In other words, a close relationship exists between the two. The activity they are engaged in should be something enjoyed by both of them: Cycling in the country, volunteering for a house-build, perhaps gardening, or marching for a cause. The important thing is that they are physically active and engaged.
2. Even though it is an activity both are engaged in, they have a disagreement that exists within the framework of enjoyment. They could disagree on which bicycle route to take, want to use a different

tool for solving an engineering problem in a build, or disagree about the placement of a plant.

3. Write a scene in which this misalignment plays out. Don't let them out of the disagreement easily! Have it resonate. ("You always get your way, it's my turn!" or "Don't you remember last time this happened." Try to delve deep into what's at the heart of the misalignment, despite the affection the two characters have for each other.

HINT: Keep the action going. Even if what's happening is mostly dialogue, have it happen within the very physical context of what the two characters are doing.

HINT 2: Never write in a vacuum. Setting and physical action always matter.

HINT 3: Put other people in the scene if you like. It doesn't have to be a folie à deux.

Example

Four enormous papier-mâché puppets of judges floated past. The people supporting them, carrying their frames, were invisible in the crowd. Sheila shifted her shoulders. A backpack was necessary for these things, but it made her sweat more. She looked around. It was impossible to see either end of the march. A good sign for such a hot day and short notice. Sheila always insisted they come out for these protests. If it could only have been a different day, any other day. She sighed. This was just too close.

There was a loud cheer from up ahead. Jennifer said, "Are we finally going to start this march after all?" A banner with a drawing of a wire hanger and the words "Never Again" snapped in the breeze in front of where they were standing. "How long have we been here anyhow?" she said.

Sheila turned to look at her, "I'm sorry, what did you say?"

"I asked how long we've been standing here. Your head has been in the clouds all morning. What's going on?"

"It's just so hot," Sheila said. "Can you get my water bottle out?"

Jennifer opened the pack, handed her the bottle. "Maybe we shouldn't have come out today. You don't do so well in the heat."

"No, this is important," said Sheila. "I'll be all right."

There was another cheer and the crowd started to move forward. Sheila handed the water bottle back. She tried to smile. "I'll be fine. Really." They began walking.

A chant drifted back: *Stop the violence. No more silence. Women fight back.* Everyone took it up. The march turned onto a street lined with apartments. People, mainly women, leaned out the windows, waved, and cheered. Jennifer waved back. She nudged Sheila to look up, up at all the faces, to wave as they walked along.

The march stopped. "What's going on?" said Jennifer. "I bet it's a stoplight or something."

"So, Jen," Sheila said, "I've been meaning to tell you . . ."

"Tell me what?"

There was a roar up ahead. Jennifer strained to see what was happening. "Can you see anything?" she said.

"No, no I can't," said Sheila. "There's just a lot of people yelling and moving back and forth. Look, Jen . . ."

"It's probably the fucking cops." She started chanting: *All cops are bastards.* People around them picked up the chant. The crowd started moving forward again. They kept up the chanting for a couple of blocks. Then the march stopped.

Sheila said, "What I wanted to tell you, was that I got a letter yesterday."

"Right, who even sends letters? Can you see what's happening now?"

Around them, a new chant started: *Not the church, not the state, women must decide their fate!* Jennifer joined in. The crowd shuffled forward another dozen feet, stopped. Jennifer said, "You're taller. Are you sure you can't see what's going on?"

Sheila strained up, craning her neck. "No, no, I can't see. This letter—"

"Oh wait, we're starting up again."

Sheila bit her lip, hitched her backpack up, and moved to keep in step with Jennifer's jubilant stride. There were loud horns, cars honking in support or rage. A loud whoop drifted back from the head of the march and another chant started as the mass of people moved forward.

They say no-choice We say PRO-CHOICE!

They say no-choice We say PRO-CHOICE!

Sheila didn't join the voices raised around them. Everyone was screaming about choices, as if choices were always easy to make. The march moved into downtown. Few people were in the glass, steel, and concrete buildings, but some weekend workers leaned out the window, cheering in support. More people lined the sidewalks here, waving, and yelling. There were bright signs, many handmade. A man held a little kid on his shoulders. The child held a pink sign that read—"My Daddy Is Pro-Choice!" There was purple glitter on the sign and in the man's hair. Jennifer laughed and pointed at him. "Isn't that great? Another generation for abortion rights. Women choose!"

"About choice," Sheila started. But Jennifer had turned to wave at the man and child. The crowd, still chanting, was moving forward steadily now. It was so hot. Sheila pushed her hat back to wipe her forehead. The sidewalk opened into a small square, where a women's drum band played Afro-Latino polyrhythms. Some marchers began to dance.

Jennifer turned to Sheila. "Aren't they great?" She looked at her closely. "Are you okay?"

"Look, it's nothing. I'm just hot. It can wait."

"After twenty-five years with you, I know it's not nothing. What . . ."

"I was pregnant." Sheila said it abruptly.

The drums got louder. The crowd cheered.

"What!"

"I said I was pregnant!"

"You were what? When?"

"Years before I met you, before I came out."

"You never—"

"That's what the letter was about. The kid, the child I gave away. She wants to meet me."

Every child a wanted child!

Every child a wanted child!

—RENÉE PERRY

Advice

This writer made an interesting choice: to have the two characters— long-term partners—engaged in a political activity: a pro-choice march. This is something both clearly believe in and think is important. Yet the main character (the character into whom the narrator gives us insight) is troubled. Not only is the fact that she gave a child up for adoption a deeply personal choice she made, but it has political ramifications as well. When she tells her partner, she opens up multiple avenues for exploration in future scenes. Notice how this writer kept the action going—we are constantly reminded of the activities and noise around them, which of course influence the course of the conversation. This brief piece has many rich possibilities for further development.

81.

Failing and Flying

As a reminder that failure isn't all it's cracked up to be, Jack Gilbert wrote in his poem "Failing and Flying" that Icarus wasn't necessarily a failure. After all, he did manage to fly—for a time. Gilbert then talks about magical moments from so-called failed marriages, and other "failures" that could plausibly claim a sense of victory. He ends his poem with "I believe Icarus was not failing as he fell, / but just coming to the end of his triumph."

Exercise

1. Think of a time you (or a character) failed at something. Make it concrete, not abstract. Not "love" but "the relationship with Clare."
2. Write a short piece about that failure. Be concrete! Use sensory details to put the reader there.
3. Include a dramatization of how that failure was also, at a very deep level, a success.

HINT 1: Note the word is *how*, not *why*. Show how that success was manifested in the physical world.

HINT 2: Try not to simply write a "lessons learned" piece ("and thus I was older and wiser as a result of this failure") but about a failure that had true beauty in it—beauty that will never die.

HINT 3: If you're having trouble, think of a glorious moment within the failure—perhaps when you were thinking you'd succeed, or you had succeeded, briefly—and describe that precisely.

Example

The grass was still damp from the rain the night before. Hakeem noticed. As Ms. Gleason pointed out the cones that marked the running course, the other kids were mostly disinterested. Only Suzy and Lynn were looking at Hakeem, pointing and smiling. Hakeem turned away from them.

It was a mile-long course through the school grounds, the first event in the big spring track-and-field day. Hakeem was mature for fifth grade, a head above all the other kids, stronger and faster as well as blacker. He was already sprouting dark, fuzzy hair under his arms. All this embarrassed him most of the time, and he even felt guilty about it, moving slower than he could in basketball pickup games so as not to show up his classmates. Everyone treated him nicely because he was a natural athlete, but sometimes he felt very alone.

Someone yelled, Hakeem, you got this! from the sidelines behind him.

Everybody lined up and then they were off. Some kids didn't even pretend to run, they just walked from the start.

Suzy and Lynn held hands, loping and laughing.

Hakeem took off at a quick pace, pumping his arms backward and forward, fingers in light fists. By the time he rounded the corner of the baseball diamond and saw the quarter-mile sign, he had pulled ahead of everyone. Approaching the ridge behind the school, he looked back. The closest runner was a hundred yards behind him, moving quickly, a girl in a pink dress he didn't recognize. Hakeem took off, his long gait opening up. His heart was beating in time with his breathing and felt light, each muscle moving in perfect rhythm. He could feel the air moving through his lungs, capillaries expanding, blood rushing to his limbs. He passed the three-fourths-mile mark, his breathing now labored and his lungs burning with the ascent. At the top of the ridge, things would level off and he would open up his gait again in the straightaway to the finish. He would be flying again.

He heard kids cheering, and then a rustle behind him. He turned to look. It was the girl. He now identified her; she was new this year, although not in his class, the only other non-white person in the school. She had the same name as that singer, the one who had died. Aaliyah.

There was no one else for a hundred yards behind her. She was moving her dark legs in quick, delicate leaps, and he saw now she wasn't wearing sneakers but running barefoot. As she moved past him, she smiled at him, her short, curly dark hair standing almost on end, and then she pulled past him. He tried to speed up, pushing himself up over the crest behind her. On the straightaway she moved farther ahead, her tiny frame light and agile. He was breathless again, but this time with admiration.

She crossed the finish line nearly twenty yards ahead and turned to wait for him, holding out her hand.

Advice

In this piece, we see that despite not winning the race, Hakeem has triumphed because of the joy he felt in running and also in his lack of animosity or competitiveness toward the girl who did win. We were told that, in fact, Hakeem was shy about displaying his physical prowess and maturity—that he felt uncomfortable with it. We get the sense—not told to us outright, but through the language and the actions of the characters—that he and this girl are going to become friends. Given that Hakeem appears to be a loner, that is another triumph for him.

82.

A Brief for the Defense

Juxtaposition, according to Merriam-Webster, is "the act or an instance of placing two or more things side by side to compare or contrast or to create an interesting effect."

Juxtaposition is an important technique in writing—whether fiction, nonfiction, or poetry. Often, you will want to juxtapose a quick association in a character's (or persona's) mind next to something that is happening in the present. This could be a memory (flashback), an association of language, of imagery, of thought, of feeling. Anything.

Sometimes you will want to directly compare the things you are juxtaposing. Sometimes you will want the differences between the images (or ideas) to speak for themselves, without explanation. Whatever effect you are trying to attain, your piece should be made stronger because of the comparison.

In his poem "A Brief for the Defense" Jack Gilbert writes about the horrors going on in the world all the time:

> *Sorry everywhere*
> *Slaughter everywhere. If babies*
> *are not starving someplace, they are starving*
> *somewhere else. With flies in their nostrils.*

However, Gilbert says, we (implicating us) go on living our lives, because "that's what God wants."

The poem goes on, making a defense for how we, as members of the human race, can—and should—go on, and be happy, but without forgetting the suffering that is taking place elsewhere, all the time.

Exercise

1. Capture a moment (using all five senses if possible) that you enjoyed recently. Describe it thoroughly and precisely. Do *not* worry if it's boring.
2. Now describe something horrific happening now in the world. Be precise! Think small (a moment), and don't go for easy, low-hanging fruit (if you choose children in cages, go deeper and get more telling details). Do some research on the Internet if you have to get details. Describe this horrific thing thoroughly and use all five senses if possible and (again) do not worry if it is boring.
3. Now write a third piece. Use the following form: "As [X] is happening, [Y] is also happening. Compare and contrast the two moments, directly or indirectly, whatever you like. Do not attempt to judge or pontificate on what it means. Just compare and contrast the details.

Example

1.

Claire made the oatmeal, heavily scented with cinnamon. Leo had just promptly flung it across the floor when the sun came up. Claire pads across the kitchen, the bottom of her slippers sticky with the goo, drinking coffee out of a mug that read YODA ONE FOR ME in large red letters. Claire wonders where the mug came from. Like so many other things in this house, objects appear and disappear. The coffee goes down too hot and too fast, scalding her tongue.

About fifty meters from the house, the smooth tender grass breaks into precise rows, carving channels in the loamy soil that hold seeds of peas, carrots, tomatoes and strawberries. In a few months they will be smeared on small faces and stain tiny fingers. Claire imagines the seeds under the soil no bigger than pinpricks, their shoots stretching upward, bursting away from the waxy hulls. Above-ground, Claire admires the flowering dense thyme and callow marigolds that interrupt the rows: placed intermittently to attract the bees that subsequently came and are steadily humming as they go about their business.

Claire bends down close to the ground, skimming the damp earth with her left hand, coffee mug still held in the right, and smiles as the first delicate basil leaves unfurl toward her. The sweet, poignant scent mixes with the bitterness of the coffee, and Claire smiles.

2.

The UN food agency has warned that thousands of families in southern Madagascar are on the edge of starvation as the country faces its worst drought in four decades. The country is parched, dust-ridden, thirsty beyond what language can describe. The people have been eating raw red cactus fruits, wild leaves, and locusts. Children still play, but their bloated bellies and weak limbs prevent them from picking up and throwing balls, or running after each other with sticks as they normally would. One little girl has lined up a row of dead locusts—they're much larger than what we're used to, at least five inches long. This is her family's dinner, and she knows that, so she's careful with them as she pretends that they are a little family, with father, mother, and children. Above all, she is thirsty, so she picks a leaf off a withered plant and pretends it is full of water as she gently holds it up to the mouths of each of the dead locusts, urging them to drink. Mandrosoa, misotroa, mahasoa anao izany. Come on, drink, it's good for you, she says softly.

3.

As Claire is walking through her verdant garden, brushing her hands along the tops of the plants and feeling the dew on her fingertips, a little girl is hungry and thirsty in Madagascar. Claire is vaguely aware that climate change is already dramatically affecting people in other parts of the world, that it's not just bigger and wetter storms or hot or cold extremes, but something that is putting lives at risk. But amidst the green magic that she grew from seeds, she finds it hard to believe and therefore hard to care. Her own son, Leo, is now happily playing in the dirt behind her, digging a small hole to bury a LEGO in. How would she feel if he were hungry, if she had to watch him waste away? That makes her stop and take a sharp inward breath. She would never allow that to happen. But what if it were beyond her powers? She shakes her head to dispel the thought. Her plants and vegetables and flowers are thriving, despite the Brood X seventeen-year invasion of locusts. To save her garden, she'd covered the entire thing with a thin mesh blanket, to let sun and water come through but keep the locusts out. Mostly she'd succeeded. She spots one, dead, near her roses. He must be an outlier; the rest had died or flown away two weeks ago. You couldn't walk on the sidewalks without crunching their carcasses. Clare hunches down and looks close at the insect. Ugly. And big—bigger than any other insect she'd ever seen. What would it be like to eat them, as she knew people in drought-ridden countries had to, to survive. She involuntarily pursed her lips and shuddered. She'd rather starve. But then, that's easy to say, her stomach full of oatmeal, her thirst fully quenched by natural spring water, and her child safely playing beside her.

Advice

This writer has chosen to juxtapose two specific scenes next to each other. One is a young mother contemplating her growing garden— peaceful and calming, despite the oatmeal thrown on the floor and the hint of the chaos of a young family. It is contrasted with the plight of a family in Madagascar, which is suffering from the effects of global climate change. Notice that the writer uses opposites, which have tension. A wet, verdant garden where small green things are coming up, compared to a parched, dry, dusty country where the people are always hungry, and, especially, thirsty. In the third vignette, the narrator tries to care about the suffering that is going on elsewhere, but has trouble doing so. Her own life is so safe from such suffering that she can't imagine being driven to eat locusts or otherwise compromise her first-world experiences. This beautifully illustrates one of the hardest things to endure in privileged modern life: the suffering that exists elsewhere in the world.

83.

Honoring the Shmita

Six years, you shall sow your land and gather its yield; but in the seventh you shall let it rest and lie fallow. Let the needy among your people eat of it, and what they leave let the wild beasts eat. You shall do the same with your vineyards and your olive groves.

—EXODUS 23

The above text refers to the Shmita, a yearlong break from farming that is supposed to be taken every seven years, according to the Old Testament. It is a slowing-down time for growth, creation, tending things left undone.

Depicting characters in the midst of the Shmita is a wonderful way to figure out both character and plot.

Exercise

1. Write a list of five (5) things that you or a character would do if you/they took a yearlong break from your/their job (your/their vocation). Or, if you prefer, from your (or their) avocation. Be very specific. Only one sentence per item is needed.
2. Specifically, what actions would you/they take to do things left undone?

HINT: To avoid this turning into a sentimental fantasy ("I would move to Bali and write my novel on the beach") try to write down things that are grounded in the physical, financial, and emotional reality of what is actually doable for you/your character. "Clean out my garage," "Finish the painting of my girlfriend I started five years ago," or "Dig up the garden and plant daisies."

> **3.** Then, write a piece dramatizing you/your character actually doing one of these five things.

HINT: How does it feel to you/your character to be honoring the Shmita? What is challenging or even unpleasant about it? What is exciting? Joyful?

Example

The pandemic would have been a good time to do it. Look through it all, organize what he wanted to keep, but mostly recycle the contents of all those boxes. Poem starts, ideas for song lyrics, scraps of plays, novels and memoirs William had fantasized about writing. But also, long out-of-date to-do lists, gig contracts that should have been filed by year but weren't, business cards of people he'd never followed up with, letters from people he'd forgotten, fading photographs, the proverbial napkin-with-deathless-lines scribbled on it—the jumbled-together variety of ephemera astounded him when he opened the first box.

Yes, the pandemic would have been a good time to do it. All his concerts canceled, no point making booking calls, plenty of free time—but that first box stopped him cold. And the thought of all those boxes in the attic . . . and the slush of loose papers on his bedroom floor . . . in the hallway . . . in two corners of the living room . . . and the precariously piled stacks of papers on, under, and all around his desk . . .

And then his son, who had been unable to visit from Australia for two years because of the virus, called to say he finally felt safe to fly. Within minutes of arriving, he said, "Dad, I don't want to be rude, but have you heard the Swedish term döstädning? It means death cleaning. I don't want to deal with all these papers after you're gone."

"There's lots more up in the attic."

"That's very comforting. Seriously, Dad, I'm here for a week. Can I help you sort through all this?"

"Your mom, of blessed memory, she was going to build a chute from the attic directly to a dumpster and go up there with a push broom. No, look, you're here for a week. I don't want to spend it sorting musty papers. But I'll make you a promise; as soon as you leave, I'll begin the sabbatical I've never taken . . ."

"And you'll keep starting new songs and poems and God knows what else and throw every new draft on the floor! I mean, it's admirable, in a way, how prolific you've stayed, but Dad, you're drowning in this stuff."

Being a writer, he'd decided early on it was vital to honor words, especially his own. The afternoon his son left, he picked up an old-looking pile on the far side of the bed. Perhaps there might be low-hanging fruit because it was from ten years ago, soon after his wife had died; she would never have allowed him to put papers on her side of the bed.

He looked through every sheet, shaking his head—what was he thinking?—and ended up tossing them all in recycling. Thinking about his wife, it became too depressing to start on another pile by the bed. He moved to his desk and started on a mound beneath it. Right away it was harder going. There was the letter from his father disowning him for marrying out of the faith. After all these years . . . save it so his son could see how much better a father he was than his father had been? In the end, he started a burn pile by the fireplace.

When it got dark, he lit a fire with these secrets he didn't trust with recycling. A strange joy rose with the flames turning old regrets and angers into smoke. The years had given him a good ride. It was time to unload the baggage. He flashed on an image of his son scattering ashes.

—LAZLO SLOMOVITS

Advice

Honoring the Shmita in this case was both an obligation and a penance for this character, who is the middle of three generations of men who have been unable to hold on to women and who are battling among themselves for recognition and love. The Shmita in this case, for this character, is facing up to regret and anger from years past and arriving at a place of acceptance.

84.

Interrupted Journey

Going on (or having your character embark upon) a journey is always a good generative device. Think of Joseph Campbell's "Hero's Journey," which is the prototype for many of the stories we enjoy.

Here are the typical stages of the classical hero's journey:

1. The ordinary world.
2. The call to adventure.
3. The refusal of the call.
4. Meeting with the mentor.
5. Crossing the threshold.
6. Tests, allies, and enemies.
7. Approach to the innermost cave.
8. The supreme ordeal.

It can be fun to play with those steps. You may want to try it sometime. For this exercise, however, you're going to do something different. You are (or your character is) going to embark on a journey—going someplace with a specific goal or place in mind. But you/they are going to encounter obstacles (of course). How do you/they react?

This is a great plotting device to use when your characters are too static and you don't know what to do next to advance your narrative.

Exercise

1. Launch your character on a journey with a specific event/object in mind about which they have strong feelings.

2. Have them get "stuck" while on the journey (something prevents them from progressing).

3. Have a stranger do something small that evokes a strong (surprising and complex) reaction in your character.

Example

Sitting cross-legged in a room with a handful of strangers, each in turn sipping a bitter liquid from a metal camping cup, Clara tried not to make eye contact.

When the cup for the "medicine" came around the circle to Clara, the woman leading the encounter, who calls herself Bliss, poured a small amount of the liquid and held the cup to Clara's lips. Clara took a deep breath. She felt the cup handle slip and the liquid spill down the front of her, soaking her socks,

There was a tittering around the circle.

Maybe better if you do it? Bliss said, pouring Clara more.

Clara hesitated, looking down at her socks, then drank the liquid in one gulp.

Last week, Clara had received a message from Bliss with a list of practical things to bring on the retreat: shower flip-flops, a notebook, hiking boots, a waterproof jacket, and a comforting item. Comforting item?

Clara had looked around her room, then picked up a pair of worn wool socks her sister Elizabeth had left the last time she visited, and threw them into the bag on the bed.

Now, Clara was feeling everything contract around her. She closed her eyes. Her thoughts were kaleidoscopic, events appeared, overlapped and disappeared. She felt dizzy.

The journey was starting. Why don't you lay down here, Bliss said, smiling, motioning to a daybed in the corner of the room. Clara took off her wet socks and got up. A woman sitting across from Clara started to sway, shaking her head and moaning slightly. The man next to her was staring, vacant-eyed, his mouth slack. Each person's assigned "guide" sat behind them.

Clara hadn't noticed her guide before. It was a bearded man, small and wiry. He slowly closed his eyes as she examined him.

It's a circle within a circle, Clara exclaimed, waving her arms as she moved toward the daybed. She suddenly was full of insight into the physical world. Sun was streaming in through the open windows. Her guide walked silently behind her. He handed her a pair of headphones and Clara put them on. Bach unaccompanied cello suites were playing. Everything else was silenced. Clara lay down and closed her eyes.

Lurid pictures started playing inside her head. They grew closer. And closer. She tried to scream but nothing came out. She felt her guide's hand on her shoulder. It steadied her. He removed the earphones from her head.

Keep your eyes closed, he instructed her. Then: What do you see?

A car accident. Clara was shaking.

Okay, walk toward it, he said.

I can't.

Yes, you can. What do you see?

Clara was crying. My brother. He was the driver. He killed them all.

Advice

The writer of this piece chose to take her character on a psychological journey, which is always interesting—as long as you ground it in concrete details. Too many times, when we're trying to depict what's going on in a character's head, we end up with clichéd abstractions. The writer avoided that here by focusing on the sensory things that were happening in the world. Clara's journey is interrupted by the bad vision she has. We don't know if it is a true memory or a result of the drug, but it agitates Clara to the extent that she can't continue.

85.

Not Ashamed

Here is a lovely piece written by Madison Smartt Bell for the City Lights Bookstore series, "Signaling Through the Flames," as a response to the pandemic and the accompanying uncertainty and fear.

If you wake up alive, you're ahead of the game.

You might say, This is the day which the Lord has made.

Not everyone has more free time in this situation, many will have more difficulty meeting their obligations. You still gotta do what you gotta do, and it may have become harder to do it; still try to do at least one thing every day that you're not ashamed of, at least one thing for the good of someone else.

You might say: we are not promised tomorrow.

But if you wake up tomorrow, you're ahead of the game.

Exercise

1. Write a scene (something happening in a particular place at a particular time) in which you or your character does something that you/they are not ashamed of. Think of the words carefully: not necessarily proud of but *not ashamed of*.
2. Note the implication: the character frequently does things they *are* ashamed of.
3. Try to avoid sentimentality and easy gestures. Think of the feeling of shame. It is a deep and complex

emotion. If you can capture it, manifest it on the page with sensory details, then you really might have something.

Example

Dear Charles,

I'm not sure you know, but I took the black-and-gray painting with the aerial view of the spiral staircase. It used to hang on the wall behind my chair. I'm sure you saw it every time you came to my office for advice or a chat. You may not have realized it is gone because we were all working from home on my last day. It was bizarre to pack my office of seventeen years without anyone around to say goodbye, good luck, thank you for your contribution, we valued you as an employee.

I know I was leaving at the beginning of the pandemic when no one really knew how to engage in the face of a changed business landscape and fear of contamination was high and unknown. I know that, in other circumstances, you would have been there, done the right thing. You always did, or tried to. But in the isolation of that moment, after I had packed my box and surveyed my desk, chair, pencils and yellow notepad for the last time, it felt as if the office stuff belonged to you, but the painting belonged to me. I had found it in the basement, covered in dust, abandoned years ago. Tom, in Facilities, dusted it and hung it on the wall. I admired it every day. Not in that casual way that grows old as the novelty wears off. The ascending spiral drew me.

It reminded me of hope and beginnings. Leaving it behind seemed wrong. Leaving the office after so many years without any form of acknowledgment felt inappropriate. So I took the painting, mounted it on the wall behind the chair of my home office. I looked at it every day for two years, sometimes wondering how I worked up the courage to take something that did not belong to me. But things are different now. Time erased the importance of owning something from your office, some sort of acknowledgment of all the years spent there, some sort of goodbye. I'm in the safety of my home, surrounded by my own stuff, and recently I received a pencil drawing of the face of an African woman. Her face is old but unlined, her eyes feel wise. I can imagine my friend, in her living room, spending hours producing this piece of art for me. I've taken down the spiral staircase and replaced it with this drawing. It fits perfectly in the space and matches where I am and who I am. There's no space for anything that was not gifted to me.

I am returning your staircase painting. If you noticed that it was gone, thank you for not calling me to ask about it.

—ZURINA SABAN

Advice

This quirky response to the exercise tells through a letter how someone had stolen a painting at the beginning of the COVID-19 pandemic, as a sort of memorial for all the time she had spent in the office. Now she is returning the painting, not needing it anymore as she comes to terms with the new way the world will be from now on. It is not something she is proud of but not something she is ashamed of either.

86.

Heat

In her poem "A Parking Lot in West Houston," Monica Youn writes, "Angels are unthinkable / in hot weather," speaking about the impossibility of experiencing joy or believing in anything when the temperature is too hot for our bodies to be comfortable.

This is a good plotting/generative exercise to put physical (and psychological) pressure on your character to make them reveal their true soul.

Exercise

1. Imagine yourself (or put a character) in a hot place. That is, a place where the temperature is high— beyond what you can comfortably bear. It can be a day outside in the sun, or a sauna, or in a hot kitchen—anywhere, as long as it feels unbearable.

2. Describe the sensation of heat. How do you (or your character) feel it physically? Describe the physical sensations precisely: the sweating, the tingling sensation on your skin, and so on. Try to use all five senses when doing this.

3. Now write a scene in which your character is in the middle of performing an obligation—can be work, can be personal—but is being thwarted by the heat. That is, they have a goal, but the heat is affecting their ability to reach it. Play the whole scene out, including the initial feeling of heat, the goal or obligation, perhaps even the seeking of relief (success-

ful or unsuccessful). Whether your character reaches
their goal is up to you. Follow it through to the end.

Example

Fry-an-egg-on-the-sidewalk hot, the man at the bus stop says to me
as I search for a place to sit.

I do not look at him and continue making my way to a place at
the other end of the bench. He is holding a bottle in his left hand and
smoking a menthol cigarette with his right, and the mix of tobacco
and mint makes me nauseous. I sit down. My back, slick with sweat,
sticks to the white Plexiglas. I thought it would be a relief to sit down,
but it occurs to me now that the seat is like a magnifying glass for the
sun. I once saw someone catch a newspaper on fire using his metal
watch to reflect off the sun. My uniform is soaked with sweat and
I can smell my own odor mixed with the smell of fried fish from
the shop immediately behind me. I am looking forward to the bus,
although it will probably be too cold, it always is, the artificial chill
gnawing at my elbows and ankles by the time I get off uptown.

The last bus had no AC. Hasn't been a bus for an hour, and I about
out of this, the smoking man says. I hadn't noticed, but he must have
sidled over to near where I was sitting.

My exhaustion lifts and I become enraged by him: the smoke, his
presumptiveness. A sudden burst of energy ignites.

Do you think I give a . . . I say loudly, standing up and turning
toward him.

It is then I notice he is sitting in a wheelchair. He is missing his legs
and an arm. The bottle he is holding up with his only limb is water.
He is my age, in his late twenties. I can see the A-46 bus is coming.

The man looks at me, blinking away sweat.

Do you think I can use $5 for the bus? I say instead, fumbling for
my wallet.

He nods, watching me.

I move toward the curb, lugging my bags to get away from him, from the image I now have of him that is closing in on me, my breathing is labored. Anticipating the rush of the cold AC, how my trickling sweat sticks my back and thighs to the plastic seat, cooling my body, closing my eyes for the long ride.

The bus pulls up and the driver comes out to let down the handicap ramp.

Hi Louie, he says.

Hi, boss, Louie says. Louie looks at me. Ladies first.

Bus can only take one more, ma'am, the driver says to me. Another coming in half an hour.

I stand there, silent.

Louie shrugs and rolls himself to the back of the bus, where the driver helps him on the ramp.

I fan my face with my hands, then pick my bags up, and go back to sit on the bench.

As the bus pulls away I see Louie raise his water bottle. Smiling down at me, he mouths, *Bye, girl.*

Advice

It is hard to be our best selves when we are physically uncomfortable. Being overheated is especially challenging because there's so little we can do. If we are cold, we can put on more garments, put our hands in our pockets, or huddle with others. In heat we generally suffer alone—in fact, we feel antagonistic if someone gets too close with their body heat (and scent). The piece exploits these types of reactions while building the narrative.

This piece also plays with a number of assumptions on the part of the narrator. The first (a valid concern for women) is that she is being harassed by a stranger. The second, false, assumption was that the smoking man was a drunk, possibly homeless, certainly not an upstanding member of society. When she is proven wrong—with the extra shame of having been rude to a disabled person—she is literally speechless, unable to make the situation better through an apology or even a gracious "No, you get on" to make up for her rudeness.

The writer has now "set the scene" for something of dramatic significance to happen—which are always those moments we look for when writing. It would be very interesting to see what happens next to this character whose defenses have been weakened by the heat and the interlude.

87.

Grief

"Grief is love with no place to go" is a resonant phrase that has reached the far corners of the Internet. It came from an unlikely place: a *Doctor Who* novel written by Jamie Anderson.

The full quote is:

> Grief, I've learned, is really just love. It's all the love you want to give, but cannot. All that unspent love gathers up in the corners of your eyes, the lump in your throat, and in that hollow part of your chest. Grief is just love with no place to go.

Unfortunately, the full quote is full of clichés: the corner of an eye, the lump in the throat, the hollow chest . . . This is the sort of prose we want to avoid.

So concentrate on that last line, which has more than a little truth in it, to do this exercise. It is meant to help you take a strong but abstract emotion, grief, and ground it in the sensory world.

Exercise

1. Imagine yourself/a character in a place of grief. It doesn't have to be for a death; it can be for a broken relationship, a lost opportunity, a friendship gone sour.
2. Write down the source of grief in a single sentence. Don't try to overexplain it. Just write down the circumstances.
3. Now write a piece in which you displace the love

you would have given to the thing you're grieving
for—and give it to someone else, something else.

4. Be subtle! We can show love in many, many ways,
and small, fresh gestures work better than large ones
(such as proclamations of love in dialogue).

Example

Source of grief: Losing a baby in a miscarriage in the fifth month of pregnancy

David said he could stay somewhere else if Nicholas and I needed time alone, but I am happy that he is here. He gives me a bear hug as I walk through the door. We stand in the hall for several minutes like this, I rest my forehead on his broad chest until the heat of midday makes my skin feel dry and hot where it touches his.

I need to get clean, I say, turning away.

Upstairs, I stand under the cool shower for a long time. The water fills my eyes, my nose, my mouth, until I can't differentiate what is water and what is me. I am filled with amazement as I lather in circles between my legs, watching the rivulets of blood turn the water pink. I get out and dry off before I slip on an extravagant gift from Nicholas, a white linen nightgown I have never worn. I look in the mirror, the nightgown is elegant and crisp, unsullied by living. I notice a bee with a broken wing buzzing, making a circle on the windowsill behind me. I pick it up gently and hold it in my palm.

I am sorry. I whisper.

Honey, lunch is ready, Nicholas calls up the stairs.

I let the bee go, and it flies falteringly out the window, circling slowly away in uneven bursts.

Nicholas made an endive salad, my favorite, and set the table on the terrace in his meticulous way: napkins and placemats at right angles, fresh bread and butter, olives, and flowers in a vase. David opens an iced bottle of Albarino. I have not had a glass of wine since I found out I was pregnant. I close my eyes and take a long sip.

This is delicious, I say, opening my eyes.

We don't talk about the miscarriage. Instead, we laugh when David tells us he has come directly from Detroit. He lives in London. For some reason we find this hilarious.

What's so funny? he asks, raising his hands and smiling. I find his gesture immensely endearing, and I reach out and grab his right forearm and hold it, tight.

He had been visiting Detroit with his friend John from college. They meet up in a far-flung city every year to take mushrooms and catch up while walking the streets all night. They have been doing it for ten years: Venice, Rome, Merida, and this year, Detroit, John's turn to pick.

Detroit is nearly abandoned, and painfully hot this time of year, says David. It wouldn't have been my choice for a trip. He lets out a guffaw at his own pun, throwing back his full head of hair, and we join him, heady with wine, laughter, and grief.

Advice

In moments of intense emotion, including grief, our awareness of the things around us can be heightened. In this piece, the narrator, in the midst of her deep sorrow, has an appreciation for the marvelous kingdom of the living. Even mundane things are imbued with wonder, such as the shower washing the blood from the miscarriage away, the injured bee, the new linen gown. Other people can help with grief too. Not necessarily by talking about it directly, but just by being there, as David is in this lovely vignette.

88.

Forgotten

Forgetting is a very human thing to do (more so as we get older). We all forget things—both minor things and important things. Sometimes forgetting can be psychologically expedient—you forgot the final exam was at eight a.m. because you were so scared you would fail it, you were still studying. Sometimes the results of forgetting something can be serious and can even hurt relationships or careers.

Forgetting also makes a great plot point—realizing that you have forgotten something can stir up characters and situations in a way that forces you to take your narrative in a fresh and surprising direction.

Exercise

1. You're going to write about a time that you (or a character) forgot something. Think of something. Try to keep it small! It can be your keys, or a name of a person, or a birthday.
2. Write a scene that places your character at the moment that they remember what they forgot.
3. First, set the scene. Where is your character? What are they doing? Who are they with?
4. Write about the repercussions of forgetting. You can use dialogue, imagery, thoughts, descriptions, associations, memories—or all of the above—to keep it concrete. See where the forgetting takes you.
5. One additional constraint: Your character remembers what they forgot in a moment when they are engaged in a strenuous physical activity. It could be

lifting boxes for a move, playing basketball or working out, or energetically scrubbing the toilet.

Example

All of the boxes are now in the back of the U-Haul. Every last glass and book we own is wrapped in last week's newspapers, placed in a box, labeled, and stacked up in a 12 x 12 x 16-foot silver windowless cube. I pull down the heavy back door to the truck.

The furniture is already gone. My grandmother's dresser, our IKEA bed frames, the old velvet couch we should really let go of. They are sitting on a dock somewhere in New Jersey, alongside containers holding other people's lives.

I sit down on the porch admiring the clipped hedge and hostas planted alongside the front walk where Giles used to draw in chalk for hours. I get up and open the front door. Inside the now-empty house the evening light is waning. Without our things inside and lamps to illuminate it, the house feels like a barren vessel. Someone else's life will fill it soon. They will replace our family dinners and arguments with their own, paint over our chosen wall paint, erase the smells of garlic and ginger that we imposed on the house.

In Giles's room, I'd noticed the wall is dark where his posters had hung all these years. Tiny triangles of the taped corners remained stuck on the walls where he had hastily taken them down.

Giles! Oh no!

I look at my watch; it is almost six. He has been waiting for nearly an hour by now at the mall. It is getting dark. He couldn't call. We'd stopped our US phone services on Monday to avoid paying another month. Getting new SIM cards would be a first stop in France. Suddenly, I am horrified at what we are doing, ripping up our roots and taking off across the sea. What were we thinking? I rush out to the car, jangling the keys.

I hesitate out of habit: Did I lock up? I get in the car and start the engine without going back.

Advice

When you find yourself getting bogged down in a scene—perhaps putting in too much description or otherwise not adding much of interest to the narrative—you should always make something happen. Whether that's a stranger coming to town, or just having your character forget to pick up her son at the mall, this is a way to jolt life into a story. In this piece, the sudden panic of realizing she had forgotten her son makes the narrator question the big move the family is making from the United States to Europe—a major emotional moment.

89.

Accepting Yourself

In this first stanza of his poem "Love After Love," Derek Wolcott instructs us to imagine a time when we will accept ourselves fully, "with elation." This exercise isn't about accepting an idealized aspect of yourself, but yourself who you really are, without pity or judgment or anger.

> . . . *you will greet yourself arriving*
> *at your own door, in your own mirror*
> *and each will smile at the other's welcome*

Exercise

1. Imagine that you (or a character) hear a knock on the door, and you open it to greet yourself.
2. Imagine that you are "elated" to see yourself.
3. Describe exactly what you see. Don't worry about it being boring. Express your elation using the language, but describe precisely. For example, don't say, "I see a beautiful boy" but "I see a boy with shining brown hair that falls to his shoulders in undulating waves." Try to avoid clichés about delight, but observe with generosity. Think of ways to delight in ordinariness and things that are more than skin deep. See yourself who you really are, without pity or judgment or anger.

Example

Welcome, my long lost!
My Little One, my
Beautiful Adult No-Self.
I thought I'd never get
to see you again! How did I
not see that you were here
all along? Come in,
come in! Skin furrows of the earth!
Hair sunshine waterfall!
We are each other's shadow,
each other's star, each other's
twin. I couldn't see you until now—
couldn't see
past my own face. Passed it.
I'm over it now.
Sweet mirror, sweet ancestral
archaeological dig. Please mentor
my love for you. This
buried treasure, unearthed,
in-mooned, up-sixed,
here, right now, overcome,
undergone, in sight, insight.
This language almost lost—
at last we speak one
and the same tongue.

—JENNIFER BURD

Advice

This joyous response to Derek Wolcott's poem celebrates this person
finding herself, after a long time, as a "buried treasure" who is loved.
This writer chose to write a poem, and to use metaphor and language

to exclaim her joy at realizing that looking in the mirror—what she calls "an archaeological dig"—is showing her something not to be ashamed of but to be celebrated. She talks about how she couldn't see "past her own face" to the soul that was in front of her all along. A lovely, exhilarating creative response to the Wolcott poem.

90.

A Month, Described

There's a poem for every month of the year. Just Google it. We picked January, February, and October for this example, but you can do any month, and try to capture its essence in a poem or piece of prose.

This is what Margaret Atwood did in the opening of her poem "February": "Winter. Time to eat fat / and watch hockey."

Here's W. S. Merwin's end of his poem "January 2001": "So after the cold rain / looking up at the stars together."

And Bill Berkson wrote that October "ecapes the year. It is not only cold, it is warm / and loving, like a death grip on a willing knee."

Exercise

1. Read the excerpts of the three "month" poems above.

2. Write a piece that describes your experience of January, February, or October (or any other month of your choosing). What are the sensory details, the emotional nuances, the memories, the associations? Important: make it personal. What does the month mean to you? Show us.

Example

In the August of My Life

I'm a spicy hot tomato,
harvester at harvest time—gatherer, reaper,
collector of all I've sown and watered,
lap bounty-full. I'm jam-packed,
brimming with scent and ripe—
sweet corn, peaches, basil,
eggplant's purple gloss,
pervaded and occupied with sufficient,
supplied with satisfied. Un-hungry.
Peppered with seeds, ready for ratatouille,
greedy for gazpacho.
Body built of an ambrosia
of all that's round, sweet, salty.
I'm fecund, tropical, lush August;
and I'm august: majestic, regal,
namesake of the Roman Empire's first leader—
a peaceful ruler—resting on my deck-chair throne,
inspired, filled up: surveying backyard trees,
scads of morning glories, the garden jungle.
I'm leafy, leafed-out, dark green,
and shadow-cool, absorbing all that's ripe and sweet,
mouth full of blueberries staining teeth and lips.
I'm for gazing up at the Dog Star
in the nights of the dog days,
measuring inches rising in the rain gauge,
dreaming of beneficial nematodes burrowing
into wet soil to banish Japanese beetles.
I can steer in dreams, fly high, luminous,
balance on a tall bike, numinous.

My sails are filled with visions and imaginations
of what's half-hidden.
And fall will be my fall—
glorious, blazing, cool, and long.

                                      —KATHERINE EDGREN

Advice

Trying to describe a month is fraught with pitfalls—we already have
a lot of now-clichéd assumptions about times of the year, and associations with them. The way to avoid them is to be hyper-personal and
specific. This poet uses vibrant, witty language to compare herself to
August, and to harvest season in general. It's a joy to read.

91.

Beginnings

The beginning of a story is often the hardest part to write. Sometimes it just comes to the writer as if from a muse, but most often it is agonized over. Do you begin your story at the start of a linear narrative? Or do you, as many advise, start in the middle? You have many (too many) choices.

Great beginnings intrigue readers. They insinuate what is to come. They entice. They set the tone and the framework for the story (or novel). They establish basic things like point of view, historical place in time, and geographic location.

There are no rules, except this one: a good opening will make the reader care what happens next.

Exercise

1. Write five story openings (can be just two or three sentences or up to a paragraph each). Don't worry about whether you can continue. Just make each one intriguing without being melodramatic.
2. You don't even have to know what comes in the next sentence. Just craft five openings to five different stories that you, personally, would like to continue reading.

Example

1. To know someone alive is not the same as to know them dead. To know someone is dead and to see them dead are very different.

2. The tinnitus started as a soft hum in John's left ear, not altogether unpleasant, but when he sang it grew higher in pitch.

3. The summer our cat, Shy, ran away, we were living in Kate's empty house on Settler's Road and sleeping on blowup pool floats on the floor.

4. Martin stood in the foyer of the professor's house, his pale hands agilely taking apart the old grandfather clock.

5. Edward was surprised there was so much water. Was it safe?

Advice

Each of these openings promises something to the reader. The question is, can you, the writer, deliver? The last thing you want to do is employ a lame plot device—a shot rang out!—unless it is absolutely central to the story.

Your openings must simultaneously attract the reader into the narrative and not prove to be a red herring in the end. You don't want your readers to feel tricked in any way.

92

Expanding on Beginnings
(2 of 2)

Now it's time to see if there were actual stories worth developing behind any of those openings. Sometimes you'll find that you start out strong but peter out eventually because there was nothing of substance behind the hook you sunk.

This exercise forces you to explore what you know about one of the narratives. This is the exercise that keeps on giving, because you can keep coming back to it and starting more stories! I have done these two exercises (#91 and #92) many times in my writing life—and gotten whole novels out of them.

Exercise

1. Choose one of the openings you wrote in the last exercise. Choose the one that resonates the most for you—that you think you have something to say about.
2. Begin writing a story based on that opening.
3. There is no need to finish the story. Just see how far you can get in 500 to 1,000 words.

Example

Edward was surprised that there was so much water. Was it safe?

In the in-flight magazine on the plane he read that the Dutch had invented elevated wooden clogs to wear when the streets flooded. The mud on the streets could be as deep as a foot. But what he saw when riding in the bus from the airport was different than he imagined, less medieval and muddy, more ethereal. The buildings seemed to float along the canals.

Edward had not thought about the Netherlands as an actual place with cities and culture but rather just envisioned it as a low-lying field thick with tulips, like in a children's book of illustrations: fields of tulips; multicolored, striated, and uniform.

The low horizon of the sky was filled with voluminous clouds that reflected in the grey canals of water and then again from the water into the arched windows of the peaked medieval buildings. Everything was convoluted, curved. It made him dizzy.

The world is not flat, he thought, getting out at the bus stop.

That made him smile because in New York City the skyline rises up but the land underneath is bedrock, at sea level. His neighborhood, his world, up until last month, had been flat.

He made his way along the Reie, turning on to Wollestraat, crossing the small bridge to the Cruyce Hotel. On the bridge he hesitated. The clouds surrounded him, floating above him and below him in the water. Long canal boats were anchored along the canal, covered over for winter. On the other side of the bridge he was surprised to see people drinking pints of frosty beer outdoors at a café's small, round tables despite the cold.

Edward suddenly was exhausted. He felt his shoes rubbing and needed to sit down too.

The hotel was situated directly on the dog's leg of the canal.

Two tall narrow medieval brick buildings with lead-glass gothic-arch windows glittered, rising up, as if from kneeling in the water. The hotel was lit with gas lamps and the walls were lined with dark wainscoting inside. At the desk, a woman took his name and handed him an enormous key from the room keys hanging on hooks behind her, then directed him to the third floor.

Edward was too tired to even glance at the dining room.

He could sense that what he sought was close, but he would have to wait to look for it. He had come this far; it could be delayed another few hours. Besides, he thought, he mustn't be too obvious.

Advice

There does seem to be some substance behind this opening that the writer has chosen to more fully dramatize. Edward is on a journey, to somewhere he's never been before—we even wonder if he's ever been out of New York; his thoughts are those of someone seeing the world for the first time.

The opening of a story or novel has to imply a lot of questions and build suspense while slanting at the central mystery, not spelling it out, and we certainly have a lot of questions. About Edward, about why he has traveled to the Netherlands, about why he "mustn't be too obvious." All this is good. Whether in a short story or a novel, your job is to open up lots of possibilities for dramatic development from the beginning sentence. That is the case with this piece.

93.

Crushed

Certain human situations naturally have awkwardness built into them. One of these is being physically crowded in a limited space with (mostly) strangers—perhaps in an elevator, or at a concert, or on the El or the Underground. Placing characters in situations where they feel uncomfortable is the job of the writer, after all. Many interesting things can happen in such situations.

Exercise

1. Write a scene in which you (or a character) get into a situation where you are being physically crowded by others.
2. A person whom your character doesn't know tries to start a conversation.
3. Write out the dialogue that ensues, as well as all the sensations that accompany being in such a situation. Remember, silence is a part of dialogue!

HINT: You (or your character) might be reluctant to get into a conversation but feel pressured by the close environment to interact in some way.

HINT 2: You must make the setting matter significantly in the piece—write the scene so that it couldn't realistically take place anywhere else. In other words, make the setting count.

HINT 3: Try to use all five senses when describing the situation.

Example

The shower at Priya's sister's house in Oslo was just a little wider than Priya's hips. When she shampooed her hair, she had to keep her elbows tucked in. When she turned, she turned on a tight axis, never veering an inch left or right.

She had considered suggesting to her sister that maybe this time when they visit, they should stay in a hotel, what with the seven kids between their two families, and the grandparents, and visitors, and the dog. But Indians don't do that. Staying in a hotel would insult your host. Creating distance when there should be only closeness. Besides, Mom always says, "You just need room in your heart."

She stepped out of the shower and tried to dry herself. Her elbow knocked the towel bar. As she bent over to wipe her legs, her butt hit the sink. Water puddled beneath her feet. This bathroom made the airplane one look cavernous.

Priya wrapped herself in a towel and grabbed her clothes. She would just have to brave the crowd in the living room as she beelined to the study, where she, her husband, and Anjali, their five-year-old, had been put up. Mom also said Indians don't go parading around in towels. But what choice did she have?

The half a dozen people in the living room were mercifully transfixed on their phones. Priya rushed into the study, trying to keep her wet feet from slipping on the wood floor. She shut the study door behind her.

Her husband was on a conference call again. Didn't that man ever take a day off? But Priya did appreciate his ability to multitask. He mostly kept the phone on mute, so he could fold his laundry, brush his teeth, make his coffee, all while listening to his colleagues discuss the market. Priya peeked at his screen to make sure his video was off. Phew. She dropped her towel and started to lotion.

Knock-knock.

"Go away," Priya whispered sternly. She knew it must be Anjali. Why does that child need me in the most inopportune moments?

Still, a part of her was impressed that her youngest was knocking before barging in.

Knock-knock. More insistent this time.

"Anj, stop," she whispered a little louder.

"Can I come in?"

"No! Go away!" Her stage whisper was getting tired.

Bang-bang.

"Stop!"

Bang-bang.

Her husband glared at Priya, his phone stuck to his ear. *Do something*, he pleaded with his eyes.

Bang-bang.

Priya heard the door creak. Soon it would be flung open. Outside that door milled aunts, uncles, nieces, nephews. Some of them were sure to get an eyeful of Priya's unclothed body. Inside, her husband was talking to his work people. But at least he was on mute.

"*Stop*, I'm naked!" Priya shouted.

Her husband looked horrified. And a little amused. He pointed to his phone. He had just taken it off mute.

—VIBHA AKKARAJU

Advice

The sense of too many people, a small and crowded home, and too much exposure is palpable in this lively scene of a woman attempting to get out of the shower with too many family members around.

94.

Earworm

As humans, we're always multitasking. We're rarely focused on just one thing at one time. This can infuse complexity into narratives, as different thoughts or emotions can be juxtaposed in interesting ways. Better still if the thoughts that keep intruding are involuntary, so that there is a struggle within a character's mind to gain control.

In this exercise, you (or your character) will be stuck with a piece of music playing in your/their ear. See what happens when you or your character's thoughts are being interfered with in this way.

Exercise

1. Imagine that you (or a character) have got a tune *with lyrics* stuck in your head.
2. First, write out the lyrics of the song itself.
3. Write a scene in which your character has an important task to perform that requires their full mental concentration. But the earworm keeps interfering. Write out the scene so that the reader experiences the earworm interrupting the proper train of thought—don't just describe it—dramatize it. In other words, tell us how the interruption plays out in the physical world of the senses.
4. Write a conclusion in which your character tries to do something to rid themselves of the earworm. Whether they succeed or fail is up to you.

NOTE: If you hope to publish one day, please be aware that you would need to secure permission from the song owner if you use more than two lines in your piece.

Example

I've been through the desert on a horse with no name
It felt good to be out of the rain
In the desert you can remember your name
'Cause there ain't no one for to give you no pain
La, la, la lala la la la, la, la . . .

The song automates his movements. When he places his fingers on the keyboard, the chorus swells in his ears again. He shakes his head and blinks hard at his computer monitor, then looks out the window at the parking lot. The sun is just coming up.

La la LA la lalala la lala la La la

He is working on a deadline. In three hours, it will be done. He will press send, turning this story over to his editor at the paper, Dana, and the song will disappear. Jonathan will go to Tres Amigos for one last beer with Hugo, the bartender, then get on the road to El Paso to make the evening flight. By this time tomorrow, he will be drinking hot coffee with his estranged wife in Brooklyn. She will be reading his story in the paper instead of talking to him.

He taps the keyboard and refers to his notebook, and then sings, half shouting:

In the desert you can remember your name
'Cause there ain't no one for to give you no pain.
La LA la lalala la lala la La la

It is the LA la LA la la la part of the chorus that is a tic, wearing a groove in his concentration. He gets up and turns on the radio. A Hank Williams song blares. He shuts it off and immediately the horse with no name is back. He slams the desk with his fist.

Jonathan has investigated this story for months: driving back and forth along the Texas border, studying the patrol logs in scribbled and often illegible books, meeting with families in Roma and Ciudad Juárez, and eating beans out of a can in this motel in Clint. At this moment, he is discouraged. He feels that all his work has amounted to fuck-all.

He will receive a Polk for his work and create an international scandal in which a president will resign and the U.S. government will pay billions in reparations. When he dies forty years from now, Jonathan White's obituary in the same paper he is writing this story for now, will refer to him as the journalist who "broke the kids out of the camps, broke the heart of America, and broke the biggest government coverup since Nixon."

Right now, on this July third morning, Jonathan doesn't know any of this. He is just a young freelance journalist who has been up all night drinking coffee with a song by the band America stuck in his head, missing a wife who is determined to abandon him.

Advice

A song's lyrics can infuse meaning into a scene, as long as it's not too obvious. "A Horse with No Name" is appropriate because the main character, Jonathan, has been in the desert for months, chasing a story about child immigrants.

Breaking the concentration of a character with an external stimulus like this can trigger interesting plot developments as well as reveal character. In this case, we find out that Jonathan, who is, unbeknownst to him, about to be celebrated for his work, feels like an unlovable failure, and that he is so driven he will do what he has to do, no matter what the cost (his marriage, his health).

95.

A Visit to an Unpleasant Place

Everyone hates going to a place that is going to cause them pain. When the boss has called you in. When it's time for your annual dentist appointment. When you've failed a test and the teacher is going to reprimand you.

This time you'll use dread for dramatic effect. You will write a piece about anticipating that an ordeal is about to begin. This exercise will teach you how to dramatize anticipation of a future event (this one happens to be negative) by focusing on concrete details and using imagery, thought, action, and association to drive the scene forward.

Exercise

1. Place yourself (or a character) in a waiting situation. In the foyer of the dean's office, in the dentist (or doctor's) waiting room, or a similar place.
2. Convey how the character feels about being there, using a combination of thought, action, imagery, and association. (What do they do when they're waiting? Fidget? Flip through magazines? Play with their phone?)
3. Your character's name is called. They enter the situation.
4. Describe what happens in detail. Do not worry if it is boring!
5. Whatever happens, your character ends up being amused by the whole experience and ends up walking out of the room laughing.

Example

I am early, I am always early, even for unpleasant things. I look through the magazines from last year. Impossibly thin, impossibly beautiful models are showing off fashion that is already out of date. I remember wanting a dress like that, but it was too expensive.

I close the magazine and let it slide from my lap onto the floor.

Why do I have the pleasure of seeing you today, young lady?

The dentist, now standing in the doorway of the waiting room, is tan for this time of year, with a full head of dark hair. Younger than me by a decade at least. Young lady indeed. I am already angry with him, already traumatized.

I recognize his expression. It is the clean-shaven confidence of a man who is aware of his effect on people, his charms. He gestures for me to follow him into his examining room.

He sits down on a rolling stool next to me and then expertly scoots the stool around with his crisp chino legs so that the headrest I am lying on is positioned between his knees.

I am acutely aware of my graying temples and the tuna fish sandwich I had for lunch.

I have a terrible toothache, I think it may be an abscess? I have been in excruciating pain for twenty-four hours.

I warble slightly when I talk, and point to my right cheek, which is swollen at the jaw.

He is upside down above me now, and instead of looking him in the eyes, I am looking at the cleft of his chin. He is not nearly as handsome from upside down: his mouth moves up and down like an enormous blinking eye and his neatly trimmed eyebrows form a sort of hairy mouth. He resembles a squid sucking in seaweed.

Let me have a look.

He smiles and picks up a silver instrument, poking around gently in my mouth with it. A sharp pain ripples through my body and I close my eyes.

Yes, it looks like an abscess. We can give you some anesthesia and drain it.

He calls for his assistant and she brings him a plastic retainer to hold my mouth wide. The noise of the tiny suction and a long needle, and within seconds the pain dims and I fall asleep, exhausted.

When I wake up the dentist is still leaning over me, his mouth smiling.

You're all set. His eyes close for a moment and the squid is back.

I feel better, I say, unable to control a giggle. Thanks.

Advice

In this piece, the patient (the narrator) is feeling insecure about her age and general physical appearance, and finds the dentist intimidatingly handsome until she sees him as something else.

The exercise is meant to put a character in a point not only of vulnerability but of anticipating pain. This is a very uncomfortable position for most humans (real or fictional). They are exposing a point of weakness to another person, who has power over them. Small wonder dentists are often depicted (humorously) in literature and film as sadistic types! This writer avoids that cliché, however, and manages to give us a fresh take on the dentist appointment.

96.

Silver Linings

It's a cliché, of course, that every cloud has a silver lining, but it's an interesting concept to explore. How can you manipulate events, emotions, and actions so that a bad situation gets transformed into a positive one?

Warning: it can be difficult to avoid clichés of sudden epiphanies or other sentimental transformations. Just keep things concrete and let your instinct take over as you write.

Exercise

1. Write a list of five unpleasant things you (or a character) have experienced. Keep them concrete and specific: Have them be things that happened at a specific place at a specific time.
2. Now write a short piece in which you enlarge upon one of the unpleasant things you identified in Step #1. Write down the circumstances minutely and completely. Do not worry about whether it is boring.
3. Somehow, through your writing and manipulation of the story, make something good come out of the bad experience. I guess you could call it an epiphany, but I try to avoid that word. Try not to be sentimental or to write what would normally be "expected." (That's hard, I know.)

Example

1. Last year, a cop threw my ID on the floor when I was buying chips at the deli and said, "Get out of here, boy."
2. After my mother died she never came back to me, not even in my dreams.
3. My cousin's beautiful daughter, raised Baptist and much loved, died of a Fentanyl overdose in her bedroom at fifteen.
4. Seventeen-year-old Trayvon Martin was walking home from a convenience store wearing a hoodie and carrying a bag of Skittles when he was killed by George Zimmerman, a neighborhood watch volunteer. Martin was Black and unarmed. Zimmerman was acquitted.
5. The M-13 gang members in my son's school are killing one another for expensive sneakers.

I am leaving the deli, crinkling chips in one hand, taking the first cold sip of Coca-Cola with the other, when I hear someone behind me say, Stop.

I turn around. Three officers are standing there, and one of them holds up his hand to signal *I got this* to the others as he walks toward me, his eyes squinting.

We need to ask you some questions. He smiles, one hand on his gun and the other on his hip.

Bill is waiting for me in the cab of the truck with his hard hat still on. Like most guys on this job, he doesn't say much. I notice, for the first time, a Make America Great Again and Trump 2020 sticker on his bumper.

His blond head is moving back and forth eating his sandwich in enormous bites, like a turtle. He has his phone held up in front of him close to his face, seemingly engrossed by something on the screen.

You live over there? The cop motions to the Brickland Projects.

No, I do not, I say.

We have a complaint that a man of your description has been working on his girlfriend this morning. Broke her arm.

I've been at work all day, sir. Just in here to grab a drink. I wave my hand, holding the chip bag down toward the deli and then down at my pants and sneakers, which are covered with cement dust.

You need to come down to the station, boy. Let me see some ID, the man says.

I am just getting my wallet, I explain as I get down on my knees, moving slowly to place my chips and soda on the ground. I keep my eyes on the officer, fumbling in my wallet for my driver's license, and hand it up to him.

He looks at it for a moment, then throws it down in front of me.

Get outta here, boy, he says to me, and then kicks me in the stomach.

I stay on the ground until the police leave, then scramble to my feet and run back to the truck.

Bill hands me a napkin and starts the engine.

I was filming, he says. I got it all. You okay, buddy?

Advice

Good things can come from bad things. In this case, the narrator was being harassed, presumably because of his race. He endures what is now a familiar scenario to anyone following the news.

There is considerable tension because of the existence of the gun, and because we know from current events that these scenes often turn deadly. But two good things do come out of it: the officers are caught on video, and Bill, a Trumper, shows his humanity. Notice how carefully the actions of the narrator are choreographed: We know he's holding his chips in one hand, and his soda in other. That means he can't get his wallet. The description of how he gets down on his knees is both logical and intentionally showing subservience to the officer with the gun. All very well done.

97.

Bad Sex

Since 1993, *The Literary Review* has annually selected and published what it considers the worst sex writing of the year. Amid a barrage of end-of-year lists, theirs is a uniquely amusing one.

Now, writing competently about sex is very, very difficult. Typically, the mistakes that writers make fall into four categories: (1) too clinical, using words like *vagina* and *urethra* to describe a rather cold and sterile act; (2) bad metaphors, comparing aspects of having sex inappropriately to other things; (3) mechanically improbable, meaning you can't imagine such things happening during the sex act because our bodies just don't work that way; and (4) way too sentimental and flowery, like in a Hallmark card.

Here is an excerpt from a finalist for the Bad Sex Awards 2018, from the book *Scoundrels: The Hunt for Hansclapp* by Victor Cornwall and Arthur St John Trevelyan that manages to commit all four errors:

> "Empty my tanks," I'd begged breathlessly, as once more she began drawing me deep inside her pleasure cave. Her vaginal ratchet moved in concertina-like waves, slowly chugging my organ as a boa constrictor swallows its prey. Soon I was locked in, balls deep, ready to be ground down by the enameled pepper mill within her.

So how *do* you write well about sex? Usually, by slanting at things, describing shoulders instead of genitalia (shoulders can be very sexy) and by using associations—our brains don't stop thinking during sex; in fact, the contrary (why am I thinking of my ex at this moment?).

Exercise

This is a two-parter.

1. First, you will write a purposely bad sex scene, using one or more of the techniques discussed above. Make it bad. Make it really bad.

2. Then you will write a well-written scene depicting bad sex. Note the wording. This is a very different kind of thing. Someone is having sex and is not enjoying it.

Example

Badly written sex scene

Raina came up behind Sarah. Don't be scared, my darling.

Raina grabbed Sarah in a passionate embrace and then threw her to the ground. Sarah's hip almost was dislocated, but she didn't care. They kissed like two kissing antelopes, gently and shyly. Raina tossed her hair and it flowed down onto Sarah's face like a waterfall, like Niagara Falls. then straddled Sarah's hips, holding her breasts like two pale fresh eggs in her palms. The eggs were creamy and delicious.

Oh God, I want you, Sarah cried out in the woods, and they shuddered and collapsed together in climax in the golden autumn light.

Scene depicting bad sex (something completely different!)

The smell of sap, spicy and dry, closed in on Sarah. She felt uncomfortable, as though someone might be watching. She knew what Raina had in mind, and she wasn't sure she felt up to it. Through the pine grove the broken logs and leaves on the ground were illuminated by the afternoon sunshine, a golden cemetery of felled trees. Many things had died here.

What is it? Raina asked, pulling Sarah by the hand. Raina's

hand felt coarse and too large, and held hers with a tight grip. It felt like bullying.

Sarah shook her head and sat down in the pine needles, inhaling deeply, and then lay down on the cool earth. Raina knelt in front of her, pushing Sarah's legs apart gently and lifting her skirt up.

The warmth of Raina's body, the prick of the pine needles on her back, the smell of earth, and the dizzying brightness of the sun in the distance through the dark pines. Sarah tried to concentrate on that. The weight of a body holding her still, Raina's weight. She lay, unresisting, but the familiar warmth between her legs didn't come. She took a deep breath, let Raina in, and waited for it to be over.

Advice

There's a big difference, as you can see, between writing badly about sex and writing about bad sex.

The badly written sex scene commits every sin in the book: it is flowery and sentimental, it has absurd metaphors, it uses clinical language, and so on. The bad-sex scene is well written, and suggests more than it shouts, but it is about sex that is not good for at least one of the participants in it.

In general (not a rule, but advice) it is best to listen to Emily Dickenson and "slant" at things like sex, rather than look at them too directly. We have to avoid hyperbole and cheesy language and images to try to get at its essence.

Sex can be interesting, especially when it explores emotions as well as the physical aspects of the act. But it can be very risky. Watch out, or one day you could be on the *Literary Review*'s list! Some very good writers have committed enough sins to be included.

98.

Unwelcome

Virtually everyone knows the sensation of not being wanted somewhere, of not fitting in. This is a good situation to put a character in,
as it has many possibilities: one can be overdressed or underdressed,
the wrong skin color, the wrong sexual orientation . . . the list goes
on and on of all the ways the world cruelly separates people.

Exercise

1. Put yourself (or a character) in the position of needing to ask for something. It can be anything—a
   cup of sugar from the neighbors, a stapler from a
   coworker, anything.
2. Have the request be refused. And not just subtly but
   rudely, even crudely.
3. Play out what your character does. Do they give up?
   Keep trying? Be rude back? How your character
   responds will reveal a lot about their character under
   stress.

Example

Imani sighed. That rubbed area on the left sleeve had finally worn
through. Her favorite sweater was fine for being at home, but there
was no way she could teach a class wearing it. Imani turned the
sweater over to look at the back. Yes, moth holes too. She was going
to have to get something warm, another cardigan maybe. All the
classrooms in Wynne Hall had terrible heat. She checked her watch.
She needed to go downtown to pick up her car from the mechanic

in an hour anyhow. She could see what was in the stores around the square. She usually went out to the mall, but this was a good opportunity to shop locally. She pulled her dreadlocks back and wrapped a scarf around them. She picked up her bag and walked out the door, locking it behind her. The fall air was sharp. She definitely needed a new sweater; maybe she'd get two. She walked up Madison. Imani kicked at the leaves underfoot. She loved that sound and the smell of the leaves as they slowly decayed. What a great day this was for a walk. She should do it more often.

She turned onto Main and walked into the first clothing store she saw. A woman looked up and frowned as she walked in. The woman looked over to a coworker who was arranging scarves and gestured toward Imani with a tilt of her head. The second woman looked at Imani, shook her head, and went back to folding the scarves. Imani stood in the doorway of the shop for a moment, then turned and walked out. She frowned and walked down the street. There was bound to be another store nearby. In a block and a half she found another clothing store. The display window was full of knitted goods—sweaters, hats, gloves, scarves. She walked in. She walked down the aisles looking for the sweaters. She stopped at a rack of jackets. "Can I help you?" The voice behind her was sharp. She turned. A woman in a dark-gray woolen dress looked at her. Imani said, "I'm looking for the sweaters. A cardigan." The woman sniffed. "I'm not sure we have anything here for you. The sweaters are over there on the left." Imani started toward that part of the store. She noticed that the woman in the gray dress was shadowing her, watching her, staying a couple of yards back. Imani looked at her. The woman looked back, silent, her face impassive. Imani turned, walked to the door, her bootheels clacking as she marched, fuming, to the door. She'd go to the damn mall.

—RENÉE PERRY

Advice

We know from the way Imani describes herself that she's not wealthy—
or perhaps she just doesn't care about material things. Her sweater is
frayed and eaten by moths, and she doesn't have a spare one; her older
car is in the repair shop; and she usually shops at the mall—where
presumably the chain and less-expensive stores are located. Still, she's
a member of the intellectual class, teaching at a university. We get a
sense that she's a thoughtful, responsible person. Her description of
her dreadlocks imply that she's a person of color—certainly someone
who presents herself in a non-mainstream way.

She's not made welcome at either of the boutique shops she
enters. In subtle and not-so-subtle ways, the retail clerks make sure
she knows they don't trust her in their stores. She is quick to grasp
their meaning. Understandably, it makes her angry, as summed up
economically by the last line.

99.

Dueling Responsibilities

A good way to move a story forward is by giving your character conflicting tasks to do. They then have to make a decision about how to proceed going forward. This is good because it grounds your character in the present, and ties plot (what happens next) to character—something we're always striving for.

Exercise

1. Put your character in a scene (something happening at a particular place in a particular time).
2. Start in the middle of an action. In other words, already have your character in motion doing something.
3. Now have your character confront the fact that they have two (2) tasks to perform, and only time enough to do one of them.
4. Play it out. How does your character choose? How do they respond to the challenge in front of them? Are they decisive and resolute, or undecided and chaotic? Put a little pressure on your character and see what they do.

Example

Vanessa left the Home Depot not sure how she was going to finish everything before six when she had to leave home to go to the meeting. The broken sidewalk felt too narrow close to the busy road, and she could feel the air in her bangs as each car swooshed by. The new garbage-disposal parts were heavy in the bag, and she felt stupid for not thinking to bring a backpack. Her shoulder hurt already, and she still had almost two miles left.

She zigzagged over the cracks and broken concrete trying to avoid bird shit, rabbit shit, and some kind of unidentified shit that appeared every few feet. Walking had made her hungry, which was unfortunate, because all she had in the house was a can of mushrooms and a bag of baby carrots. There wasn't going to be time to drop the Home Depot bag, cut up food for the turtle, and walk to and from the grocery store before dark. If there was even enough food for Ferguson to begin with. Shit. This was exactly what the pet-store idiot had been talking about when he had gone through his lecture on pet-owning responsibility.

Vanessa shivered. The air smelled like gasoline, and she started to worry about inhaling fumes from the passing cars. What would happen to Ferguson if she dropped dead before mile two from gas particles in her brain? She tried holding her breath, but that made her dizzier than the fumes.

—DANIELLE STONEHIRSCH

Advice

This piece immerses us into a character who is stressed and conflicted. She needs to go grocery shopping, to take care of (amusingly) her pet turtle, but is under time pressure to get home and prepare for an important meeting. What's good about this writing is that we are simultaneously in her mind, worrying, yet also very much on a busy city street. Very well done.

100.

Hauntings

There are many ways to be haunted. By people who have passed, certainly, but also by old events that won't let us go, old decisions that still bother us with what-ifs, and people we used to know whom we have lost touch with.

Exercise

1. Think of someone (or something) that has haunted you (or a character).
2. Write a short piece (500–1,000 words) in which you detail all the ways you/your character have tried to lay this ghost to rest.
3. As part of the piece, write a scene (something happening at a specific place at a specific time) in which an attempt is made to finally exorcise this ghost for good.
4. Whether your character succeeds or not is up to you.

Example

I would have had a child who was seven years and eleven months old.

It's the tiny shoe lying on the side of the highway between the cigarette butts and the Burger King wrappers and the weeds that does it. I see a ghost toddler, running through the desert, all chubby legs and padded diaper bottom, laughing.

Be careful of the cactus! Ouchy! Don't touch! Come to mama!

I've pulled over after my car overheated, driving from New York to

Arizona with all my possessions in my old Volvo. I am alone. I am forty-seven years old. I was not supposed to be alone. This was never the plan.

I'm waiting for the AAA tow truck in the desert, peering down the yellow lines and black tar road that recedes into a point in the wavy distance that is too far for me to see. The desert, too, sprawls out in every direction, interrupted only by the cacti that lift their spiny arms in surrender. Its barren vastness scares me, like it could swallow me up and nobody would know. It's hot, and I fashion a visor out of my hand and walk a bit into the strip of desert next to the road, looking for turquoise rocks. About ten feet off the highway, I see the shoe. America's highways are littered with single shoes, but this one catches me off-guard.

It's a tiny sneaker, a white sneaker with blue stripes. Eight years and one month ago, I had a sneaker. I had two. I had a box full of tiny sweaters and pants, and a pair of tiny sneakers, purchased for a life that never happened, a life that only existed on a black-and-white printout of an ultrasound handed to me by a nurse. That life had been pinned to a corkboard above my desk, where it stayed for eight years, fixed in time in my other life, my current life, which carried on in another direction. I had collected the baby clothes right up until the abortion, right up until the day that John fell to his knees and begged me, begged me to choose him, said if I had it he would leave. I chose him. I looked at the pinned ultrasound every time I walked into my office, shoved the box of baby clothes to the back of the closet, unwilling to release that life from purgatory. My plan for them was "someday." Two failed rounds of IVF with donor sperm later, and they remained. Last week, I had put it all in gray garbage bags for Goodwill. Not just the ghost life with the baby clothes, but the ghost life with John, who was gone almost as soon as I walked out into the waiting room afterwards. I chose wrong.

The ghost baby toddles out into the desert and vanishes. But the shoe remains, covered in a thin layer of dust, pinned to the desert floor. In the distance, I can see the tow truck emerge from the wavy air radiating off the highway, headed toward me. I walk back toward the car. Then I stand on the road, the shoe in my pocket, waving my arms for help.

—NIRMY KANG

Advice

In this piece, we see how an infant's shoe left on the side of the road triggered memories of this person's "ghost"—her decision to end a pregnancy rather than lose her romantic partner, and how the decision, at least from her current vantage point, was wrong. Notice how concretely everything is manifested: she doesn't just "remember" her decision and its consequences, she is jolted by the physical things she deliberately kept—almost to torture herself—the image of the ultrasound she keeps on her office wall, and the baby clothes she only reluctantly gave to Goodwill last week. Especially strong is the dramatization of how this narrator keeps trying to close this episode of her life, yet at the end, she waits for the tow truck with the baby shoe still in her pocket, indicating she is not quite ready to let go.

As I often tell students (of all ages): everyone has their own process, their own way of getting into their material. Some—maybe even most–people require quiet, even isolation. Others, like me, could get their best work done in the middle of Chicago O'Hare Airport on Thanksgiving eve. The more noise and chaos around me, the better. Put me in a beautiful green forest with nothing but time and birdcalls, and I'll produce nothing. Whereas a deadline, a plane connection to make, and a baby howling in the seat behind me will allow me to generate page after (hopefully decent) page.

So you can see why I'm always hesitant to give advice about process. The main thing to do is to actually write. The metaphor I use is that of fishing. If you got in a boat and began rowing around the bay to try to find the perfect place to drop your line—say you were determined not to drop your line until you actually could see a fish—you could spend most of your time splashing through the water and never catch any fish. You must at some point put your line in the water and see if a fish will take your bait. This is also the only way to write. Sink your line—and here's where the metaphor breaks down—and work it. Put your heart into it. Maybe you'll catch something. But if you hold off putting words down until you get a sign that there's something important to write about—well, then, you're likely to be sitting motionless for a very long time.

Of course, there are writers who "write" in their heads and don't put anything down on paper (or screen) until the poem, story, or novel is finished. Then it flows out. They do exist—and if you're one of them, count your blessings and try not to feel too bad about the dirty looks you'll get from other writers. But most of us are like the writers that B. F. Skinner described in his essay "How to Discover What You Have to Say: A Talk to Students."[1] The writing doesn't happen in the head, it happens in the fingers, Skinner argued. The physical act of writing calls into play all the intuition, unconscious thoughts and feelings, and wisdom that is buried under the layers of ordinary living. You are, in effect, learning and discovering as your fingers type (or write by hand). Skinner argues that if this sort of transformation and sense of discovery doesn't happen—if you just write down precisely what is on your mind—you're just taking dictation from thoughts already fully formed in your brain. This almost always results in prose that is logical, "expected" and, yes, boring.

Of course, there are also writers who are outliners, and planners, or plotters. I don't happen to be one of them, but again, if that's how you work best, go for it. But even for those types, this is the book you can pull off your shelf when you're stuck for a plot point, or when a character isn't speaking to you.

This is precisely why I wrote this book. For the majority of us writers who need structure when writing. Who need a little kick in the ass. There's nothing wrong with this. When I write my novels, I'm always putting something in notes in the margins to explore a scene or section of narrative—usually little exercises that came up and went quickly in the story.

And constraints are not only for beginners. Look at Michael Cunningham, who began his Pulitzer Prize–winning novel *The Hours* as an exercise in imitation of Virginia Woolf's *Mrs. Dalloway*, constraining himself to using her language and her plot points in building his own narrative.

There's nothing to be ashamed of in using constraints. It's not cheating, and it's not an easy way out. It's a time-honored way to unleash the inherent creativity of your mind. Go to it!

Acknowledgments

Thanks to my husband and daughter, David Renton and Sarah LaPlante Seidner, for putting up with me during the writing of this book during COVID. And enormous gratitude to the members of the Tramontana Writers' Workshop, who were my guinea pigs for trying and refining these exercises via Zoom while we were on strict lockdown: Carol Jackson, Shirley Kirby James, Jeanette Russo, Kirsty Duffield, Maureen Gallagher, Paula Power, Sarah Barnett Bernelli, and, in memoriam, Ann Morgan. Your generosity was remarkable. The team at Norton was spectacularly insightful and efficient: Jill Bialosky, Drew Elizabeth Weitman, and Rachelle Mandik, thanks for all your efforts that made this a better book. My agent, Victoria Skurnick, of the Levine Greenberg Rostan Literary Agency, thank you, as always, fully and affectionately, for your friendship, support, and hard work to transform an idea into an actual book. Thanks for the inspiration and wisdom contributed by my dear childhood friend, the poet Jennifer Burd. My invaluable editorial assistant, Nora Della Ferra, kept me on track to get the details right. And a big shout out to all the writers—new, emerging, and professional—who contributed examples of the exercises in this book to help and inspire others.

Glossary of Literary Terms
Used in This Book

Ambiguity: For writing purposes, we will say an ambiguity is a mystery—but not one that can be solved. It describes people, events, and situations that cannot be resolved. No matter how much you analyze, there will always be two or more legitimate interpretations. W. S. Merwin once said "poetry is the exact rendering of ambiguity." Likewise, Flannery O'Connor advised, "Don't attempt to solve your mysteries. Render them." These two quotes say it all. If you manage to accurately capture an ambiguity with your words, you have really achieved something.

Character: A character is an entity within a piece of writing. It doesn't have to be human. It doesn't even have to be alive (see personification). You have numerous ways to depict the "personality," for lack of a better word, of characters: description, how they speak, how they think, how they act, how they react to others . . . Most of today's so-called serious or literary fiction focuses on character over plot or action.

Cliché: An overly familiar phrase, typically a metaphor that has been overused. Clichés do not mean the writer is using bad or inappropriate language to describe something. In fact, clichés usually start out as superb turns of phrases that ring true, and therefore get used until they sound tired to our ears. Case in point: many of Shakespeare's metaphors and phrases, which were delightfully fresh in Elizabethan times, have been used to the point where you literally can't deploy them anymore because they are such clichés. Take, for example, "green-eyed monster" to refer to feelings of jealousy. Although it certainly still rings true, it is off-limits to serious writers because it is so familar.

Dialogue: Dialogue is the words characters speak within a scene. Always keep in mind three things when writing dialogue: (1) gesture is a part of dialogue; (2) silence, or pauses, are very important aspects of dialogue; and (3) dialogue is something characters *do* to each other—much like the body blows in a boxing match.

Epiphany: In religious terms (the origin of the word) *epiphany* meant the revealing, or showing, of the Christ child. In literary terms, this has come to mean that a character (or group of characters) has had a major realization. "Suddenly she realized" are the words that commonly precede an epiphany. Many, many stories and novels in the 1970s and 1980s were built around characters experiencing epiphanies as the climaxes of their plots. It got to the point where some people thought that a piece had to have an epiphany to be a complete story. Charles Baxter debunked this myth with his essay "Against Epiphanies," in which he argued that stories can take many forms, and the epiphany story is just one of a multitude of narrative structures. (I agree with him.)

Flashback: A scene or section of narrative that takes place before the time of the current action, usually to explain background to the current drama or to prepare us to understand something that is to come.

Flat character: A flat character is one that has no depth, no surprises. Stereotypes are always flat, although not all flat characters are stereotypes. They're dull and drag your story down.

Foreshadowing: A sense that something of dramatic significance is about to happen in a narrative. Foreshadowing can be achieved in many ways, but is usually conveyed by dropping sensory clues into the text, or hinting in descriptions that something important (good or bad) is going to eventually take place.

Frame story: A frame story is a story within a story. It is set in one timeframe (typically, the so-called present of the story) that frames a second story, usually from the past. The pattern of a frame story is thus typically Present (opening); Past (most of the story); Present (coming back to the opening timeframe). However, there are many, many types of frame stories, including stories about one person or event that frame a story about another person or event. But the point of the frame story is that the two stories are stronger together than they are as individual, separate stories. Something about the juxtaposition of the stories together is especially powerful.

Imagery: An image, in literary terms, is anything that is described using one or more of the five senses. Writers too often depend only on visual images, when images that evoke two, three, or even more of the senses can be much more powerful.

Juxtaposition: Juxtaposition is the placing of people, places, things, or events next to each other to provoke associations and meaning that otherwise might go unnoticed. For example, juxtaposing a scene in the present at an amusement park next to a scene at a funeral parlor could make for an interesting thematic exploration of character. Some stories are "plotless"; they consist only of individual vignettes juxtaposed against each other in a certain sequence as determined by the writer. "In the Heart of the Heart of the Country" by William Gass is a famous example of this kind of "modular" story in which the juxtapositioning of vignettes drives the tension.

Metaphor: A metaphor is a direct comparison of two unlike things. A good metaphor will thematically fit into the mood or plot of a story and provide insight with its lucid vision. Metaphors are difficult to pull off. It's hard to find a fresh way to express a comparison, for one thing—many of the metaphors we instinctively reach for are overused to the point of cliché. Another issue is the comparison must be appropriate for the narrative. If you are writing about the death of a child, for example, you probably would not create metaphors with happy or positive connotations. Finally, the comparison must make sense. You wouldn't compare your dog to a teakettle, unless you had some very clever explanation of why the comparison worked. (When you have to explain your metaphor, that's usually not a good sign, although it can be done successfully by skilled writers.)

Narrative: Narrative is the other essential element in addition to scene. All fiction (or creative nonfiction) is made up of either scene or narrative. Either something is being dramatized or shown (scene), or something is being told to us by a narrator or persona (narrative). Sometimes the two are mixed within a sentence—that's how closely they are intertwined. But whenever something is told rather than shown (think of what you could actually experience firsthand, as in a stage play or movie, versus a voiceover explaining things to you), you have narrative.

Personification: Personification is giving human characteristics to a nonhuman thing or entity (including things as well as animals). This can be an interesting literary technique to play with—to have buildings watching (as James

Joyce does in *Dubliners*) or imbue horrible humanlike behaviors onto ordinary objects (as Stephen King does in *Christine*).

Plot: This is a tricky one. We could write volumes about what plot is and what it does. But for the purposes of this work (and for generating new writing in general) let's use this definition: A plot is a sequence of events, put into a specific order, to get a desired effect.

Point of view: Point of view refers to the type of narrator you have (the narrator is the intelligence behind the telling of the story). First person: the narrator is speaking as "I," and is usually a character who is an active participant within the story, although there are exceptions to that, as in frame stories. Second person: the narrator speaks to a "you," which is typically used as inverse first person. Second person is a complex point of view—see the three exercises devoted to it in this book (Exercises 48, 49, and 50). Third person is when the narrator (the intelligence telling the story) is not part of the story but is separated—disembodied—from action. Third person can be omniscient (godlike), or extremely limited (direct observer) or anything in between. Third-person narrators thus have varying degrees of knowledge into what's happening that they can tell readers about. Need more? See *The Making of a Story*, in which I explain point of view in exhaustive detail.

Round character: Round characters, as opposed to flat characters, are fully realized—they have depth of emotion and thoughts that are complex and even contradictory, and are always surprising us. That's why the phrase "in character" is a difficult one to apply properly. You want your characters to be believable, but you also want them capable of surprising us—and themselves. E. M. Forster in *Aspects of the Novel* says that round characters are "surprising yet convincing," which is actually a mantra we should apply to all our writing.

Scene: A scene is one of two essential elements for fiction (or creative nonfiction) and is made up of a number of components: dialogue, gesture, setting, characterization . . . the list goes on. But for the purposes of this book, a scene is something that happens at a specific place and specific time. When a scene starts, the narrative "clock" starts ticking—we are aware of time passing. If a scene is paused for any reason—say to give backstory, insert a flashback, or provide a description—the narrative clock stops until the scene resumes again.

Sentimentality: I always define this as clichéd emotion—that is emotional reactions induced by a story plot that are so familiar to us that they have become stale and trite. I've heard other writers describe this as "emotion that has not been *earned* by a story." Either way, a sentimental story is one that depends on tiggering pre-existing cultural or societal emotional reactions that are rote and don't surprise.

Setting: Setting is the place that a narrative occurs in. A story may have just one setting or numerous ones. What matters are two things: (1) that the setting is described in such a way to evoke a strong feeling of place for the reader; and (2) that the setting matters to the narrative. Why the latter piece of advice? Because too many stories are set, and plot points are created, in a void. Two characters are arguing in a laundromat, but it may as well have been a fancy restaurant—in fact, if the scene were moved to a different setting, nothing would change. This is a bad sign. Use your settings to full advantage so that what happens there couldn't happen anywhere else.

Simile: A simile is also a comparison of two unlike things, but is less assertive (and often less powerful) than a metaphor, as it uses "like" or "as" to make the comparison. "My love is like a red, red rose" is a simile. All the same cautions go for similes as for metaphors.

Stereotype: A stereotype is a clichéd character—a "type" that we've seen before. They only do or say expected things. The prostitute with the heart of gold. The all-loving mother. The devoted servant. We want to avoid these.

Subtext: Subtext in dialogue is what is meant versus what is said. A character can say, "Will you please pass the butter?" to her partner, and it could mean, with the right context and some writing skill, "I'm sick of you and breaking up with you." We always strive to have our dialogue exist on those two levels: the actual words versus what they really mean.

Symbol: Something that stands for something else. Typically, this is a physical object (something that can be perceived with the senses) standing for something abstract. Like a cross standing for Christianity, or a flag standing for a country. In writing, I strongly advise against the conscious planting of symbols. It can come across as pretentious and heavy-handed. Symbols are best "discovered" after you've written something, when you realize you've established enough emotional context and sensory evidence to have earned turning an object into a symbol. Tread carefully here.

Tense: This is a grammatical term that has enormous consequences for narratives. Is the story being told as it happens, now (present tense) or relayed as something that has already happened (past tense). The choice of tense is one of the most important decisions writers make when they sit down to write. Tense must be skillfully used when "time traveling" within a story (see the Exercise 14 in this book).

Theme: Theme is another literary device that I would wield with caution. As I say repeatedly throughout this book, think small. Thinking about theme—what your story means on a macro level—can cause you to lose focus on the details and go abstract or, worse, clichéd. Let the theme arise from the story. Best of all—let someone else tell you what your theme is after you've finished a piece. Sometimes the best writing happens when we are unconscious of its larger meaning.

Notes

SECTION I: Using Constraints to Generate Creative Work

1. Heydar Aliyev Center, "Azerbaijani Mugham," Google Arts & Culture, accessed May 15, 2022, https://artsandculture.google.com/story/azerbaijani-mugham-heydar-aliyev-center/bwWR35r5G6adIA?hl=en.

2. "Styles of Jazz," *A Passion for Jazz*, retrieved May 20, 2022, https://www.apassion4jazz.net/jazz_styles.html.

3. Christoph Heinrich, *Monet* (New York: Taschen, 2000).

4. David Bevington, Terence John Bew Spencer, John Russell Brown, et al., "Shakespeare's Sources," Britannica.com, accessed June 4, 2022, https://www.britannica.com/biography/William-Shakespeare/Shakespeares-sources.

5. Roland Penrose, *Picasso: His Life and Work* (Berkeley: University of California Press, 1981), 345.

6. "Bull's Head," PabloPicasso.org, accessed May 21, 2022, https://www.pablopicasso.org/bull-head.jsp.

7. Hilda Kossoff, "Arthur Koestler Calls Creativity a 'Bisociation' of Idea Codes," *Stanford Daily,* January 22, 1965, accessed May 1, 2022, https://stanforddailyarchive.com/cgi-bin/stanford?a=d&d=stanford19650122-01.2.4#.

8. Mihaly Csikszentmihalyi, *Creativity: The Psychology of Discovery and Invention* (New York: Harper Perennial, 1996).

9. Mihaly Csikszentmihalyi, "Flow" TED Talk, 2004, accessed March 2, 2022, https://www.youtube.com/watch?v=I_u-Eh3h7Mo.

10. Oguz A. Acar, "Why Constraints Are Good for Innovation," *Harvard Business Review,* November 22, 2019, https://hbr.org/2019/11/why-constraints-are-good-for-innovation, accessed May 24, 2022.

11. Ravi Mehta and Meng Zhu, "Creating When You Have Less: The Impact of Resource Scarcity on Product Use Creativity," *Journal of Consumer*

Research 42, no. 5 (February 2016): 767–782, https://doi.org/10.1093/jcr/ucv051.

SECTION 4: Afterthoughts

1. B. F. Skinner, "How to Discover What You Have to Say: A Talk to Students," *The Behavior Analyst* 4, no. 1 (Spring 1981): 1–7, accessed March 28, 2022, https://www.ncbi.nlm.nih.gov/pmc/articles/PMC2741992/pdf/behavan00072-0003.pdf.

Works Referred To in This Text

ATWOOD, MARGARET. "February." In *Morning in the Burned House*. Houghton Mifflin Harcourt, 1995.

BALDWIN, JAMES. "Nothing Personal." *Contributions in Black Studies* 6: The Blues Edition (2008).

BELL, MADISON SMARTT. "Signaling Through the Flames." Presentation given at City Lights Bookstore, April 8, 2020.

BERKSON, BILL. "October." *Portrait and Dream: New and Selected Poems*. Minneapolis, MN: Coffee House Press, 2009.

BERRY, WENDELL. "The Peace of Wild Things." In *The Peace of Wild Things and Other Poems*. Berkeley, CA: Black Oak Books, 1968.

CAMUS, ALBERT. *The Plague*. New York: Vintage Books, 1991.

DAVIS, LYDIA. "I'm Pretty Comfortable, But I Could Be a Little More Comfortable." In *Can't and Won't*. New York: Farrar, Straus and Giroux, 2014.

DI PIERO, W. S. "Aubade." *The New Yorker*, March 30, 2020.

ELLMANN, LUCY. *Ducks, Newburyport*. Biblioasis, 2019.

ELSON, REBECCA. "Antidotes to Fear of Death." In *A Responsibility to Awe*. Manchester, UK: Carcanet Press, 2018.

ERDRICH, LOUISE. *The Painted Drum*. New York: HarperCollins, 2005.

FORSTER, E. M. *Aspects of the Novel*. Harmondsworth: Penguin Books, 1964.

GILBERT, JACK. "A Brief for the Defense." *The Sun*, July 2013.

————. "Failing and Flying." In *Refusing Heaven*. New York: Alfred A. Knopf, 2005.

HUGO, RICHARD. "Triggering Town." In *The Triggering Town: Lectures and Essays on Poetry and Writing*. New York: Norton, 1979.

JOHNSON, DENIS. *Jesus' Son*. New York: Farrar, Straus, and Giroux, 1992.

KENISON, KATRINA. *The Gift of an Ordinary Day: A Mother's Memoir*. New York: Grand Central Publishing, 2009.

LARKIN, PHILIP. "Home Is So Sad." In *Collected Poems*. New York: Farrar, Straus and Giroux, 2003.

———. "The Pleasure Principle." In *Required Writing*. London: Faber and Faber, 1983.

———. "Sad Steps." In *Collected Poems*. New York: Noonday Press, 1993.

MAMET, DAVID. *The Museum of Science and Industry Story*. In *Five Television Plays*. New York: Grove Press, 1994.

McKIBBENS, RACHEL. "Poem for Three Dead Girls of Last Summer." In *Into the Dark & Emptying Field*. Small Doggies Press, 2013.

MERWIN, W. S. "January 2001." *Poetry*, January 2001.

MONTILLA, YESENIA. "Maps." Academy of American Poets, Poem-a-Day, March 28, 2017.

MUNRO, ALICE. "Post and Beam." In *Hateship, Friendship, Courtship, Loveship, Marriage*. New York: Vintage, 2002.

NYE, NAOMI SHIHAB. "Kindness." In *Words Under the Words: Selected Poems*. Portland, OR: Eighth Mountain Press, 1995.

O'CONNOR, FLANNERY. *Mystery and Manners: Occasional Prose*. Edited by Sally and Robert Fitzgerald. New York: Farrar, Straus, and Giroux, 1969.

OLDS, SHARON. "His Terror." *Poetry,* September 1991.

OLIVER, MARY. "I Worried." In *Devotions: The Selected Poems of Mary Oliver*. New York: Penguin Press, 2017.

———. "The River." In *Evidence: Poems*. Boston: Beacon Press, 2009.

———. "The Uses of Sorrow." In *Thirst*. Boston: Beacon Press, 2006.

PARKO, KIM. "Bitch Is a Word I Hear a Lot." *Poetry Now*, 2019.

PAVESE, CESARE. "Passion for Solitude." In *Disaffections: Complete Poems 1930–1950*. Copper Canyon Press, 2002.

PLATH, SYLVIA. "Tulips." *The New Yorker.* March, 1962.

RANKINE, CAMILLE. "The Current Isolationism." In *Incorrect Merciful Impulses.* Copper Canyon Press, 2016.

SAUNDERS, GEORGE. *A Swim in the Pond in the Rain.* New York: Random House, 2021.

SHAUGHNESSY, BRENDA. "Visitor." *Poetry,* September 2011.

SNYDER, GARY. "Looking at Pictures to Be Put Away." In *The Back Country* (New Directions) 1971.

SOLNIT, REBECCA. "Apricots." In *The Faraway Nearby.* New York: Viking, 2013.

STRAYED, CHERYL. "The Ghost Ship That Didn't Carry Us." *The Rumpus,* April 21, 2011.

STRAND, MARK. "Keeping Things Whole." In *Sleeping with One Eye Open: Poems.* Stone Wall Press, 1964.

THOMAS, DYLAN. *Under Milk Wood.* New Directions, 1954.

WILLIAMS, WILLIAM CARLOS. *Paterson.* Cambridge, MA: New Directions, 1949.

WILSON, KEITH S. "Invisibility." In *Fieldnotes on Ordinary Love.* Copper Canyon, 2019.

WOLCOTT, DEREK. "Love After Love." In *Sea Grapes.* Farrar, Straus and Giroux 1976.

WOLFF, TOBIAS. "What Is a Short Short?" In *Sudden Fiction: American Short-Short Stories.* Edited by Robert Shapard and James Thomas. Salt Lake City: Gibbs Smith, 1986.

WOOLF, VIRGINIA. *The Waves.* London: Hogarth Press, 1933.

YOUN, MONICA. "A Parking Lot in West Houston." In *Barter.* Graywolf Press, 2003.

ZAGAJEWSKI, ADAM. "Try to Praise the Mutilated World." In *Without End: New and Selected Poems.* New York: Farrar, Straus & Giroux, 2002.

Contributors

Vibha Akkaraju writes personal narratives that touch on, among other things, her bicultural heritage and her family life. Her work has been published in *Big Apple Parent, India Currents, HerStry*, and *The Dillydoun Review*. She is working on a memoir about her search for identity as she moved from India to America as a young girl.

Stories by **Jeanne Althouse** (she/her) have been published in numerous literary journals, most recently in *Catamaran Reader, Connotation Press, The Penman Review, Digging Through the Fat, Potato Soup Journal*, and *The Plentitudes Journal*. She is grateful her work has won several awards, been collected into a chapbook, and twice nominated for a Pushcart Prize. She loves reading, wordplay, and her husband, but husband first, usually.

Ben Black is an assistant fiction editor at *AGNI* magazine. He holds an MFA from SFSU and teaches English and creative writing in the Bay Area. His stories have appeared in Best Microfiction 2022, *The Southampton Review, New American Writing, Wigleaf, Harpur Palate*, and *The Los Angeles Review*, among others. See more at benpblack.com.

Jennifer Burd is the author of *Body and Echo, Days Late Blue, Receiving the Shore*, and *Fringe* (poetry). She is also author of *Daily Bread: A Portrait of Homeless Men & Women of Lenawee County, Michigan* (creative nonfiction). Her website is jenniferburd.ink.

Cynthia Cima-Ivy is a lifelong Californian and amateur historian. In her fiction-writing life, she likes to explore the roles of the varied people who have migrated to the state—both their relationships with one another and with the land itself.

Matthew Clark Davison is the author of *Doubting Thomas*, a novel (Amble Press, 2021); and of *The Lab, Experiments in Writing Across Genre*, coauthored with Alice LaPlante (W. W. Norton, 2023), the latter of which is partially based on a generative writing workshop Matthew started in San Francisco in 2014. He's also faculty in creative writing at San Francisco State.

As the son of a librarian, **John Didday** has loved reading all his life. His speculative and allegorical fiction is inspired by RPG video games, fantasy novels, and his day job as an attorney. John and his wife live in Petaluma, California, where they care for their son, Clark, their Texas Longhorn Cleo, and their goat, Billie. www.johndidday.com.

Shirley Jo Eaves lives in Loveland, Ohio, and has creative-writing certificates from UCLA and Stanford University. Her work has appeared in *T-Zero Quarterly*, *Short Story America*, *Kaleidoscope* magazine, and others. She writes to explore and share her responses to life with its crazy mix of beauty, pain, and joy.

Katherine Edgren's latest book, *Keeping Out the Noise*, is scheduled to be published by Kelsay Books in 2022. In addition to her book *The Grain Beneath the Gloss*, published by Finishing Line Press, she also has two chapbooks: *Long Division* and *Transports*.

Mieke Eerkens is a Dutch-American writer with an MFA from the University of Iowa. Her book, *All Ships Follow Me: A Family Memoir of War*, was published by Picador in 2019. She teaches creative writing in Amsterdam.

Maureen Gallagher has spent the last two years working in a residential home, caring for people with dementia. Having previously cared for her father, who died from vascular dementia, she is passionate about removing the stigma surrounding this disease.

Lillian Giles is a Black, queer writer and educator living in Oakland, California. She has completed an MFA in creative writing at San Francisco State University, been published in *The Rumpus,* and was awarded the Nomadic Press Award for fiction.

Nirmy Kang is a British-Punjabi writer. Her work explores her plural heritage and the universality of our common experiences irrespective of origin.

Surinder Dosanjh Kang, British-born Punjabi and longtime California resident, has had careers in the medical field, foster youth advocacy, and design. She enjoys reading, interior design, fashion, cooking, and entertaining.

Patra Kasturi's stories and essays have appeared in *Jaggery, Litbreak,* Strands International Flash Fiction Competition, *TMYS Review,* and others. Her debut novel won a pitch competition and was published in 2021. She currently lives in Luxembourg with her husband and four rescued pets.

Lydia Mathis graduated from Agnes Scott College in 2019 and has a BA in English literature. She is now pursuing an MA in creative writing at New York University. She currently resides in Atlanta, Georgia, with her family, where she is constantly dodging tumbling book stacks.

Cassund Olivier is an author from Brockton, Massachusetts, with a bachelor's degree in health sciences and a minor in chemistry. She is getting her master's in creative writing at New York University. She works as a lab technician in Manhattan and lives in Brooklyn, New York.

Renée Perry writes short fiction. She lives in California's Central Valley.

Teresa Pham-Carsillo is a Vietnamese American writer based in the San Francisco Bay Area. Teresa's fiction and poetry has been featured in numerous publications, including: *Poetry, The Southern Review, Salt Hill Journal, The Minnesota Review, Smartish Pace,* and *Passengers Journal.*

London Pinkney is an MFA candidate at San Francisco State University. She is the founder and editor-in-chief of *The Ana.*

Charlotte Pregnolato has taught research and academic writing, and presently she is a freelance writer of food- and lifestyle-related articles. Her first love is reading and writing fiction, and most of her fiction is inspired by classes, workshops, forums, and the dedicated writers at Writer's Village University.

TreVaughn Malik Roach-Carter is a queer, Black writer born in Modesto, California. He is a novelist and fiction editor with *The Ana.* His Afrocentric fantasy novel, *The Aziza Chronicles,* is published with Deep Hearts YA.

Zurina Saban, born in Cape Town, is an author and poet. Her writing is inspired by her experiences growing up on the Cape Flats, her passion for survival and growth and her love of Africa.

Saikrishna Sarveswari is a short-story writer with publications in several literary journals. She looks forward to a day when she can write without interruptions.

Lori Savageau is a technical writer by trade and aspiring novelist at heart. Though her time and affections are split between East and West Coasts, she currently lives in Warwick, Rhode Island.

S. Shaw is the author of *The House of Men: Poems*, and his poems have been published in *African American Review, Rhino 2021, Rattle Literary Journal, Taint Taint Taint Journal*, and upcoming in *Obsidian*. He also has a short story in *Mighty Real: An Anthology of African American Same Gender Loving Writing*. He is a Cave Canem Poetry Fellow as well as a Pushcart Prize–nominated poet.

Laszlo Slomovits is one of the twin brothers in the award-winning children's music duo Gemini. Singer, songwriter, and multi-instrumentalist, Laszlo has also set to music the work of many poets, both ancient and contemporary.

Danielle Stonehirsch lives in Silver Spring, Maryland. Her fiction has appeared in several places, including the anthologies *This Is What America Looks Like* and *Roar: True Tales of Women Warriors*.

Marisa Vito is a queer Californian, Filipinx poet who has published with *Crab Fat, The Spectacle, Mixed Mag, Phyll*, and the *Los Angeles Magazine*. They are based in Brooklyn, New York.

Alanna Weissman is a writer and editor from New York City. Her work has appeared in *The New York Times, The Guardian, The Rumpus, Bellevue Literary Review, San Francisco Chronicle*, and elsewhere. She holds an MFA in fiction from New York University, an MS from Columbia Journalism School, and a BA in English and art from Colgate University.

Brigitte Whiting lives in Maine and uses settings from her backyard and from rides throughout northern New England in her writing. She has been published in *Village Square Literary Journal* and *Literary Yard*.

Anna Zagerson is a writer, educator, and occupational therapist who loves embroidery, dancing, and animals. She spends her free time rewatching reality TV with her rescue cat, Wolfie.

Emma Zimmerman's journalism has appeared in *Outside, Runner's World*, and *Women's Running*, among other publications. Her literary nonfiction has received honors from Lighthouse Writers' Workshop and PRISM International. She is currently completing her MFA at NYU, and she lives in Brooklyn, New York.

Permissions